Grace in the Gulf

by
Jeanette Boersma
with
David DeGroot

To God be all glory
Jeanette Boersma
II Cor 2:15

The Historical Series of the Reformed Church in America
No. 20
Primary Mission Sources

GRACE IN THE GULF

The Autobiography of
Jeanette Boersma,
Missionary Nurse in
Iraq and the Sultanate of Oman

by

Jeanette Boersma

with

David DeGroot

Wm. B. Eerdmans Publishing Co.
Grand Rapids, Michigan

Copyright © 1991 by Wm. B. Eerdmans Publishing Co.,
255 Jefferson Ave. S.E., Grand Rapids, Mich. 49503

Printed in the United States of America

ISBN 0-8028-0603-1

Dedicated to my parents
who loved and prayed for us.

The Historical Series of the Reformed Church in America

This series has been inaugurated by the General Synod of the Reformed Church in America, acting through its Commission on History, for the purpose of encouraging historical research and providing a medium wherein this knowledge may be shared with the academic community and with the members of the denomination in order that a knowledge of the past may contribute to right action in the present.

General Editor

The Rev. Donald J. Bruggink, Ph.D.
Western Theological Seminary

Contents

Illustrations

Editor's Preface

Khatune Naeema was Jeanette Boersma's Arabic name, literally translated "Respected foreign lady Grace." Certainly, God's grace was evident and present in Jeanette's gifts of healing, Christian nurture, encouragement, instruction, and ministry.

Before she was born, Jeanette's mother prayed for a child and vowed that the child would be given to God. *Grace in the Gulf* is the story of the fulfillment of that vow, of God's grace in Jeanette's life, and how she was used to show God's grace in her lifetime of service in Iraq and Oman.

Jeanette's desire to allow God's love and the leading of the Spirit to permeate her book has been fulfilled. At the same time she has made a valuable contribution to the Primary Mission Sources of the Historical Series of the Reformed Church in America.

When compared with the two prior works of Primary Mission Sources: *Pioneers in the Arab World* by Dorothy Van Ess, and *Sharifa*, by Cornelia Dalenberg, it will be obvious that the Reformed Church in America has sent to its mission fields persons of varied personalities and gifts. Together, they have provided a rich tapestry of devotion and service to the cause of mission and to the people of the Gulf.

In addition to those committed people are also those gifted laity who share the commitment to mission and have worked very hard to make it possible for the commission to publish this volume. Special thanks are due to David and Barbara Vander Woude, Beverly Renz, the people of the Mount Greenwood Reformed Church, and to David DeGroot.

The Historical Series of the Reformed Church is grateful to all of those who through the series share their gifts with the church, and in particular in this volume for Jeanette Boersma, who has so openly shared her life, and her understanding of God's grace, as she has sought to live out that grace.

Donald J. Bruggink

FOREWORD

Jeanette Boersma's life was intertwined with my family's throughout thirty-nine years in the Arabian mission. We were colleagues, neighbors, and friends—part of the "mission family," a term understood only by those who have lived and worked in a community bound together by one loyalty and one purpose.

Jeanette arrived in Basrah, Iraq, in 1944 (the year I went out to Iran). There she studied Arabic with another newcomer, Jay Kapenga, and with Ed and Ruth Luidens. In the summer of 1946, at a conference for young missionaries in Hamadan, Iran, Jay and I became engaged. One of the things I was told was that if Jeanette had not approved of me, our engagement wouldn't have happened! The next time I met her was in the summer of 1948 when we were all in Kodaikanal together on vacation—Jay and I, Jeanette, Ed Luidens, and Jake Holler. That was the summer our Peter was born in an emergency Caesarean section performed late at night. Jeanette was present in the operating room, and I woke to find her sitting by my bedside with Peter in the baby crib. This was my first experience of her very personal loving care.

Her first furlough and ours came the same year. Then, in January of 1948, we returned to our assignment in Muscat and were already living in the Zenana house over the school when Jeanette moved into the mission house with the Rev. Dirk and Minnie Dykstra. She lived with them until they sailed off for retirement in the spring of 1952. All that separated these two houses was a narrow road, barely the width of a jeep, and the small, one-room church building known as Peter Zwemer Memorial Chapel. From our second floor apartments, we could see each other through the open windows, and I could hear her Black Forest cuckoo clock every hour of the day and night.

Jeanette and I were not at all alike and probably would never have chosen one another as friends had we remained in the USA. But mission colleagues, like natural brothers and sisters, are given, not chosen. We had to live closely with one another, work together, and learn to respect and love one another. Jeanette was one of the most hard-working and self-giving missionaries I have known in nearly forty years of mission life. Jay and I have often said that living next door to Jeanette was like living next door to Mother Theresa! Both of them are dedicated, loving, compassionate, hard working, strong, and determined. To live so close to all this energy can be tiring and, sometimes, even exasperating. Someone has to save them from the incessant demands of others, to keep them from wearing themselves out.

The difference in our temperaments created some tension. Jeanette always reacted to any given circumstance from the heart, and gave herself unstintingly to the service of her fellow men and women, while I tended to begin with the mind, figuring things out and then deciding what to do. She loved everyone, even those whom I found difficult or even impossible to love. We could be part of the same event and interpret it differently. These differences led to plenty of discussion and argument at our daily afternoon teatime. She was involved in the school and the church and we were involved in her hospital, so we always had a lot to talk over.

Jeanette seems to have entered into the thought patterns of her Omani friends and tends to speak and think as they do. Every few sentences she will exclaim, "Praise God," or, "Thanks be to God." Giving God the credit for everything that happens is a biblical concept, but it is articulated more often by Muslims who believe everything that happens is preordained by God. Where I might consider someone to be mentally ill, Jeanette sees as the Arabs would and believes that person to be possessed by evil spirits. Because of this, she has often been able to help such persons when western medicine has failed. Jeanette always thought the best of everyone (including ourselves) in every situation. She could be optimistic when we were pessimistic, and she never doubted her missionary call or her vocation.

Through all her hospital service as a nurse, trips to the Bedouins, and relationships with Arab people, Jeanette has been a faithful and consistent witness to Christ. Mission methods and mission theology may change with the times, but there is no substitute for living with, loving, and serving one's fellow human beings in Christ's name. This book is a subjective account of what happened in the Arabian mission while Jeanette was on the field, as well as being a record of her own missionary service in Arabia. It is the Arabian mission as seen through her eyes. If she were living here in Florida, instead of way up north in Chicago, we might well be spending our tea times evaluating, interpreting, and reflecting on all these memories of events and persons that we have in common, but that is not possible.

All of us in the Arabian mission believed ourselves to be part of a great fellowship of missionaries who went out to one of the most difficult mission fields in the world. It is no easy task in any place to live a life that radiates to others the love of God in Christ. May this modest account of a life of devoted service inspire new recruits from the Reformed Church in, America to go out to Muslim lands and be a presence for Christ.

Marjory Kapenga
Penny Farms, Florida

Preface

After a worship service in the Mt. Greenwood Reformed Church in Chicago, on a warm Sunday evening in August of 1988, Dave and Barb Vander Woude approached me saying, "Sit down, Jeanette, we'd like to talk to you." After sitting they said to me, "We'd like you to write your story."

Bewildered, I replied, "But I have never written a book. I wouldn't know where to begin."

Dave said, "We have just the man to help you. Dave DeGroot, who helped write *Sharifa*, Cornelia Dalenberg's life story, is willing to help you. And he is a friend of ours."

I recalled how individuals throughout the years had written to me after receiving my letters, "Jeanette, your life is so interesting. Some day it must be written." Since retirement I have spoken at many churches. As I stood greeting at the door at the close of a service some would say, "You should write a book about your life." At these times I wondered if these could be promptings of the Spirit because of the occasional and yet continued nudging over a span of years. I quietly kept these remarks in my heart. Here it was again. Truly this must be from the Lord.

Dave and Barb were enthusiastic. It was suggested that we use the same procedure as was used for Cornelia's book; thus a committee would have to be formed. Dave and Barb would be part of that, of course, and I also suggested Beverly Renz. I had met the Renz family one afternoon while walking home from the post office. I stopped at their home because I had read in the church bulletin that Mr. Renz was not well. This call was to be the beginning of a friendship and relationship of prayerful support. I recognized in Beverly an ability and intelligence that must be used and encouraged her in it. I thus suggested that she serve on the book committee. This proved to be a wise selection. We were now four members. The Mt. Greenwood consistory was informed of what we were about to do, and we received their whole-hearted support and blessing.

My parents, and later sisters and brothers, had saved the letters I had sent them through the years. And there were many letters, because while my parents were living I wrote them every week. These letters were stored in my basement. Sorting them and other written material would entail hours of work. The committee met approximately every week over the next two years. Hours were also put in at our homes late into the night for the ministry of the book. The committee worked unstintingly. When I showed concern, Dave said, "It's a ministry God has called us to. It must be done." We recognized God's help, his special grace and strength, and even miracles. In fact, from the beginning we knew that God was in it.

David DeGroot came four times to interview me from Tucson, Arizona. He had the letters, articles, and some books and spent a tremendous number of hours studying the material at hand to compile the contents of this book. Meanwhile I continued to feed him material and added some while editing as well. The final writing was his. He put the book together. I am most grateful for his professional and experienced help. I am also grateful to Dave, Barb, Bev, and her mother, Mrs. Renz, for listening, advising, and praying; and to Julie, Andrew, Kristie, Jonathan, and Phillip Vander Woude who sacrificed because their parents did. God faithfully continued to pour forth his Spirit, grace, strength, and help to each of us during the writing of the book. This book could not have been written without the help of our God, the help of Dave DeGroot, and that of the committee.

God tells us over and over in his Word, "Give thanks to the Lord, call on his name; make known among the nations what he has done. Sing to him, sing praise to him; tell of all his wonderful acts" (Ps. 105:1,2). First Peter 2:9 tells us, "But you are a chosen people, a royal priesthood, a holy nation, a people belonging to

God, that you may declare the praises of him who called you out of darkness into his wonderful light." (All quotations of scripture are from the NIV unless otherwise noted.) The purpose of this book is to tell all people what God has done with one insignificant life through the prayers of her parents. There is one thing that must shine through this book and that is the power of prayer. This book portrays the fact of God fulfilling the prayer of a humble, immigrant farmer's wife and his holding of her, and me, to this prayer. The purpose of telling my story is to show the sovereignty and leading of God in each of our lives. Our God reigns. To God be the glory.

I give thanks to the pastors of the Mt. Greenwood Reformed Church, who faithfully stood by me those forty-two years with their prayers, loving support, and giving. The pastors who served during this period were the Revs. Everett De Witt, Lambert Olgers, Henry B. Poppen, Harris Verkaik, Robert L. Bast, Franklin Spoolstra, Jacob Dykstra, and Philip Grawburg. For the writing of this book the congregation and our present pastors, the Rev. Dan Van Houten and Mr. Don MacDonald, supported me with their prayers, giving, and encouragement. I am also indebted to my cousin and friend, Gert Beintum, who throughout my years of service addressed and stamped more than 200 envelopes each time the RCA's department of promotion, communication, and development sent her a pack of my "Dear Friends'" letters—an event that occurred three or four times a year. Her husband, Clarence, assisted her in posting them. They too are members of my home church.

During my span as a missionary in the Middle East I was accountable to God and to the General Program Council (G.P.C.), the program agency of the Reformed Church in America, with headquarters in New York City. I give God thanks for them. They worked for our good and were there when we needed them. There was constant contact, even personal visits, and a good relationship between them and us. They were our support body and source of security. I give God thanks for my supporting churches (listed in Appendix A) who, like my home church, took a personal interest in me and supported me with their prayers and gifts. I give God thanks for the churches within our denomination for their interest in mission, prayers, and giving. I saw for myself the generous giving of our people, when I was out speaking amongst the churches. The G.P.C. and these churches together stood by loyally to support the ongoing programs of both the home and overseas mission work, so we could be on the mission field. We were in this together. Without the prayers and support of these good people we could not have served our God. I can only commit them to a faithful loving Father and say, "God bless you."

"And our God met all our needs, according to his glorious riches in Christ Jesus" (Philippians 4:19, my paraphrase).

I am grateful to the prayer chain (and it's a long one) of the Mt. Greenwood Reformed Church. How often in my need I ran to them for prayer. I am grateful to the special women who meet to pray on Monday mornings for their support and understanding while the book was being written. I am grateful to family and friends throughout the States for their prayers and help in financing this book project. I am grateful to my many friends in Oman and India who remained faithful in their prayers for me during the writing of this book and for their letters of encouragement.

I thank my colleagues: Jay and Midge Kapenga, Harve and Hilda Staal, Anne De Young, and Don and Eloise Bosch for their prayers, help, suggestions, support, encouragement, and understanding during the writing of this book. In times of frustration I would run to them, call them by phone, or write to them.

I thank Henry Boersma, grandson of Uncle Sietje and Tietje Boersma (whom readers will meet in these pages), for teaching me to use a computer. He and his wife, Joyce, also came to my aid when I sent out an "SOS" in times of special need. I thank Dave and Barb who also came to my "computer" needs. I thank Roger Vander Woude, father of Dave, who kept the account records and was treasurer of the book fund. I thank Ruth Bretveld for her encouragement and hours of typing at the beginning of the project. I thank Elsie Mitkus and Angie Fisher, who stood faithfully by in special ways.

Above all, my thanks to Almighty God who led us to write the book; who enabled it to be written; who heard and answered the prayers and cries for its writing. We thank and praise God.

This book speaks of the leading and faithfulness of a great God in my life even from the time before I was born to the present. To God be the glory and praise. If this book will be an inspiration to all who read it; will strengthen the faith of all who read it; will increase the giving of the churches to mission; will lead many to a new life in Christ; and will lead others to give of their lives in service, then it will have fulfilled its purpose. Jesus said, "The harvest is plentiful but the workers are few. Ask the Lord of the harvest, therefore, to send out workers into his harvest field" (Matt. 9:37,38).

Out of my friendship, love, and concern for my Omani friends, names have been changed.

Jeanette Boersma
July 28, 1990

I
Mother's Prayer

Before I formed you in the womb I knew you,
before you were born I set you apart.
                                              Jeremiah 1:5
All the days ordained for me were written in your
book before one of them came to be.
                                              Psalm 139:16

Both of my parents were born in Friesland, a northern province of the Netherlands, in 1890. They arrived in the United States with their families in 1905, when both were fifteen years of age. They did not come to know each other until their families settled in the southwest section of Chicago in an area called Roseland. Both families attended the same church, the First Reformed Church of Roseland, which was located on 107th Street and Michigan Avenue. Three other Reformed churches existed in this area. By God's grace and leading the Boersma and Anema families both chose to attend the First Reformed Church of Roseland.

My father came from a poor family. Dad and his two brothers were hired out to local farmers at early ages to provide income for the family. More than once dad recalled hearing, through the walls of his bedroom, his parents agonizing over how to feed their children the next day. In order to leave the Netherlands, grandpa borrowed money from his brother, Sietje, who preceded him to the United States by some years. Sietje Boersma settled in the Mt. Greenwood section of Chicago, which some years later became our home.

My father and his two brothers, Christian and Henry, first worked in a factory and then began vegetable farming or "truck gardening" in Roseland. They worked hard, spent little, and saved much; they were able to return the borrowed money to their Uncle Sietje after just one year in the States. My mother's family, on the other hand, had funds to come to the States. Grandpa Anema repaired shoes, delivered milk, and was the undertaker for the town of Minnertsga in Friesland.

Mom and dad completed the sixth grade in schools in the Netherlands. Mom was evidently a very good student, because the schoolmaster asked her father to permit her to go on to higher education. Her father, however, decided it would not be necessary for a girl to pursue additional studies. Had she been a boy, it might have been different.

Mother's trip to the United States was not very pleasant. Her baby sister, a beautiful girl, was given a wrong injection by the doctor during the voyage across the Atlantic and was buried at sea. Then, on Ellis Island, a medical officer examined mother and observed that her eyes seemed to be smaller than normal. He immediately placed the fifteen-year-old girl in an isolated quarantine area. It was several hours before her parents were able to locate her. Later she was given a clean bill of health, and the family was allowed to proceed to Chicago.

Both families gave God thanks for the chance to build new lives in America. Dad and his brothers were grateful that their traveling debt could be paid after only a year of hard work. As their lot in life improved, the three bachelor brothers began courting young women from local churches. All three brothers married within a year of each other.

The brothers worked on the farm with their dad. They were given room and board, but no salary. Everything went into one pot, and as each one married he was given a special lump sum. Dad, being the youngest, had to wait his turn at marriage (and obtaining his marriage money) even though he had courted mom longer than the others had courted their brides. After his older brothers were married it was his turn.

Dad's brothers and the two couples who were my parents' best friends—Darius and Jennie DeVries and Harry and Annie VanBolhuis—were soon blessed with children. My parents were not so blessed. Mom and dad were patient; they had faith and a strong feeling that God was in control of their lives. They prayed and waited. In those days, families in Roseland were often large. Young immigrant couples took seriously the injunction to "be fruitful and multiply." Then, too, the young couples looked to their children for help on farms and for security in later years.

Still my parents waited for a child. Months passed. The babies born to the other couples became toddlers. My parents prayed constantly—one time my mother spent an entire night in tears and prayer. Like Hannah, the mother of the prophet Samuel, my mother vowed, "Should you, oh Lord, be pleased to give us a child, we will give the child to you in special service."

She did not ask the Lord for a baby boy, but she probably thought that if God answered her prayer he would send a male child. The Dutch immigrants held church leaders in very high regard, and my mother probably had in mind a boy who could grow up to become a pastor, teacher, or missionary.

A year later, in 1918, I was born. There was no doubt in the minds of my parents that I was an answer to prayer. They were prepared to dedicate me to a life of special kingdom service. But there seemed to be an unanswered question: "How can we prepare a girl for the Lord's work?" (Remember, this all happened before women even had the right to vote!)

Other questions probably arose. Their vow was pushed to the back of their minds. The pressures of farm life and the concerns of daily living almost caused the vow to be forgotten. God, however, did not forget. The Lord holds us to the vows we make. God remembered my mother's prayer.

As the years passed, my parents were blessed with other children: Harriet, born in 1919, sixteen months after me; Ted, born in 1921; Mildred, born in 1922; and Mel, born in 1926. The Roaring Twenties swirled around us, but like other Dutch immigrants, my parents focused their attention entirely on their home, their children, church, school, and farm work.

For the first five years of my life we only spoke the Friesian language in our home—mainly for the sake of my paternal grandparents, who lived near us. Grandpa and his sons worked the farm together. My parents actually learned English quite soon after arriving in America, as dad mingled with English-speaking factory workers and mom did housework in wealthy suburbs. When I started attending school in 1923 they began speaking English at home.

In 1925, we followed my uncles and moved to Worth, a rural village about six miles southwest of Roseland, beyond the Chicago city limits. My father bought twenty acres of good farmland.

Dad was progressive, always trying new ideas that would improve the farm and thereby help the family. Needing water for his family and home, dad brought in men to dig a well. It was quite a project for those days, as they had to go down 225 feet before they tapped into usable water. The water was rich in minerals and had an odor of sulphur which did not bother us, but did disturb most of our visitors, who described the smell as "rotten eggs." Some went as far as to hold their noses while drinking a cup of water. As I write these lines, at seventy-one years of age, I still have my own teeth, as do my brothers and sisters. I can't help but think that the well water and vegetables from the farm were responsible for the good teeth of our family.

Later dad added an electric generator to run a water pump and to give us electricity for lights. Next came a wonderful new indoor bathroom. Until then, the toilet was outside in the barn not far from the cow's stall, complete with a Montgomery Ward's catalog that wasn't used to order merchandise. It was a long walk from the house to the barn in the cold of winter!

God blessed the farm and prospered us. Dad grew a great variety of vegetables on his twenty acres. He rented other land, too, working up to sixty acres in truck gardening. This meant seeding with a hand instrument and planting small plants by hand, which took much work, time, and patience. Some of the work was done on his knees. He was conscientious and spent long hours every day in the fields.

During the winter months hotbeds were prepared for spring planting. Vegetable seeds were put into the hotbeds as early as January. And there was always maintenance to be done and improvements to be made to the buildings and property. In the spring dad would hitch our horses to the plow, turn over the black dirt, put out the young plants, and pray that God would provide a harvest. Later in the summer, when the vegetables were ready for market, he would load his wagon (or truck, in later years) in the evening. At three o'clock the next morning he would drive to the South Water Street Market near the Chicago River. My brothers often accompanied dad to market. It was a treat for my sisters and me to go with dad to market once a year, to see vegetables unloaded at the warehouse. We also enjoyed stopping at a restaurant for a sweet roll.

My sister Millie worked in the fields more often than Harriet or I. However, there were times Harriet and I would go out to pick beans in season, weed after a rain, trim cauliflower, or bunch asparagus in the shed. Mom would often join us in the shed. There was always plenty of pleasant conversation, laughter, and chatter as we worked together.

We had a Jersey cow for milk, chickens for eggs, a horse for plowing (later replaced by a tractor), and always a dog and some cats.

During winter months the seed man would come to the house and sit with dad in the warm kitchen to discuss next season's crop. We children peered around doorways from adjoining rooms and sometimes sat at the table watching dad choose his seed for the next year. A home visit from a person not connected to the family or church was a rare occurrence.

Dad took seriously God's Word, the Bible. He well knew God's command and promise in Joshua 1:8: "Do not let this Book of the Law depart from your mouth; meditate on it day and night, so that you may be careful to do everything written in it. Then you will be prosperous and successful." Many times I heard him read from Psalm 1: "Blessed is the man...(whose) delight is in the law of the Lord, and on his law he meditates day and night....Whatever he does, he prospers."

Dad would open and close each meal with prayer and we children each had a little prayer to recite after dad's "amen." The oldest child began the litany, and the order descended downward to the youngest. We always ate together, and the Bible was read at the close of each meal. To make sure we were listening, we had to repeat out loud the last word of scripture that dad read during these devotions. Mom and dad also had a time of prayer together before going to sleep. I am certain that a main priority in their prayers, after giving thanks for the day, was the spiritual health and the well-being of their children. I am convinced that these kinds of prayers build strong families and are instrumental in helping children do well in life. The children are kept and led by the hand of God. Parents and grandparents have a great responsibility and wondrous opportunity to pray for their children. The prayers of our parents follow us even today. As a family, we were remarkably blessed. We humbly give God thanks for our parents and for God's continued grace in each of our lives.

Mother kept the house and her children clean and neat. She sewed many of our clothes and darned our socks. She was a talented seamstress. I enjoyed wearing the dresses she made and felt well dressed and comfortable in them, even as a teenager. Mom could be compared with the "wife of noble character" spoken of in Proverbs 31:10-31. Mom always worked hard and, like dad, put in long hours. I have to confess that there were days when I was less interested in a clean house than she was, and I sometimes was not as helpful as I could have been. Today I am grateful for the training she gave me. I appreciate and enjoy keeping a clean, neat home.

Family picture: (top row) Millie, Dad, Mel, and Ted; (bottom row) Mom, Jeanette, and Harriet.

Dad was an elder in the First Reformed Church of Mt. Greenwood for many years. He was respected by the people of the church and took his church duties seriously. The elders were required to oversee the spiritual welfare of the people, visit the sick, discipline straying members of the flock, and visit members regularly in their homes. On Sunday mornings dad would take two of us to the Dutch language service with him. It was good for us to attend worship services, and by taking some of the children with him, dad gave mom a break from child care. Although dad had little formal education, he was a conscientious student of the Bible. The men of the church, including dad, took turns leading the Bible study each week. I remember dad's immediate family and their children coming to celebrate my folks' twentieth wedding anniversary and giving them a set of Matthew Henry's *Commentaries.*

After a Sunday noon dinner prepared by mom, we would attend the English service at two o'clock, which was followed by Sunday school. We would often take friends home for the evening meal or go to their homes and then attend another service in the evening. Later, after the Dutch service had been eliminated, the English services were held in the morning and evening with Sunday school following the morning service.

When we were teenagers, we invited friends to our home after the evening service and "made a joyful noise." And loud it was! Harriet and I played duets on the piano, Ted played the trumpet, and Millie played the piano accordion. We sang the great hymns of faith around the piano in the living room, while my folks sat in the kitchen. Dad and mom also enjoyed the music and fun. Cake and cocoa followed.

The Mt. Greenwood Reformed Church had a special interest in missions, which continues today. One of the highlights of the year was our Fourth of July mission fest for the Chicago area, when all the churches came together for fun and fellowship and to hear visiting missionaries tell about their work. We met from morning until evening in Render Aggen's beautiful grove. Our church's Soli Deo Gloria band, under the direction of Martin Knipper, played hymns, marches, and patriotic music. It was a festive occasion in which the spiritual and physical met. The highlights were the speeches given by missionaries. People were in a generous mood and gave liberally to the work of missions. Program booklets were paid for by advertisements placed by community businessmen.

Everyone, even the children, would look forward to this day of food, fun, and fellowship.

One of the missionaries who made a deep impression on me was Dr. Paul Harrison. Dr. Harrison was a highly respected surgeon and evangelist from our denomination's Arabian mission field. He was recognized internationally for developing new surgical techniques. Originally from Nebraska, Dr. Harrison had received his training in the prestigious Johns Hopkins School of Medicine. Although he could have practiced almost anywhere, he heard a call from the Lord to go to Arabia. Not only was he respected in the medical world, but he was also a spiritual leader and an effective speaker. I was only eight years old when I heard him for the first time. I don't remember any of his message, and I did not know about the power of the Holy Spirit, but the Holy Spirit used Dr. Harrison's message to touch me. When we returned home that evening, I said to my folks, "I would like to be a missionary."

The same week Dr. Harrison visited our home to solicit funds for the Arabian work, as was the custom in those days. Dad asked him, "What would be the best preparation for a girl who wants to be a missionary?" Dr. Harrison's reply was, "By all means, let her become a nurse." At that time, as today, there was a great need for nurses on the mission field.

My parents now remembered the vow they had made years earlier to dedicate their first-born to special kingdom work. They did not tell me about it until years later, when I was on the mission field. But they recognized God's reminder and were embarrassed and sorry they had forgotten. They were amazed that God had not forgotten and that God would hold them to the vow they had made several years before.

In Genesis 28:20-22, Jacob made a vow: "If God will be with me and will watch over me on this journey I am taking and will give me food to eat and clothes to wear so that I return safely to my father's house, then the Lord will be my God. This stone that I have set up as a pillar will be God's house, and of all that you give me I will give you a tenth." In Genesis 31:13 God appeared to Jacob and said: "I am the God of Bethel, where you anointed a pillar and where you made a vow to me. Now leave this land at once and go back to your native land." In Deuteronomy 23:21-23 God says: "If you make a vow to the Lord your God, do not be slow to pay it, for the Lord your God will certainly demand it of you and you will be guilty of sin. But if you refrain from making a vow, you will not be guilty. Whatever your lips utter you must be sure to do, because you

made your vow freely to the Lord your God with your own mouth."
In Ecclesiastes 5:4,5 God says: "When you make a vow to God, do
not delay in fulfilling it. God has no pleasure in fools; fulfill your
vow. It is better not to vow than to make a vow and not fulfill it."

Although they didn't tell me of all this, my parents confessed
their sin to God and renewed their vow, promising to do all they
could to provide me with training for mission service.

The Great Depression of the 1930s hit my family as hard as
everyone else. My parents lost all their savings when the Wiersma
State Bank in Roseland failed. I finished eighth grade in the public
school in Mt. Greenwood in February, 1932. The family planned to
send me to Chicago Christian High School (CCHS), where I could
receive good academic training as well as religious instruction.
This meant paying tuition plus street car fare from Worth to
Englewood, where the school was located. (Should I have attended
a public school, there would have been no cost.)

Despite their financial difficulties, dad and mom held on to their
plan to send me to CCHS. It was a struggle. Each winter dad had
to borrow money to keep up with the tuition payments. During the
summer vegetable season he managed to pay off the winter loans,
only to begin the cycle again the following winter. The family
sacrificed to keep me and my sister Harriet in the Christian
school. Ted was not interested in attending high school after he
finished eighth grade. His decision proved to be a blessing for us,
because he helped dad full-time on the farm. As a family we are
indebted and grateful to Ted for his contribution and help at that
time.

My mother, who appreciated music and enjoyed singing in the
church choir, had the foresight to see that Harriet, Ted, and I were
given music lessons. Later Millie also took lessons. When I was in
the sixth grade in school, my parents sent me to take piano lessons
with Martin Knipper for fifty cents a lesson. Mr. Knipper had lost
a leg in a train accident and was quite crippled, although he never
called attention to his handicap. His problems did not deter him in
any way from using his talents for the Lord.

During the Depression dad always was generous in sharing his
vegetables with others, including the pastor. When relatives and
friends came to visit, they would leave carrying fresh vegetables
with them. The poor were also remembered. One such person did
not even have enough money for street car fare, and he walked six
miles to get food from dad for his family.

At the age of fifteen I made my public confession of faith in Christ Jesus before the people of my church. I found it difficult to stand before the congregation, although I was certain of my commitment to Jesus.

During these years I was painfully shy. In high school I was taller than my classmates and much too thin. I suffered from adolescent acne and stuttered. I also lacked self-confidence. But I did have supportive girl friends. It turned out that my best friends were outside the "inner circle" of girls from the families of large churches that sent children to the Christian school.

While in high school, I took a general science course in preparation for nursing. I was conscientious about my classwork. I often studied late at night after the family had gone to bed. Typing was not part of the curriculum. When my mother suggested that I add an extra course in typing, I fought the idea. I knew that departing from the general plan of study would mean taking the initiative to go to the school administrator who handled schedule changes. As a timid person, that was the last thing I wanted to do. Mother, however, kept pushing me. Finally, with difficulty, I drummed up enough courage to see the administrator and ask him to change my schedule. The goal was accomplished. Looking back, I can see that mother knew typing would help me in my career. This was another leading of the Lord in preparation for kingdom work, although I did not know it at the time.

The night before my senior class picnic, in 1935, my folks didn't have the twenty-five cents necessary for the bus fare from school to the park, the site of the picnic. I was disappointed, but I could see that the money simply wasn't available. I resigned myself to missing out on the fun.

At noon the next day I was surprised to see dad at school. He left work and drove ten miles to Englewood to give me the money. He may have borrowed the quarter. I attended the picnic that afternoon.

I graduated from high school in 1935. I wanted to get a job doing what my peers were doing—housework in wealthy homes. The people who could afford to hire housekeepers lived in Beverly and Morgan Park, about three miles from our home. My parents were not happy about this decision, but I got my way and went to work for three dollars a week. My mother had done this type of work when she first came to the States and did not want her children to do it. I cleaned houses for about a year. Then dad said to me one evening, "Jeanette, shouldn't you be making inquiry into nurse's training?"

I shrugged my shoulders and said, "Dad, I'm not interested."

But his question did not leave me, it kept tugging at my heart. One day I said to my sister Harriet, "Will you go with me to the Roseland Community Hospital?" Harriet agreed to go with me on her afternoon off.

At that time, the Roseland Hospital was the only place I knew that had a nurses' training program. It was relatively close, only six miles from my home.

When we got to the hospital, we inquired at the reception desk and were sent to Miss Bergquist, the director of nurses. She gave me a critical look, asked my age, and said, "You're too thin and too young. You need to be at least nineteen years old."

But then Miss Bergquist relented a bit. She gave me an application and said, "Fill out the form, return it to me, and I will see what I can do for you."

I did what she asked, and was accepted despite my shortcomings. I entered nurses training, by God's grace and leading, in 1936. In those days, beginning students were put on four months of probation, during which time we were observed and the students who couldn't "make the grade" were eliminated. One girl, I recall, had problems early in the school year and had to leave.

One of the harder courses that first semester was anatomy and physiology. We had to learn the names of the bones in the human body, the names of all the muscles, the parts of the circulatory system, and other systems of the body. I studied hard, but at the end of the semester I failed the final examination. Miss Bergquist, however, allowed me to take the exam a second time.

Again I failed. I came back to my roommate that afternoon crying uncontrollably. Other girls came into the room and tried to console me, but to no avail. My fear was that I, too, would be dropped, even though I had done well in the other courses.

Miss Bergquist, however, must have seen potential in the youngest member of the class because she let me have one more chance. This time I passed with a grade of 90. What a relief! How grateful I was! As I reflect on this, I can say, "It was truly the Lord's doing." It was God's will that I continue in nursing. Without his help I could not have done it. I also learned some spiritual lessons about prayer and persistence, both of which I would need later in life.

So I continued. The months sped by and at last the probationary time was over. At that point we had the formal capping ceremony and we "Probies" were allowed to exchange our black shoes and stockings for regular nurse's whites.

I was immersed in my own little world, so I hardly took note of the tension building up in Europe. Germany, led by Adolph Hitler, took over Austria and Czechoslovakia. No one realized it at that time, but the German dictator was also making plans to invade Poland.

Miss Bergquist led us each morning in prayer, scripture, and the singing of a hymn. I was asked to play the piano for the singing. We would then leave the nurses' quarters and walk the three blocks to the hospital with Miss Bergquist bringing up the rear. It was a beautiful sight as the first-, second-, and third-year student nurses, clad in uniforms with caps in hand, walked two by two in orderly fashion up Wentworth Avenue to the hospital.

Miss Bergquist also arranged chorus practice for us one evening each week, at which both the director and pianist were accomplished women. The "All Nurses Glee Club" sang classical and religious numbers and we were popular in the community. Miss Bergquist was an excellent director of nurses, and we learned much from her. Along with the intense studies and the ethics of nursing, she was strong on practical bedside nursing. She was also an officer in the Nurses Association of Illinois. She was loved and respected by all.

During nurses training I was not able to attend worship services regularly, and I would have to say that my spiritual growth was hindered. But the Lord stood faithfully by.

When I did have a Sunday off, I took the street car to my church in Mt. Greenwood and spent the day with the family. Dad would bring me back to the Nurses' Home before the ten o'clock curfew.

One day, Grandma Anema told my folks about a special mission program to be held in her church in Roseland. Dad called to ask if I might be interested in going; he would pick me up at the nurses' dormitory. I agreed to go with him. The speaker was Dr. Mylrea from the Arabian mission. I did not know Dr. Mylrea at that time, and I knew little about the Arabian mission. The Lord spoke to me again during his message. As dad took me back to the nurses' dormitory, I said, "I would like to be a missionary, but I don't know how to go about it."

Dad turned to me in the glow of the automobile lights and said, "Don't worry, Jeanette, the Lord will show you the way."

Since our school of nursing was affiliated with the big Cook County Hospital on the near west side of Chicago, we were assigned to a "contagious unit" and later to pediatrics during our third year of training. After a period of night duty at Cook County, we were given twenty-four hours off. During one stint of this night duty in January, I made plans to use my day off to go ice skating near our home. After working all night I caught the first street car toward Mt. Greenwood in the morning. It was a slow ride, about an hour and a half, as the vehicle stopped at almost every intersection.

When I got off at the end of the line between the two Mt. Greenwood cemeteries, I was met by a group of women: my mother, Mrs. Aggen, Mrs. Toppen, Mrs. Beukinga, and several other women of the church. "We're going to Moody Bible Institute," they said cheerfully. "It's Founder's Week and they have some fine speakers today. How about joining us?" It was obvious that they had been waiting for me.

This was the last thing I wanted to do! I had worked all night and already had spent an hour and a half in the street car, and I wanted to go ice skating. But I didn't dare refuse these fine, respectable ladies either. Mom and the others encouraged me to join them. I know they saw my hesitancy. Finally, out of respect for them and in obedience to mom, I consented to go with them.

So back into the street car I went. Later I was to know that God was in it, but at the time I was angry and upset. I sat by myself peering out the window, not speaking or conversing with anyone! It was a two-hour ride into the city to the Moody Bible Institute, so I had a long time to pout and ponder this unfortunate turn of events.

These good ladies had chosen Wednesday, "Missionary Day," which featured many missionary speakers. I sat with the women in the auditorium, listening to speaker after speaker and feeling more miserable as time went on and missionary after missionary spoke.

But then my feelings changed. I wasn't feeling sorry for myself any more. The Holy Spirit was getting to me, speaking to me, and I was uncomfortable and uneasy.

As the minutes ticked by and tears began to flow, I became more and more uncomfortable. Finally I said, "Lord, I'll go where you want me to go. I'll do what you want me to do. I'll be what you want me to be."

A beautiful peace swept over me and I felt joy within my spirit. It was to be a long time before I shared these feelings and this experience with anyone. I kept these things inside of me, and

when we returned to the farm late in the afternoon, no one knew
what had happened except the Lord and me.

As months passed I remembered that promise, but I was in no
hurry to act on it. After graduating from nurse's training at age
twenty-one, I donned my white uniform. I was now salaried and
worked as a graduate nurse. Six months later, along with many
others, I passed the grueling State Board examinations.

Jeanette in nursing uniform

During the two years that ensued as a graduate nurse, I worked as a supervisor in the Roseland hospital and later in pediatrics in the Little Company of Mary Hospital in Evergreen Park. I also did some private duty nursing, which paid very well.

By now there was a new director of nurses at Roseland Community Hospital, Miss Putnam. Miss Putnam placed me in supervisory positions. I worked the 7 a.m. shift two days, the 3 to 11 p.m. shift two days, and the 11 to 7 a.m shift two days every week. While working the morning shift I was supervisor of the surgical floor; during the evening and night shifts I was superintendent of the entire hospital. I didn't mind the odd hours. One night there was an emergency appendectomy on a child. I prepared the child for surgery, awakened the "on-call" surgical staff, and helped prepare the theater for surgery before Dr. Pape arrived. He seemed to be pleased that all was in readiness for him to begin surgery and said to me later, "Miss Boersma, you must always remain with us in this hospital."

I received a good salary of $60 per month; I had matured since the awkward high school years, and I found that my social life was improving. There were picnics, boyfriends, shopping trips, church group outings, and work at my dad's farm stand on my time off.

Summers we would go to Lake Winona, Indiana, to a Bible camp. One time dad took mom, Mrs. Heersma, our Sunday school teacher, and the entire Sunday school class of girls to spend the week. Besides swimming, bicycling, playing shuffleboard, and hiking, we attended various meetings and heard some fine speakers. Traditionally, there was a "hilltop service" in the evening, when the sun would be low in the sky, shining across the lake. These services were always an inspiration. They were memorable experiences for me.

Although I was not interested in learning to drive, dad taught me to drive our '37 Chevy in 1941. In later years I knew this, too, was of the Lord.

Grandma was getting older and dad saw that it was increasingly difficult for her to support herself. She had been widowed in 1922 and supported herself for many years by selling coffee, tea, and Hofstra's Dutch Bakery Goods from a wagon which she pulled up and down the streets of Roseland. She supplemented that income by boarding people in empty rooms in her house. Dad convinced her to leave her quaint and strenuous business, and she came to live with us.

We loved having grandma with us on the farm in Worth. She soon became an integral part of our family. (Since I was named for her, I had a special place in her heart.) Grandma loved helping to prepare food, working with mom. Her faith was deep and she prayed constantly. I remember that she attended almost every funeral in town, because she sensed the Holy Spirit's presence, the victory of death in the life of a Christian, the fellowship, and the comfort a Christian funeral brought.

The Depression years slipped behind us. The Wiersma State Bank returned some of the money my parents lost when it failed. My girlfriends were forming attachments with young men. Many of the young women had their sights set on getting married, settling into homes, and having babies. The young men were getting stable jobs in the improving economy. War had started in Europe, and the prospect of marching off to war was very real for the men. As war clouds gathered, some couples accelerated their wedding plans. It was an exciting, fast-paced time.

While all this was going on, my two sisters married young men from the church who were accepted and approved by my parents.

Street car was the mode of travel for us in those days. And I traveled by street car between Worth and Roseland at all hours, day and night. At the end of the car line was a three-block walk to my home, which skirted St. Casimer's Lithuanian Cemetery. One night at midnight a man in a red roadster drove up alongside of me at the loneliest part of the walk. "Can I give you a ride?" he asked. I was scared but tried not to show it. I calmly explained to him that I didn't have far to walk. He wouldn't leave me and continued to try to persuade me to take a ride. I had thoughts of running back to the Aggen home, two blocks east, but decided that would not be helpful. I had better stay on course. Still the man stayed close to me. My heart pounded, but deep inside I felt calm. I tried to keep up a conversation with him and he continued to try to get me into the car.

We finally reached my home beyond the cemetery and I cut behind his car, running to the back door of our darkened house. Everyone was sound asleep. I slid through the door and locked it behind me, then, without turning on the room lights, peered through the window. He was still out there, probably waiting to see if the home was really mine, or if I was just hiding behind it. I breathed a prayer of thanks. I strongly felt God's protection and guardian angels surrounding me.

I told dad and mom about it the next morning. From that night on, each time I worked the 3 to 11 shift, dad waited at the end of the line for me.

Such incidents aside, I should have been enjoying life. I was healthy, well paid, and getting along well with my supervisors and those under me. Doctors sought me out to help change dressings and handle other care for their patients. I was responsible for emergencies at night, supervising the student nurses, and handling set-up in the operating room, while the student nurses scrubbed and assisted the surgeon. Twice a week I supervised the medical and surgical floors. Later I also worked in the pediatric unit in the Catholic hospital near my home.

But after a year and a half in my chosen profession I was not happy.

It is hard to describe my feeling at that time. It was physical, like a heaviness in my chest. At the time, I did not see a spiritual dimension to the feeling. I was restless and couldn't feel peace within. Along with the affluence, prestige, good salary, and position, I had forgotten promises to the Lord to "go where you want me to go."

The feeling would not leave me. I tried to discuss this with a girlfriend. She was sympathetic but could not understand what I was going through. I didn't speak of it with my parents, although I should have. By the spring of 1941, I knew it was time for me to do something. I wasn't happy.

I began to realize that everything in my life up to that time seemed to point toward missionary work. The Lord was telling me to move forward.

This realization did not come in a flash of insight, but rather during months of struggling with that gnawing sense that I needed to do something different. I kept it all inside of me.

I still did not know about my mother's vow. But I did remember the promise I made to the Lord during Moody Founder's Week. I was finally driven to see my pastor, the Rev. Everett DeWitt. I told him everything, including a description of the heavy sensation in my chest. The pastor recognized my problem to be spiritual in nature. He thought about it and then suggested that I seriously consider Bible training.

The only Bible school I knew was the Moody Bible Institute in Chicago, so I applied there for admittance in the fall of 1941. Weeks went by. In August I still had not heard about my application, so I called the registrar's office. They told me that I was too late to enter in the fall, but they would find a place for me when the winter semester began. By then the feeling of heaviness and unhappiness was so great that I felt I couldn't live with it for another six months. I hung up the phone, quietly praying, "God, I cannot go on like this any longer. I just can't wait that long!"

On a warm evening a few days later I was helping dad at his farm stand, selling vegetables to people driving down Crawford Avenue. Pastor DeWitt pulled up in his car. He came right to the point.

"Jeanette, my niece, Cornelia DeWitt, from Kansas is visiting me en route to the Reformed Bible Institute in Grand Rapids. Why don't you consider attending RBI?"

The next day I wrote to the school. Miss Johanna Timmer, RBI's first director, responded immediately. There was one bed left in the dormitory, and if I would enroll as soon as possible, I could start classes the following week.

I applied and was accepted. I then gave notice of my resignation to the director of nurses. The doctors and the nursing director tried to talk me out of attending Bible school and even offered me a pay raise. Several tried to dissuade me by saying there was a mission field at home in the hospital.

But I knew I was doing what God wanted me to do. I put away my starched hat and uniform and packed my bags. My parents drove Cornelia and me to Grand Rapids the following week.

Amazingly, the moment I walked through the door of RBI's two-story, Victorian building the heaviness left my chest. What a relief! Joy filled my heart, as I now knew that this was God's will for me. It was one of the happiest moments of my life. *This* was where God wanted me to be!

I threw myself into the school work. RBI was still in its infancy—beginning its third year of operation—and we students felt as if we were still breaking new ground. We faithfully set aside time for prayer, devotions, community service, chapel attendance, and study. Miss Timmer was very happy to learn that I was a nurse. Having a nurse available for health care, when someone in the dormitory was sick and she needed advice, was important to her. She was thrilled that God gave her a qualified nurse in each of the first three classes at RBI.

As part of our training we were assigned districts in which to do house-to-house evangelism. After each visit we had to write observation reports of our experiences. I worked in an Afro-American district with an RBI upperclassman. We enjoyed the challenge and I grew to love the people in the black community. I taught a Bible class in Children's Memorial Hospital; later I taught Bible in a mission. We continued our practical assignments along with the class work during the three years we attended RBI.

There were men in our class at first, but we later lost them to military service. During the war years, the school was made up mainly of women. Students could develop leadership skills in a congenial atmosphere. This was especially good for me, since leadership was an area that later became an important part of my life. I was elected class secretary, student council treasurer, and student body president in my final year. I served as editor of the school's first yearbook and was the school pianist during my last two years.

Miss Timmer, who helped found the school, was administrator and teacher for three years, until Dr. Dick Walters became RBI's president. The two of them worked together to bring in speakers to stimulate our thinking about God's Word and missions. Miss Nelle Mierop served as the music director. She directed our chorus, gave voice lessons, taught music appreciation and child pedagogy. The Misses Timmer and Mierop lived together. Besides complementing each other as faculty members, they were good friends. Their home was always open; they were an inspiration and a blessing to each of us.

I was especially close to three classmates: the four of us sat along a wall in class and were seen together so often that we were called the "Four Musketeers." Cornelia, my pastor's niece (later Cornelia Vander Ploeg), went on in later years to teach in the Zuni, New Mexico, mission school and later in Holland Christian High School. Mary Kuik went on to serve as a teacher for many years among the Navajo people in Rehoboth, New Mexico, not far from Zuni. Margaret Dykstra served for many years in Nigeria, teaching and doing evangelistic work.

The happy years at RBI passed too swiftly. I have warm thoughts of the school and am glad that it has prospered over the years.

As my final year began, the question looming in my mind was, "Where will I serve when I graduate?"

I began writing the Reformed church mission board in New York in January, 1944. I was ready for any field that was open. I awaited their response.

The reply came back. It was the mission board's policy, the letter stated, that an overseas missionary had to be a college graduate. Strictly speaking, RBI was not a college, and my education had not included college work. I was disappointed but not upset. I knew that the Lord had a place for me. So I left the frustration in God's hands and continued my studies at RBI.

A home missions job in the Chicago area became a possibility for me, but I didn't feel a strong leading toward it. In March, 1944, I received another letter from the Reformed church mission board secretary Miss Ruth Ransom. The board wanted to interview me during my spring break. They suggested a meeting at the Drake Hotel in Chicago.

The interview went well, by the grace of God. On April 13, 1944, I was appointed to the Reformed church mission. Then came a specific assignment. The mission board told me that there was a great need for nurses in Arabia. "Would I go there?"

God's leading was evident again. Already, God had spoken to me through missionaries from Arabia. I immediately saw that he was leading in that direction. But until the board selected that field in April, 1944, it wasn't final.

Then I learned that I would be one of six new missionaries appointed for work in Arabia. During the Depression, the ranks of Arabian missionaries had diminished. No new missionaries had been appointed, and some veteran missionaries returned to America due to financial problems in the mission. Those returnees were now going back to the field, along with the six first-timers, to swell the ranks of the mission force. Dr. Gerald and Rose Nykerk and Dr. Lewis and Dorothy Scudder went out in the early 1940s, and in 1944 there were Harry Almond, Jay Kapenga, Ed and Ruth Luidens, Harriet Wanrooy, and myself.

June, 1944, was an eventful month. For me, the month brought my long-awaited graduation from RBI. For most of the world, it was the month of the long-awaited Allied invasion of northern Europe.

In a sense, my brother Ted was helping give all of us the freedom to consider mission work and world travel. He was a turret gunner on a B-17 Flying Fortress, making flight after flight into Nazi Germany to attack military targets. We knew little about his efforts, and Ted couldn't write to tell us that he flew in one of the lead planes that went on almost every bombing run. About the time I graduated, Ted was running up twenty, twenty-five, and then thirty missions. He heard that he would be relieved from bomber duty after thirty-five missions.

Meanwhile, I was invited to a meeting of the mission board in New York, where I was formally welcomed with the others as one of the denomination's missionaries to Arabia. Three of us were

Ted, 1943

commissioned at General Synod that June in a gathering in the beautiful mountains of Buck Hills Falls, Pennsylvania. Ed and Ruth Luidens had been commissioned the year before. That summer the board sent me to a special course in rural missions in Asheville, North Carolina. The wheels were set in motion for an October departure to Arabia.

Ten weeks before I was scheduled to leave, my brother Ted was shot down and taken prisoner by the Germans. We didn't learn the details for many months, but later the story unfolded. When Ted's bomber was returning from its thirty-fourth mission, three of the

four engines went out, one by one. By the time they reached
Belgium, they had dropped so far behind the formation that the
plane was isolated and under attack by German fighter planes. The
crewmen fought for their lives. When they realized that they
would not make it over the English Channel, the men took a vote
and decided to abandon the plane. The first two and last two that
parachuted from the plane landed in forest areas and escaped
capture. The rest, including Ted, were captured.

At the beginning of his imprisonment, Ted spent weeks in
interrogation and solitary confinement in Leige, Belgium. He was
half-starved and beaten with rifle butts for refusing to give more
than his name, rank, and serial number. Later he was sent to a
prisoner of war camp in northeastern Germany near the Polish
border. For months he was locked in a room with twenty-four
other men, sleeping in a paper sack on the floor*. All this we
found out months later.

On September 7 I was at home in Worth, helping my family and
making general preparations for the trip to Arabia. I remember
the day very well. There was a knock on our front door, which was
unusual because on the farm all our friends and family members
used the back door. Mom and grandma Anema were working in
the back, so I answered the door.

A young woman from the Red Cross was standing at the door
holding a telegram. "Is this the Boersma residence?" she asked.

"Yes," I replied.

"I'm afraid I have some bad news for you," she said. "Ted
Boersma has just been listed by the Air Force as missing in action.
We don't have any other information at this time."

I broke down in tears. The young woman asked if I needed help
and I said, "No, my mother and grandmother are out back. I'll be
OK."

Mom had heard the knock on the door and wondered why I
lingered so long. She called out to me to ask who was at the door.
There were two bedrooms on the ground floor of the house. First I
went into my folks' bedroom, which happened to be the nearest, to
get my composure before having to give this news to my mother
and grandmother. I then went into grandma Anema's bedroom.

---

* Portions of the story of Ted's capture were adapted from
material written by Christin Boersma, Ted's granddaughter, in
1989. At the time of the writing, Christin was a junior at Chicago
Christian High School.

When I finally reached the kitchen, where grandma and mom were preparing dinner, I told them we had received a telegram from the Air Force that Ted was missing in action.

Mom and grandma Anema took it hard. They asked me to go to the field and tell dad. I walked out slowly to dad. Then I broke the news to him. Dad's response was amazingly swift and confident. "Ted will be OK. He'll be back."

Some time later, when I reread Psalm 112:7,8, I was reminded of dad and recognized his source of faith in God. In those verses we read, "He will have no fear of bad news; his heart is steadfast, trusting in the Lord. His heart is secure, he will have no fear; in the end he will look in triumph on his foes."

The Rev. DeWitt met with our family for prayer that evening. Relatives and friends, including Grace Togtman, Ted's fiancee, also came over. After forty-five years, as I reflect on the incident, I still marvel at the faith of my father that day.

One week before my departure my mother entered the hospital for major surgery. She had needed the surgery for some time and decided to go through with it before I left, so I could care for her. The surgery was complex and we were concerned. I spent many hours in the hospital with her as her special nurse.

In the quiet hospital room I thought long about the two parents I was about to leave and how much I loved them.

The day came for me to leave. I finished packing. Brother Mel put my hand luggage in the trunk of the car. (Larger pieces of luggage had already been sent ahead to Keatings Shipping in New York City.) Lastly, I went into the kitchen to say farewell to grandma Anema. She was tired. Instead of standing up to see me off, she remained sitting at the table. I put my arms around her and kissed her. Only the Lord knew that within ten days she would be in heaven.

Dad couldn't leave mom's bedside in the hospital, so Mel drove me to the Englewood train station on the 17th of October. When we arrived at the station, to my surprise I found Margaret Dykstra, one of the Four Musketeers, waiting to see me off. Margaret was studying in Chicago at the time. We talked until the last moment, then Margaret prayed for traveling mercies and for God's blessing on our future endeavors. Then we said farewell.

I boarded the train and settled into the seat. After a few miles the excitement wore off. I was a forlorn, lonely young woman as the train headed for New York City.

II
Into the Arab World

*After this the Lord appointed seventy-two others
and sent them...ahead of him to every town
and place where he was about to go.*
Luke 10:1

*When I was a child, I talked like a child, I
thought like a child, I reasoned like a child.
When I became a man, I put childish ways
behind me.*
1 Corinthians 13:11

The Reformed church's Arabian mission was approaching its fifty-fifth anniversary when I sailed from Philadelphia. One of the two missionaries who was instrumental in opening up the field, Dr. Samuel Zwemer, was still speaking and writing at that time.

The Lord brought together Zwemer and James Cantine, along with fellow student Philip Phelps, at New Brunswick Theological Seminary in the 1880s. There they met Professor John G. Lansing, whose parents had been missionaries in Egypt. In one of Dr. Lansing's classes the three students came to realize that Christian missions had long neglected the Arab world. The power of the Holy Spirit touched them with a challenge to reach Muslims for Christ.

At that time the Reformed denomination had heavy commitments in China, Japan, and India, and it could not take on another field. The young men visited churches and friends to organize financial backing through an independent board of supporters. A legacy in the amount of $5,000 from Miss Catherine Crane Halstead became the spark that started the fire.

Then the young men met with Professor Lansing in the Catskills and developed a plan. On October 1, 1889, Cantine was ordained and sailed for the Middle East that same month. Zwemer was ordained and followed in 1890. Phelps was unable to enter foreign missions and took a pastorate in the United States.

The Revs. Zwemer and Cantine started in Lebanon and then worked their way south and east, around the southern part of the Arabian Peninsula. At one point Zwemer was joined in a southbound boat by Bishop Thomas Valpy French, a gentleman representing the Church of England. Bishop French had served as a missionary in India for forty years, had retired, and then had gone to Arabia to explore the possibilities of opening a new mission field there. Bishop French knew eleven languages, including Arabic.

Zwemer and Cantine's first stop on the peninsula was in Aden, where a young Scottish Presbyterian missionary, Ian Keith Falconer, had organized a little mission church. Falconer had died three years earlier. While exploring the area, Zwemer and Cantine were weakened by bouts of malaria and ran out of cash. "We prayed and fasted for a day," Zwemer said, "and the answer came in a long-overdue remittance for salaries."

From Aden, they continued in a coastal boat to Muscat, where they learned that their new Anglican friend, Bishop French, had died from heatstroke while traveling in an open boat.

Cantine traveled to the island nation of Bahrain and then went up the Persian Gulf to Basrah, in what is now Iraq. In Basrah he was greeted warmly by an English physician, Dr. Eustace, who opened his house to the young missionary and introduced him to Arabs and English-speaking residents of the city. Cantine had not been in the city long when Dr. Eustace invited him along on a 500-mile cruise up the Tigris River to Baghdad. Along the way Cantine was introduced to people of the area. He also passed Amarah, which was later to become an important mission station for the Reformed denomination.

As the two men settled down in the Persian Gulf area, an agent of the British and Foreign Bible Society gave the Arabian mission responsibility for scripture distribution. Through God's grace, the men had a foothold. Then they began calling for additional missionaries.

Satan did not overlook the establishment of the new mission work. Two of the next members of the mission team, men of great promise who could have been pillars of strength, had their lives cut short by death.

A young Syrian, Kamil Abd el Messiah, came to know the Lord while studying in Beirut. He was disowned by his Muslim father and came to Basrah, where he was the first Arab Christian to join the mission. He was a good teacher and preacher, and the missionaries had high hopes for his future. Within six months, however, he became ill and died. Poison was strongly suspected as the cause of his death.

The Rev. Peter Zwemer, Samuel's brother, came to the mission in 1892. He was a talented young person who quickly made friends among the Arabs, even before he learned the language fully. Muscat, the capital of Oman, caught his attention, and in 1894 he began working there. In 1896, two boats full of slave boys were captured by the British Navy off the coast of Oman. These freed slave boys were destined to be raised in government camps in India, until Peter took them and began the "School for Rescued Slaves" in Muscat.

Peter became ill with a serious case of malaria a couple of years after founding the school and became too sick to stay in Oman. He returned to the States and died not long after. His death was a blow to the new mission effort, but the Lord helped the young missionaries continue.

When the first mission station (not including the Basrah headquarters) was established in Bahrain, our missionaries were able to take occasional "tours" to the interior parts of Arabia. The first mission hospital was built in Bahrain in 1903, a chapel and school were started in Basrah, and Kuwait became a mission station in 1910. The status of Amarah, a hundred miles north of Basrah, was raised from "outpost" to "station" in 1910. Bible distribution by colporteurs (traveling Bible sellers) also became an important part of the Amarah work. The Rev. James Enoch Moerdyk established a home for lepers in Amarah in his latter years of service.

In 1900 there were six men and three women on the mission field, by 1910 there were twenty-six people, and by 1930 there were forty. The Reformed Church in America eventually took over full responsibility for the Arabian Mission, running things capably from offices first at 156 Fifth Avenue, and then 475 Riverside Drive, in New York City.

One of the missionaries who joined the Arabian mission about the time my parents came to the United States was Dr. John Van Ess, whose father, the Rev. Balster Van Ess, was the minister of the First Reformed Church of Roseland for many years. My parents and grandparents knew the Van Ess family and always spoke of them with great respect. Dr. Van Ess had the ability to learn languages easily, and his talent with languages helped him associate with many kinds of people throughout the Middle East. He was personally acquainted with Iraq's King Faisal I and Colonel T.E. Lawrence ("Lawrence of Arabia").

George and Christine Gosselink, who served in Basrah for many years, remembered a special occasion in Basrah when King Faisal addressed a large, English-speaking audience. Van Ess interpreted for the king. King Faisal was not a good speaker, and Van Ess added many touches of his own to the interpretation to help the king get his message across. Part-way through the speech, the king grew flustered and said quietly, "Van Ess, tell them about the point I forgot to make."

"I already did, Your Majesty," Van Ess whispered back.

Van Ess and all the other missionaries were saddened by the death of King Faisal in 1933. His son, who ruled the next six years, was more of a playboy than a national leader. Oil money began flowing into Iraq in 1934, so he had plenty of money to play with.

As events in Europe moved toward the Second World War, nationalists took control of Iraq's government and decided not to cooperate with Great Britain and the Allies. In 1941 Iraq's government went pro-German. Just before America entered the war, the British sent soldiers into Basrah and fought for control of the city and the country. They won, and during the rest of the war, the British were there to protect oil supplies and transportation routes through the Gulf and up to the Russian Front. Twenty thousand British troops were stationed at Basrah. Years later, when I came to Iraq, British soldiers were still stationed near Basrah, Amarah, and other cities.

World War II had not yet ended when I sailed from Philadelphia on the S.S. *Colonial*, although the tide of war had turned against the Germans. Paris had been liberated, the Russians were pushing toward Berlin, and the Netherlands had been freed from Nazi rule. Admiral Nimitz and General MacArthur were heading for Japan. The mission board felt that safe passage across the Atlantic was possible, although we all knew there was a possibility of encountering German submarines.

Portugal was neutral during the war, and since the S.S. *Colonial* was of Portuguese registry, we felt relatively safe. On the ship I was accompanied by Harriet Wanrooy, a tall, attractive young lady from the Garfield Park Reformed Church in Grand Rapids, Michigan. Harriet served for five years as a "short-term" nurse in Bahrain. After her service she married a British young man and eventually settled in England. Theirs was a happy marriage and was blessed with children. (Harriet and I still keep in touch every Christmas.) Also representing the Arabian mission on the ship were the Rev. Edwin Luidens and his wife, the former Ruth Stegenga. Ed was the son of a Reformed church minister and had grown up on the East Coast. Ruth, also the daughter of a Reformed church minister, came from North Bergen, New Jersey. (Ruth's brother, Preston, later became president of Northwestern College in Orange City.) They had been married a year earlier and were going to the Arabian mission field for the first time. The four of us got along very well and became good friends.

I passed through customs with about thirty cubic feet of baggage, well under the maximum allowed by the passenger liner. Most of my material was checked through to Basrah, but I kept two pieces of luggage with me. Harriet and I shared a small stateroom with two other young women, Gertrud Nyce and Marie Hodges, who were on their way to India. We found out later that there were seventy missionaries on the ship—the same number of disciples that Jesus once sent out during his ministry. Of that number, twenty-two were first-termers like myself and my companions.

Before leaving, we were told to dispose of personal papers that contained family information, citizenship material, or facts about government or military matters. I promised the officer that I would send my papers back to my parents in the first package of mail, and that seemed to satisfy him.

The crossing was slow. The ocean was rough and I had my first bout of seasickness. Harriet lost her breakfast the first morning. I tried to fight off the sickness by sitting on deck in the fresh air and focusing my mind on other things besides my quivering stomach. On one of the roughest days, only about half of the passengers showed up for the noon meal. That night we were told that a hurricane might be approaching and the crew locked the portholes and hatches. The small stateroom became uncomfortable—very stuffy and warm.

A day later the danger passed and we gave God thanks. Then the temperature rose, the wind dropped, and the sky cleared. The ocean grew calm. We got our "sea legs" and began to enjoy watching the rainbows in the waves at the prow of the ship and the many hues of blue in the water and sky. "It seems as if all the bluing in the world were dumped into this ocean," I wrote my mother, knowing that she would appreciate the metaphor. Flying fish could occasionally be seen skimming above the waves, and dolphins played in the distance.

At night we could look directly into the black depths of space, illumined by the bright, shining, starry hosts above. I remember listening to Marie Hodges quoting from memory Psalm 19: "The heavens declare the glory of God; the firmament showeth his handiwork. Day unto day uttereth speech, and night unto night showeth knowledge" (KJV). It was truly awesome, depicting God's greatness.

We became acquainted with some of the other missionaries and found out they were from all kinds of backgrounds: Mennonite, Congregational, Presbyterian, Methodist, Baptist, and Lutheran, along with representatives of the Scandinavian Mission Alliance and Sudan Interior Mission. Every day we gathered for fellowship, Bible study, and prayer. After the evening meal we sang hymns. I had the opportunity to play the piano at these times. On Sunday mornings all the missionaries met for an hour of worship, which was conducted much like our worship services at home. I remember that Ed took one of these services. There were several ministers in the group, and each took turns leading us in worship.

I wrote many letters during the voyage and in Lisbon, but it was weeks before I could post them or receive the first packet of mail from my family. My brother Ted, as far as I knew, was in his third month as a prisoner of war. I fervently prayed that my mother was recovering from her surgery. My grandmother, too, was ill. At the time I didn't realize how serious her condition was.

We listened to news about the war through Portuguese broadcasts monitored and transcribed by the ship's crew. One of our American missionaries translated the typed bulletins every day, so we were able to keep abreast of most of the major developments in the war. We prayed for safety from lurking submarines. We also hoped and prayed that victory would come soon, and we feared that the final assault on Japan would take hundreds of thousands of American lives. I worried that Ted, if he were released in good health, would find himself in the Pacific theater of the war during an invasion of Japan.

The four of us studied Arabic during the voyage. Ed and Ruth had already taken a year of it at Harvard University, and they tutored Harriet and me. Arabic is a difficult but beautiful language, referred to by Muslims as "the language of angels." As I began to study the language, I thought I would never learn it. I shed tears of frustration over my seemingly slow progress.

Our ship stopped briefly at the Madeira Islands, about 800 miles west of Morocco. From quite a distance, we could see white specks against the dark rocks rising from the seashore. As we grew closer, we saw white and yellow houses, some of them extending several stories up and down the volcanic cliffs, all capped by bright orange roofs.

When our ship entered the harbor, we were greeted by boys in small canoes who were eager to dive for coins. The boys were a bit choosy, we noticed. They wouldn't dive for copper pennies, but they were in the water immediately when they saw silver. Then rowboats with enterprising businessmen came to the ship. They were not allowed on deck, so they did business by way of baskets lowered from the railing by passengers. Madeira was famous for its lace. Passengers on the ship hoisted up dozens of table cloths, doilies, scarves, and luncheon cloths. They started asking eighty-five dollars per piece, but even when the prices were haggled down to half of that amount, they were still too expensive for most of us. Eventually I did purchase some smaller items.

We left the islands at night. As the ship steamed out into the open sea, we looked back at the cliffs dotted with lights while God's constellations rose in the black sky. The ocean again grew rough and many passengers were ill. About 300 new passengers had joined us at the Madeira Islands, and they were in the same shape we had been in when we first hit rough water after leaving Philadelphia.

I continued to worry about Ted. My family was in contact with the government, but the lack of news bothered me. Someone suggested that my family should approach the Red Cross aggressively, asking for information. Someone else suggested that a Farm Bureau office would be able to get my family into better channels of information. I noted these bits of information on an unsent letter and continued to pray fervently for my brother's safety and return.

We docked in Lisbon, Portugal, November 3, 1944. We were greeted on the dock by American missionaries, some of whom I had met in July at the mission course in North Carolina. They had been waiting as long as three months for passage out of Lisbon to their mission fields.

We went to our hotel and were thankful to learn that we were assigned to the penthouse rooms. The manager explained that the hotel was full and he would provide the choicest rooms for us at the regular price. We enjoyed being served breakfast in bed (consisting of freshly baked hard rolls, jam, and delicious hot chocolate) at no extra charge! As soon as we were settled in the hotel, we walked over to the American consulate to see if there were letters for us. There were none.

Anxious to get to the mission field, we waited at the hotel day after day. At first we thought we might catch a boat to India via the Cape of Good Hope, and then go from India to the Persian Gulf, which would have taken months. Then someone said it might be possible to take a military plane across the Mediterranean. Days passed.

With extra time on our hands, we had opportunities to see points of interest around Lisbon. The famous old city had narrow streets that wound through steep hills, completely unlike the long, straight roads in Chicago. Quaint tea shops that sold delicious petite Portuguese pastries lined these streets. We visited these shops for tea in the afternoon. The city was crowded with people from many different countries. Portugal was neutral during the war, and the Germans were very visible, along with Americans and British. We passed uniformed German soldiers on the street, in the hallways of our hotel, and ate near them in the restaurants.

We worshiped in a little Scottish Presbyterian church on Sunday mornings and in a Bible church late in the afternoon. We were struck by the fact that the Scottish church hymnal contained words only, no music. Most of the tunes of the hymns were unfamiliar to us.

One of the first sermons I heard in the Bible church was taken from 1 Corinthians 13. The thrust of the message was to put away childish things; to decide upon what to keep and what to discard as one grows spiritually. I was deeply touched by the message. My formative years, I was beginning to realize, had been spent in just a tiny part of God's great world among just one group of his people. There was so much more to see and learn!

"How little I know," I wrote to my parents in one letter. "I wish I had read more and taken four years of college."

Many of us are aware of shortcomings in our schooling, but not as many are aware of shortcomings in our spiritual development. I didn't realize fully that I would be entering a life-long struggle to grow *spiritually*.

As the weeks passed, the army of waiting missionaries swelled to 500. Every day one of us would walk to the American consulate to inquire about mail. Ed, Ruth, Harriet, and I decided that whoever received the first letter would treat the others to afternoon tea.

Finally the day came. When we first checked at the consulate, the clerk told us that there was no mail. Later in the day there was a knock on the door of my room and there they were, three letters hand-delivered to my room! I tore open the letters and read rapidly.

There was some shocking news. Grandma Anema had passed away ten days after my departure. She had probably been suffering from the early stages of pneumonia when I left. I remembered that she didn't stand to embrace me but had remained seated when we said goodbye. Apparently she was not well at the time but did not tell me. My mother was recovering from her surgery, but she mentioned problems with her nursing care. How I wished I could have continued to care for her! The whereabouts of Ted was still a mystery. I hoped and prayed that he was safe. My sister Millie's husband, John, was safe and sound, serving in India and Borneo.

How wonderful it was to hear from my family, but how sad some of the news! I had a dream one night that Ted and John came home and joined the family in a big celebration.

On December 6, our marching orders came. Ed, Ruth, Harriet, and I were scheduled to fly across the Mediterranean. It seemed as if all of the other 500 missionaries were still waiting to leave Lisbon. (One missionary who left for India about that time had to take a three-month ocean journey around Africa.)

Ed Luidens

Our early departure was the work of the Lord, who used Ed Luidens as his instrument. Ed had begun making daily visits to the British Army office suggesting we go "lendlease," on a plane bound for Egypt or Iraq. Ed had the gifts of tact, diplomacy, and patience as he approached the officers each day like the persistent widow mentioned in Luke 18. He emphasized that Harriet and I were nurses who were desperately needed for the work in the Gulf. Ed didn't seem to be awed by high ranking military men. After some telegrams were sent between Lisbon, New York, and Washington, D.C., Harriet and I were told to catch a Dutch plane to Gibraltar and a British plane from there to Cairo, Egypt. Ruth and Ed would travel the same day on a separate flight and meet us in Cairo.

We packed our bags the next day and caught a Royal Dutch Airlines plane. When boarding, I tried to speak to one of the crewmen in Dutch, but he would respond only in English. After a flight of about 200 miles, we landed and were taken to an old hotel at the foot of the great Rock of Gibraltar. I was told not to put anything about the rock in my letters, as military censors would cut out such references. We heard that the rock was honeycombed with tunnels, caves, and gun emplacements. I remember the well-kept gardens, flowers, and lawns around some the buildings.

Before sunrise the following morning we were awakened by a bugler playing reveille. We dressed hurriedly, and at six o'clock a representative of British Airlines knocked. In the pre-dawn darkness we followed his flashlight beam to a waiting car. Then, to our surprise, we were driven to the edge of the sea rather than to the airfield where we had landed the previous night. A young British soldier gave us tickets and helped us take our bags to the end of a dock. There we were met by a speedboat.

As pink dawn shone across the Mediterranean, we saw our plane. It was a B.O.A.C. "Flying Boat," rocking gently on the waves. A door was opened under one of the four huge engines and we were helped up into the passenger compartment, which was like a cozy parlor in a curved metal room. Harriet and I sat in two cushioned seats separated by a little table. Across from us there were two cushioned couches separated by a longer table.

At seven-thirty the motors were started and a roaring sound filled the cabin. We strapped ourselves in the seats and listened to the water slapping against the hull as the plane circled into its take-off position. The roar of the engines grew louder. The plane began cutting through the waves. Then the water sounds were gone and we were airborne. The plane headed for the northern coast of Africa and we flew over land for the first part of the twelve-hour journey.

Crew members came down into the cabin from time to time and chatted pleasantly with us. They explained how to use the life vests stored under our seats. As we soared over the plains and deserts, they pointed out locations at which battles had occurred not long before.

The plane landed at the Island of Djerba to refuel. We were taken by speedboat to the beach, and from there by military truck to a tent bearing a sign that read "Passenger's Dining Room." We were given tea and cookies and then took a fifteen-minute walk. Then we were escorted back to the plane and the journey continued. The sun was beginning to sink in the west as we flew over another stretch of the Mediterranean Sea and then into the darkening desert. Close to eleven o'clock we crossed the lights of Cairo and splashed down in the Nile River. After clearing customs around midnight, we got on a B.O.A.C. bus and headed through the narrow streets to our hotel.

As I looked out of the bus window into the black, twisting streets, I was aware of movements near some of the buildings. There were people dressed from head to ankle in black cloaks. As we looked more closely, we could see they were women in the long, black *abbas*, the typical covering of Arab women. This was my first encounter with the black *abba*, and I must admit that it was frightening to me. (In later years I was to wear the *abba* myself, when I worked in Qatar.)

Ed and Ruth had arrived earlier in the evening. There were other hotels in Cairo, but the British airlines put all of us in the same hotel. Harriet and I found a note from Ed and Ruth waiting for us at the hotel. They asked us to awaken them, should we register in the same hotel. We excitedly knocked at their door, found them, and talked long into the night comparing our adventures and thanking our Lord for bringing us that far along our way. We stayed in Cairo five days while trying to obtain airline tickets to Basrah. The four of us visited the pyramids and the Great Sphinx across the Nile in Giza. While in Cairo we also saw the Mosque of Muhammad Ali and heard for the first time the Muslim call to prayer. On Sunday the full impact of being in a non-Christian nation fell on us. Throughout the city, it was a regular work day. We got together for our own little worship service in the hotel room that morning.

On December 14 Harriet and I left Cairo in a military plane on the final leg of our memorable journey, while Ed and Ruth made plans to cross the Red Sea by boat and then motor across the desert in a bus. Arriving in Baghdad, Iraq, that afternoon, we were welcomed by the Rev. and Mrs. Bernard Hakken, RCA missionaries who were associated with the United Mission of Iraq. They invited us in for supper. The Presbyterian Church U.S.A and the Reformed Church in America worked together in the northern sector of Iraq; while the RCA alone handled the southern work in Amarah and Basrah. I sensed the warmth and hospitality of the Hakkens, people who were wholly dedicated to the Lord.

I was thrilled to set foot in old Mesopotamia, the land of Ur of the Chaldeans, Haran, Assyria, Babylon, and Nineveh. The Garden of Eden is reputed to have been in Iraq. Later I was to see the point at which the Euphrates and Tigris rivers met between Basrah and Amarah, where stood a shaggy old tree and a sign reading "The Garden of Eden."

That night in Baghdad, a thousand and one thoughts filled my mind. I was excited to think that I would soon be in the city that was the Arabian mission's first home. There I would meet people who, Lord willing, would be part of my life for many years to come. My mother's prayer, my father's words of encouragement, nursing school, and my RBI Bible training were all coming together to launch me in the mission work I would encounter for the first time the following day.

Would the missionaries receive a good impression of me? Would they put up with my insecurity and lack of a full college education? Would I be able to learn Arabic? I tried to put everything in the Lord's hands and get some sleep.

The next day our plane took off early in the morning. Far below I could see the glistening Euphrates River, with slender native boats slipping through the water. There were vast stretches of open desert. Then we saw some of the huge marshes which, until only three or four decades before, had been unexplored by westerners. Many romantic stories were told about the marshes. For 6,000 years conquering nations (even the modern Turkish Ottoman Empire) had failed to bring the marsh dwellers into subjection. The fiercely independent people lived on hidden islands in reed huts. Some of them, it was said, were pirates, smugglers, and outlaws.

Then Basrah came into view. Along its edges were scattered huts. We saw the winding streets and close-packed buildings of the central district. There were two sections to the city: the older inland city of Basrah proper called Ashar, and a newer part of the city two miles away, called Basrah City. Basrah was built on the banks of the Shatt-el-Arab River.

We landed at the airport and called the mission. Dorothy Van Ess answered the phone and said she would drive right over to pick us up. Mrs. Van Ess had been working with Christine Gosselink in a mission-sponsored girls' club. We were sorry that the two busy missionaries had to leave their girls to get us.

The mission compound was located on six acres in Ashar, near the bazaar. In the early part of the century, the mission had erected a chapel, a hospital, two schools, and mission houses there.

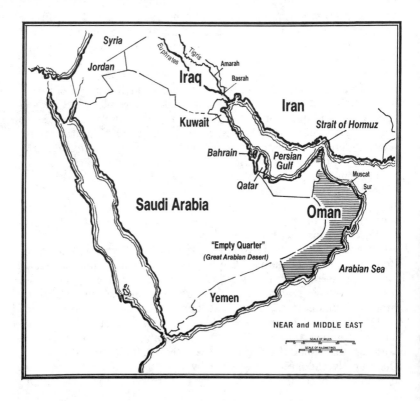

NEAR and MIDDLE EAST

We soon met Dr. John Van Ess, George Gosselink, Harry Almond, and Jay Kapenga. (Ed Luidens, Harry, and Jay all had graduated from New Brunswick Seminary in 1943 and 1944.) Harriet and I joined Harry and Jay for lunch at the Van Ess's.

I stayed in a room in the Van Ess's house and ate there every day. I also got to know the Gosselinks and their three children. George and Christine's two oldest children were enrolled in school in India, but were spending the Christmas holiday with their parents.

I quickly grew to love Arab food. For lunch we often ate rice and Arab stew, which consisted of many kinds of vegetables with chunks of mutton. Dates were a staple in the diet. We ate them fresh off the trees or mixed with other foods, such as homemade yogurt. Vegetables and fruits were readily available in Basrah. I still recall the well-prepared eggplant dishes. The food must have agreed with me, because I gained a few pounds.

During the following days, I became acquainted with the mission compound and the people who worked there. We met and were greeted by many Iraqi nationals who were friends of the mission. I visited the boys' school with its many rooms, where Dr. Van Ess, George Gosselink, Harry Almond, and several Iraqis, both Christian and Muslim, taught. I visited the chapel and saw where Mrs. Van Ess and Christine Gosselink taught the girls. The compound, located on a creek, was shaded by eighty stately date palms. The grounds were ideal for sports, games, and quiet walks memorizing scripture verses and singing. I was introduced to Adaaba and Zenoob, Iraqi women who helped Dorothy and Christine teach the girls.

The mission's book shop was located in a strategic place in the market. Colporteurs would sell a variety of books, including scripture portions, gospels, and Bibles. Some of these early Arab colporteurs were unsung heroes and became martyrs for the cause of Christ.

The mission's "School of High Hope" for boys, the name of which was borrowed from the RCA's Hope College in the United States, was the first modern elementary/secondary school in Iraq. It had achieved an excellent reputation throughout the country. When I arrived, both the Basrah chief of police and the mayor were graduates of the school. A school for girls, started by Mrs. Van Ess (at this time under the direction of Miss Kellien), was conducted in the old part of the city, two miles away. Mrs. Van Ess had weathered many storms as she established the girls' school.

Prominent Arabs in Basrah had proclaimed that the school would be a waste of time because girls were not able to learn!

Ed and Ruth arrived in Basrah a few weeks later. Harriet Wanrooy left immediately by plane for Bahrain, where the medical staff was awaiting her. Jay, Ed, and Ruth studied Arabic on the Ashar compound with Baqar, a high school senior in the School of High Hope, as their teacher. Dr. Van Ess, a linguist, supervised Baqar and us. I studied Arabic with Baqar on the girls' school compound in Basrah City, where I lived with Miss Kellien and Rachel Jackson, both veteran missionaries.

George Gosselink first came to the boys' school in 1922 as a short-termer to teach English, take charge of what was then the boarding department, and generally supervise the young men. He enjoyed teaching the Iraqi boys. After his term of service, he returned to America to continue his studies at Princeton and Western Seminaries. As an ordained missionary, he returned to Basrah in 1929 and supervised evangelistic and educational work and succeeded Dr. Van Ess in the School of High Hope. He served as the mission's field secretary for twenty years.

Christine Scholten Gosselink was a native of Boyden, Iowa, where she had served as principal of the local Christian school. She married George while he was in seminary and came to Basrah to work with Mrs. Van Ess in women's evangelism and Girls Club outreach.

Rachel Jackson and her sister Ruth first visited the Arabian mission in 1918, the year I was born. At the time of this visit they felt the call to mission work and returned to America for special training. In 1921 they were both appointed by the mission board to Arabia. Rachel worked most of her forty-year career in the girls' school in Basrah. She also served later in the girls' school in Muscat. Her sister Ruth established the girls' school in Bahrain during her forty years on the field. Girls from the royal families, merchant class families, poor families, and our orphanage attended this school. It was popular and appreciated by many in that community. Each year the school increased in numbers until it was breaking at the seams, when a new school had to be built.

Cornelia Dalenberg, who was from South Holland, Illinois, came to the mission field with the Jackson sisters. I met her at the annual mission meeting in Basrah in 1945, just as she was leaving for a furlough in the United States. (I heard later that as she crossed the Mediterranean, two of the ships in her convoy were torpedoed by a German submarine.) Cornelia served in Iraq and then for many years in Bahrain where she became well known. Our parents lived just twenty miles from each other in Illinois.

Dorothy Firman Van Ess came to Basrah in 1909 as a young, single woman, with the purpose of starting the girls' school. While studying Arabic she met John Van Ess, and the two were married in 1911. Through friends of her husband, she was introduced into a wide circle of women: Arabs, Turks, Persians, British; Sunni and Shi'ite Muslims, Jews, Catholics, Protestants; city people, marsh people, and villagers. She enjoyed visiting with the women of Iraq. She and other women of the mission did evangelistic work among women who were not able to have contact with any of our male missionaries. Social customs kept the Arab women away from gatherings at which men other than husbands and close relatives were present.

Dr. John Van Ess, whom I have already described in some detail, was tall and very thin. I found out later that his health was beginning to fail. He wore round, wire-rimmed glasses and a mustache. He greeted me warmly and wasted no time organizing my Arabic studies.

Besides studying Arabic, we were given a number of books to read and sets of papers written by the mission staff. One of the books, an Arabic grammar text, had been written by Dr. Van Ess. We were told that comprehensive tests would be administered by Dr. Van Ess after the first and second years of language study. At the end of two years, as part of our final exam, we were expected to give an evangelistic talk, in Arabic, to a group of Arab women.

Facing two years of studying a complex language was almost overwhelming. There were times when I longed to go directly into hospital work. But my young tutor, Baqar, was patient and well organized. Little by little the difficult verbs and pronunciations lodged in my brain. I always believed that my early years of speaking Frisian helped me to express Arabic better. Friese has several harsh sounds which are similar to sounds in Arabic. For example, both languages roll the r's and have the gutteral "kh" that comes from the back of the throat.

Not long after I arrived in Basrah I received a letter saying that my brother Ted was alive and in a German prison camp. That's all we knew at the time; it wasn't until months later that my family heard Ted's full story.

After his capture in Belgium, Ted had been taken to Berlin and then to a large P.O.W. camp near the Polish border. During the winter of 1944-45, Ted lived in the camp, sleeping on the floor and subsisting on rations provided by the Germans. Mail and food packages from my family were never forwarded to him, even though the others in his room received messages. Ted was convinced that we thought he was dead.

As the war turned against the Germans in the spring of 1945, the camp was abandoned and the prisoners were marched west, back into Germany. The German soldiers put the prisoners in barns each night, sometimes packing them so tightly that they could not lie down.

One night the prisoners were herded into a large barn with a loft full of hay. Seeing an opportunity to escape, Ted and some other prisoners had friends bury them deep in the hay. They stayed under the hay for two days without food or water, during which time Canadian soldiers were closing in on the Germans. Bullets ricocheted off the walls of the barn. A nearby barn caught fire and burned to the ground. The German who owned the farm stood outside the door and called to them saying he knew they were hiding in his loft. He told them that he was willing to make a deal: their freedom in exchange for a signed statement that the farmer had helped them. The German feared his barn would be burned, like the others, and as the Allies were about to overrun his farm he needed to gain their favor. Ted and his friends wrote the note but would not sign it.

The escapees remained in the barn two more days, because of the fighting. By God's grace, the barn did not catch fire.

Then the area came under the control of the Canadians. Ted and his companions left their hiding place, found a Canadian camp, and joined the line-up of Canadian soldiers in a chow line. After being without food for so many days they ate too much and got sick.

Recovering, they made their way to a British camp. The British were suspicious of the young wanderers and kept them under such close guard that it was like a second imprisonment. Eventually Ted and his friends persuaded one of the English guards that they were indeed escaped P.O.W.s. The guard allowed them to tie him up and take his gun to simulate a forcible escape. Again they were on the run. They stole a tractor from a nearby farm and ran it until it was out of fuel. They again took to walking. Finally Canadian soldiers picked them up and took them into another one of their camps. Then they were transported to a U.S. Air Force radio station. From there, an Air Force pilot took them to France. They traveled by boat to the United States, and Ted called home for the first time on Mother's Day, 1945. It was only then that he learned about grandma Anema.

All this happened as I studied my Arabic lessons in Basrah, and I learned the story through letters telling of Ted's experiences and his safe return. The Van Esses were very sympathetic. Their own son, John Jr., had died of a tropical disease while in military service about a year before, and their daughter was serving in the WAVES.

Many afternoons I would visit women of the community with Mrs. Van Ess, Christine Gosselink, and Ruth Luidens. I sat quietly and concentrated intensely on the conversations around me, trying to pick out a few words. There eventually came a time when I could follow the drift of a conversation. Then the patient and hospitable Arab women would converse with me in simple sentences.

The missionaries in Basrah usually attended two churches on Sundays: the Arabic-speaking Arab Christian Church in the morning and the English-speaking St. Peter's Episcopal Church in the evening. Most of the people who attended the Arab service were refugees from the terrible Armenian massacres in Turkey between 1895 and 1925. They were wonderful, sincere Christians who had gone through unbelievable hardship as they made their way to the Persian Gulf. Some of them escaped death by wearing the skins of goats and sheep on their backs as they crawled through fields, just like the believers described in Hebrews 11:37.

On Wednesday afternoons I would attend a prayer meeting with about fifty women of the community. Many of these women, too, were Armenian.

During these days of language study and interaction with the older women missionaries, my reactions to the city and the people were typical of most westerners. I noticed the dirt, the illiteracy, the poverty, the confinement of women, and the fanaticism displayed by some of the Muslims.

As months passed, however, the Lord enabled me to look through the surface things. As I learned to know the people, I learned to love them too. I was impressed by some of the homes we visited in which furnishings were modern and the women dressed in western clothing. The poor as well as the wealthy were friendly and hospitable.

It took me a while to get used to the different kind of worship service at St. Peter's Episcopal Church, which was more liturgical than our denomination. The services contained chants, kneeling, written prayers, and sermons that were short, in-depth, to-the-point, and very spiritual. I often played the organ for this service and found their hymns to be very different from ours. The *Magnificat* and *Nunc Dimittus* were strange to me, but in time I learned to appreciate these songs, too.

Every week the Van Esses and Gosselinks entertained soldiers in their homes and we language students often joined them. The soldiers, who were stationed at the big British base just outside of town, seemed to be lonely, and they were as interested in the young women as in the food and fellowship! However, since they were under orders not to fraternize, and since we were wrapped up in our studies, romantic attachments didn't develop. We enjoyed conversations and occasional picnics in the gardens.

In those days I was firmly committed to the Lord's work but not as firmly committed to remaining single. That decision would come later. Our Arabian mission in the 1920s and 1930s had lost many young women who joined the work, met eligible young men, and then left missionary work. Cornelia Dalenberg, in her book, *Sharifa*, recalled the pain of seeing well-educated medical women (many of whom had received two years of language training in Arabic) abandon their missionary calling.

Not long after arriving in Basrah I also met Dr. and Mrs. William Moerdyk (Bill was the brother of the Rev. James Moerdyk.) The Moerdyks were a physician and R.N. team. They had come to the mission field many years before and were serving their final years in Amarah. (Bill later took an early retirement due to tuberculosis.)

The Moerdyks called me to Amarah on a temporary emergency assignment just as I began my language studies. Typhus and bubonic plague were approaching the town and I was needed to help immunize school children. During the first few weeks I was in Amarah, we gave almost 3,000 typhus inoculations and 2,500 inoculations for plague. I also assisted a midwife in a home baby delivery on a dirt floor in a date stick hut.

I liked Amarah from the first moment I saw it. The Tigris River flowed along the west side of the town, near the mission compound, and all around it were palm trees, mulberry bushes, orange trees, roses, and vegetable gardens. The mission compound contained a chapel, hospital, two mission homes, and some gardens. Across the road from the mission compound was a beautiful, modern boys' school run by the government. Every evening men and women would walk and talk along the main dirt road. The pace of life seemed to be slower and easier than Basrah.

But as much as I enjoyed assisting the Moerdyks in Amarah, my main responsibility at that time was to learn Arabic, and Basrah was the best place to immerse myself in the language. Back I went to Basrah. I worked hard at the language. Arabic is totally different in construction from European languages. As Dr. Van Ess explained in his book, *Meet the Arab*, spoken Arabic has sounds that range "from the lightest breath to the heaviest growl." There are two kinds of T sounds, two S sounds, and three DH sounds, and many other differences in English and Arabic sounds. Written Arabic is logical. It has its own script and reads from right to left. Day after day we studied, listened, and conversed with our tutors and discovered that our communication skills were indeed improving. I began to glimpse some of the beauty of the language.

In later years, lengthy papers written by mission personnel were required reading for new missionaries. One paper, for example, dealt with ways for missionaries to approach a new culture. Another was titled, "Islamics." Another very practical paper by Dr. Maurice Heusinkveld listed many ways that our missionaries were making contacts with the Arab people every day. A quick reading of these "contact points" gives one an overview of our missionary methods at that time:

- Teacher-student contacts in our schools
- Scripture distribution in our shops
- Evangelism in church, chapel, office
- Social engagements in the community
- Women's groups
- Clinic talks in the hospitals
- Witnessing in hospitals during daily duties
- Care of the poor
- Care of orphans
- Business contacts
- Staff prayers with visitors present
- Contact with foreigners (such as soldiers)
- Home visits
- Contacts with language tutors

At the end of our first two years in Iraq, Dr. Van Ess gave the final language examination. We were accountable for written and spoken Arabic. The exam was very thorough. Ruth Luidens and I also gave the required evangelistic message in Arabic to a group of Arabic-speaking women. The more we came to know Dr. Van Ess, the more we envied his great skill in communicating with the people. The four of us (Jay, Ed, Ruth, and myself) passed the exam with good marks.

After having completed our two years of language study Ed and Ruth were sent to work in Bahrain, where they would be active in evangelistic and educational work. Jay Kapenga was sent as an evangelist to Kuwait. He married Marjorie Underwood, better known as Midge, in 1947. At that time Midge was a short-term teacher working with the Presbyterian church in Iran.

I was sent in January, 1947, at age 28, to Amarah. I would be serving as a nurse in the mission hospital. It was not easy to leave the missionaries and my many new friends in Basrah. In just two years Basrah had become my home. I now had to launch out into the unknown, among new people, into the work of a hospital completely new to me. I also worried about using my new language. We had learned the basics of the Arabic language but really had had little opportunity to practice it. I left Basrah en route to Amarah, alone, by taxi, and in tears. Yet I was not alone, because the Lord was with me.

III
Amarah

(Love) always protects, always trusts, always hopes, always perseveres.

1 Cor. 13:7

We considered blessed those who have persevered.

James 5:11

And so after waiting patiently, Abraham received what was promised.

Heb. 6:15

We work hard with our own hands. When we are cursed, we bless; when we are persecuted, we endure it.

1 Cor. 4:12

Amarah is located in the heart of Iraq, the home of Adam, Eve, Abraham, Sarah, and countless other biblical characters. While living there I often passed the site of the tomb of the Old Testament prophet Ezra. Daniel, Shadrach, Meshach, and Abednego lived in captivity not far from where we worked. After God's second call, Jonah went to Ninevah (the site of which is in Iraq) and called the people to repentance. The ruins of Babylon and Ninevah lay along the Tigris and Euphrates rivers.

I remember tall date palms, with their long fronds and clusters of yellow fresh dates, hovering over the banks of the great rivers—the country's export of dates was the largest in the world. The sky was bright blue almost every day, with few clouds. I will never forget the moon and stars shining through dark date palm trees in the depths of the night.

A westerner in Iraq, in those days, immediately noticed the absence of traffic noise, the rumbling of trains, and the droning of airplanes overhead. All was quiet on this eastern front. Outside of Iraq's major cities, life was even slower. People were not hurrying about. There were no deadlines, telephones, fancy restaurants, or bustling office buildings.

Once one left Basrah or Baghdad one was in a different world. The dirt road between Basrah and Amarah twisted and turned and was full of holes. Whenever there was a rainstorm, the road turned to mud and was impassable. Amarah would be cut off from the world. Not even mail would get through.

In the countryside around Amarah there were deserts in one direction and marshlands in another. In the deserts one could see herds of sheep and cattle, camels, and donkeys. In the villages were brown goat hair tents with small children toddling in and out of the shadows. Jackals lurked in the hills and mountains.

South, in the great marshes, were the Marsh Arabs, with their unique manner of living. They made their homes of reeds and lived on islands hidden in reeds that grew twice as tall as a person. Water buffaloes waded through the water and at night hoisted themselves up on land near the huts. Many kinds of fish were available at mealtimes.

I never adjusted to the swarms of flies, which stuck to the eyes and clung to infants and children. There seemed to be little knowledge of the basics of sanitation and health care. Chickens ran throughout many yards, attracting even more flies. It seemed that every human and animal was at the mercy of the flying, biting insects.

Amarah, when I lived in it, was the third largest city in Iraq, with a population of about 55,000 people. A third of the people worked in farming and herding, some worked in manufacturing, and some of the men traveled out of town to work in the big oil fields.

Among the men there were social classes according to work, family background, religious sect, and ethnic background. Some classes of people owned shops and were merchants. Others were farmers. Sheikhs and other landowners supervised big pieces of land. I knew several fishermen who were adept at rowing their narrow boats rapidly through the water. A favorite pastime of the men of Amarah was talking and visiting in tea shops. It seemed that everyone in town took breaks to sip strong tea and discuss the latest events. Every evening the townspeople, especially the teenagers, enjoyed walking up and down the main street of town, River Road, which skirted the edge of our mission compound. Merchants up and down the side streets were always friendly and eager to show off their wares.

Iraqi mothers and fathers were good parents. Children were generally well behaved and disciplined. There was no child abuse. If physical harm was present it was due to ignorance and superstition. The mothers nursed their babies until they were five years old. That provided ready milk for the babies at all times and it also kept the mothers from having frequent pregnancies—it was a means of birth control. The mother-child bonds seemed to be very close.

Iraq put a high value on education for its children. Thanks to oil money, the government was able to finance good schools. Boys and girls attended separate schools, following the custom in most Muslim countries. There was a government boys' school across from our mission compound and a girls' school just down the road. When I was outside during the day I would look across the street and see the boys walking about the playground studying. Their teachers were demanding and it was of utmost importance to pass difficult examinations. Once an exam was over, the pressure was off and I would see the boys enjoying archery, soccer, and other games.

Each year the girls' school performed for the public. The girls' dramatic and musical presentations were well rehearsed and the students took pride in them. We were invited to these special occasions and privileged to attend them. Some of the girls graduating from the high school became teachers; others went on to nurses' training in Baghdad.

Unfortunately, many poor girls and boys from the lower classes did not attend school. One obstacle was the expense of purchasing clothing for the school children. The daughters of poor families sometimes stayed at home to care for little ones and help their mothers with house work. Boys helped with the chores, cared for flocks, and found work about town to support poor families.

Taxi service in Amarah was by horse-drawn buggy. There were few cars there in the 1940s and much of the transportation was by *beden*, the graceful, canoe-like vessel rowed by men on either side. Donkeys hauled loads on land.

Our walled mission compound was situated on about five acres of land on the edge of town. It contained two homes, one for the evangelistic worker and one for the doctor. It also contained a chapel with a bell, our Lansing Memorial Hospital, a guard hut, a tennis court, and a vegetable and flower garden. Most of the medical and evangelistic work was conducted within the walls of the compound.

Compound in Amarah, hospital on left, kitchen in center, and missionary residence with windmill to draw water behind.

When I first came to Amarah, I lived in the same house as Dr. and Mrs. Moerdyk. I had my meals with them, too, for about a year and a half. The Moerdyks labored under a very heavy load during their last years in Amarah. During the war years Dr. Moerdyk was the only doctor in the hospital, and besides his medical duties he preached each Sunday. Many British troops attended the worship services at the compound and the Moredyks entertained them in their home. In 1948, when he retired, Dr. Moerdyk was admitted to a sanitarium in Michigan for treatment of tuberculosis. With God's help he eventually recovered but was not given a medical clearance to return to the mission field. Dr. Moerdyk was a fine internist and diagnostician, and it didn't take him long to establish a busy practice in Holland, Michigan.

The Rev. and Mrs. Gerrit Pennings were assigned to Amarah in 1946. Mr. Pennings took over the evangelistic work and soon became known all over town. He visited patients in the hospital and merchants in the bazaar each morning. He conducted men's Bible studies during the week.

Mrs. Pennings visited women in the hospital every day and conducted a *mejlis* for women every Thursday evening. Occasionally there would be as many as twenty-five women present at her groups. She was also in charge of the Sunday school, overseeing several teachers, including myself. I was very impressed by the teaching ability of the Iraqi young women who taught in that Sunday school.

A fine Armenian named Khalaf was the mission's colporteur. He sat in our book shop in the bazaar every day, talking to passers-by and selling Bibles and portions of scripture. Khalaf, a widower with two children, was also a survivor of the horrible Armenian massacres. Shortly before I came to Amarah, his wife had become very sick. Since our own doctor was on furlough, she had been sent to a government hospital in Basrah. By the time she reached the hospital, the diagnosis was a ruptured appendix. I was told that the doctor called in to perform surgery had been drinking, and when it was all over the poor woman had bled to death. Khalaf and his children were overcome with sorrow. God gave them strength to carry on. In fact, Khalaf maintained a quiet but strong witness for our Lord in the midst of a very difficult living situation, as a Christian raising two children in a Muslim country.

The mission work in Amarah still bore the stamp of four people who worked there and left before I came: The Rev. and Mrs. Dirk Dykstra; the Rev. James Enoch Moerdyk, the brother of William; and Cornelia Dalenberg. The Dykstras at the time were in Oman, and Cornelia Dalenberg was in Bahrain.

The Dykstras were childless, and they were able to do many things and go many places that were impossible for our missionary families with children. Mrs. Minnie Dykstra was an ardent, zealous, tireless worker for the Lord. She set standards that few other missionary women could live up to.

The Rev. Dirk Dykstra was also a tireless worker in evangelism. He is perhaps best remembered for purchasing a boat called the *Milton Stewart* from the British military after World War I. He outfitted it for cooking and sleeping and sailed it over Iraq's waterways on many missionary expeditions in the 1920s and 1930s.

The Rev. James Moerdyk had retired from mission work in 1941 and passed away, but they still talked about him. He originally came to Arabia in 1900, and during his years of service he bounced from mission station to mission station like a ping-pong ball. As I found out about his life, I was amazed to hear how the Lord had used him in so many different places. I couldn't help but notice that the man had been single, and it was because of his freedom to pack up and travel at a moment's notice that he served so effectively in so many capacities.

In his first term, Mr. Moerdyk had served in the old mission station on the Euphrates River, Nasiriya. From that base he had toured throughout Mesopotamia. In 1908 he supervised the mission's boys' school in Basrah. From there he went to Bahrain, where he took over educational and evangelistic work. He was mechanically inclined and supervised early building projects there. Next he went on tour in Oman and covered nearly 2,000 miles of territory never before seen by any missionary. He was also instrumental in accumulating a number of pieces of property in Muscat, which later became valuable for the mission. On one piece of property he built a guest cottage that housed sheikhs from the interior who journeyed to Oman to visit the Sultan (in the days before hotels in Oman).

Then he went back to Bahrain, and from there to Basrah, and then back to Nasiriya. He spent his latter years in Amarah, where he established a wonderful work among lepers at a time when the government had no facility for lepers. The lepers came to love the tall, quiet man dearly. People still talked about how devastated the lepers were when he died. He was buried in Iraq.

People like the Dykstras, Moerdyks, Pennings, and Khalaf the colporteur were shining examples for all of us in the mission. I was just a raw recruit. As I adjusted to everything, it seemed as if my own effectiveness as a missionary would be like a drop in the bucket when compared to the work of these veterans.

I didn't have much time to worry about adjusting, however, because I was thrown immediately into my work. The hospital was a busy place. It did not take me long to know the staff. They were overworked and badly in need of help, so they welcomed me with open arms. My taxi arrived in Amarah late in the afternoon and at seven o'clock the following morning I was at work.

I knew the basics of Arabic, but my real education in the language came as I worked every day with the Iraqis. I used many hand motions in the beginning, but the people were patient and helped me through rough spots. We worked six days a week, with long hours every day, so I was constantly exposed to the language. As the same words were repeated over and over I began first to recognize them and then to use them myself.

Work at the hospital began each day with seven o'clock prayers. The guard who was responsible for collecting the night lanterns went around from room to room to pick them up. The cook went to the bazaar to bargain with the shopkeepers for the day's food. The housekeeper got the wash tubs out of the locked supply room and gave them to the laundry woman. Another housekeeper filled the stove with crude black oil and lit it to begin heating water for all the hospital's needs during the day. One nurse set out ointments, eye drops, bandages, and medicines; another nurse sterilized syringes in preparation for the rush of patients. Two cleaning women went to work on the floors and an orderly began changing beds.

The clinics were large. We would begin to work through hundreds of cases that were lined up, waiting for attention. The benefits of admission as an inpatient were not widely understood, so most of the people walked in as outpatients. We often saw thousands of people per week in the clinic.

Then the doctor arrived. First he would see the male inpatients (a half dozen men); then he would go to the women's section and discuss the female cases (usually another half dozen) with the nurses. Orders of the day were written and carried out by us.

Then the clinic would open. Our doctor would seat himself at a table in an inside room and the patients were ushered into his room. An orderly had already distributed passes consisting of a small and large card (chits) and a number for each person. Since there were no women doctors in Amarah, Mrs. Moerdyk sat in the women's clinic and screened cases until her husband was released from the men's side.

As patients waited to be seen, Mr. and Mrs. Pennings would make the rounds among them, praying and giving a gospel message. Sometimes the waiting patients had a hard time staying orderly—especially when there was some delay and it looked like a long time would pass before they were seen. The Pennings, I remember, were very effective in easing the tension and talking to the waiting people. They knew the language well.

I was kept busy in a treatment room caring for ears, eyes, and various kinds of skin sores. Trachoma, a disease of the eyes, was a terrible affliction in many Middle Eastern countries. This disease, which was very contagious, settled in the upper and lower eyelids. Symptoms were reddened, infected, thick, papular-raised inner eyelids. The tissues inside the lid would begin to shrink, causing the eyelashes to turn inward against the cornea. Every time a victim of this disease would blink, the eyelashes would rub against the cornea, causing great pain and eventual blindness. If the eyes were treated during the first stages of the disease, we could prevent injury and blindness, but if treatment were delayed, there was little hope.

I straddled a bench while a trachoma patient lay in front of me. Sitting behind the head of the patient was an Iraqi girl who assisted me by holding the patient's head firmly. I turned the eyelids inside out and scraped the raised papules with a copper stick. Then I wiped the tears and discharge with clean cotton. A copper stick was the most effective treatment at that time, followed by soothing eye drops and ointment. (Later sulfacetamide eye drops and tablets became the most effective treatment.) Speed was important and I established a quick, effective routine in my treatments.

I syringed many an ear with peroxide and warm water to remove accumulated wax. Also there were always open ulcers and infected sores to wash, treat, and bandage. I enjoyed working in the treatment room because the results were fairly quick and satisfying.

We were fortunate to have an excellent midwife in Amarah. Her name was Rahma and she had been trained well by Cornelia Dalenberg. She was on the heavy side, and she looked like anyone's warm, huggable "auntie." She came to the hospital for supplies and sterilization of her equipment, but she was often out in the town in homes. She was a close friend of Cora Moerdyk.

In the city of Amarah, trained midwives helped in home deliveries, but out in the countryside it was another matter. "Granny midwives," who had virtually no training in obstetrics, were the only people available. Some of these women had good common sense, but others used techniques that did more harm than good.

I was also involved in evangelism. My first devotional in the clinic, I remember, was based on Acts 3:1-10. I told the people that there was a reason for everything. There was a reason why the lame men sat by the temple and why Peter and John were at the temple that day. There was also a reason why I had come from America to Amarah, why they were at our mission hospital, and why God sent 'Esa (Jesus) to the earth. I told them that God was sovereign and in control of everything.

Up until then I got affirmative nods and other responses from the people. But then I told them about the love of God and that God had sent Jesus to die on the cross for us. If we believed in Jesus, we would not die but have everlasting life.

They did not understand. How often in the years ahead I would be frustrated when people would say, "Jesus was too good to die on a cross. God would never permit such a great prophet to die such a horrible death."

If we had more discussion, the Muslims would say, "Yes, someone did die on a cross. The Koran tells us that someone who looked like Jesus died that day, but it was not Jesus."

I felt that Satan had lied to them and blinded their eyes for thirteen centuries. How badly I wanted them to know the truth!

With my missionary friends I would ponder the best way to communicate the gospel message to my Muslim friends. The people had been preconditioned to argue against the very foundation of the Christian message. How could we break through the wall of disbelief?

The Rev. Bassam Madany, a Lebanese minister who pioneered the Arabic radio broadcasts of the Christian Reformed denomination, points out that Islam is the only major religion of the world that is anti-Christian at its core. He also reminds us of the tragic fact that when Christianity and Islam came together throughout history, there was always conflict. Islam originally grew by conquering Christian lands. In the eleventh century Christian crusaders fought against Muslims to regain some of these lands. Arabs still look back at the Crusades with anger.

So how could a modern Christian missionary break down this wall of resistance?

In my files, I have an essay written by James Cantine in 1911. In it Cantine took into account all the differences between Christianity and Islam and cut to the heart of the matter. The title of his paper was "The Nearest Way to a Muslim Heart."

Like attracts like. The nearest way to the Muslim heart is to use what appeals to the heart, rather than to the intellect. Our individual attainments, or the attainments of the Christian Church, or Christian nations, in knowledge, riches, or power, are not in themselves persuasive. These things held up as the fruits of Christianity will not lead many Muslims to desire to be engrafted into the True Vine. Neither has our...theology been the way by which Christ has approached the hearts of most converts from Islam.

The Muslim heart is not different from yours or mine. What would appeal to us would appeal to him. It must be the heart that touches the heart. The things of the heart—love, joy, peace, longsuffering, gentleness, goodness, and the like—are what the heart esteems worthwhile the world over. The way then for him who would enter the door is to bring of these gifts which the heart always craves.

We have first to know the Muslim heart and the things he holds dear. We cannot know, understand, appreciate without first loving. We have to touch his heart with our hearts, to come into intimate contact with his life. For this we want no faltering tongue nor imperfect means of communication.

We want to enter into his life and forget the things in which we think our civilization is superior.

In short, we must approach him just as Christ approached the people of Judea and Galilee. It is only by such a way of self-denial and service that we can get near enough to show forth the things that commend our faith and will lead our Muslim friend, in God's providence, to accept of it as his only comfort in life and death.

From the very beginning, Zwemer and Cantine recognized the power of medical mission work in demonstrating the love of Christ for the people of the Arab lands. In the early years of the mission, the Christian hospitals freely shared medical knowledge with people who were still practicing methods learned thousands of years before.

Our job as evangelists was to show divine love, and our job as medical missionaries was to minister to rich and poor in the name of the Lord.

There were times when it was hard to be loving and gentle, especially when our Christian beliefs came into conflict with those of our Muslim friends. Muslims had a way of accepting every occurrence in life as planned by God. This, of course, was good in the sense that they could accept most things as God's will. Christians also believe that God is omnipotent.

It was not so good, however, when this belief went too far and became fatalism.

I remember, for example, parents bringing nearly blind children to us. "Why did you not bring the child earlier?" we would ask the parents. "We told you about treating the child's eyes. We could have prevented the blindness!"

Too many times the reaction would be a shrug and the statement that it was God's will.

"No, it is *not* God's will!" I groaned inwardly.

We always dreaded a death in the hospital. We sympathized with the family, but it would be impossible to quiet them. After a death family members would weep and wail and go wild with grief. All control was lost. Gone was the passive acceptance of good and bad. The women would pull their hair and tear their clothes. Sometimes women would beat their heads against walls or on the floor. The noise and tumult would be very disturbing to a hospital. For this reason, we tried to remove the body quickly before people could gather to join the bereaved family in this tumult and mourning. We would sometimes have to close the doors of the hospital and lock the outer gate of the mission compound.

One time a woman with a head injury was brought to the hospital in an unconscious condition. We obtained a history of her case from her husband. It turned out that the woman had recently been notified that her mother, who lived in another village, was very ill. The woman immediately made arrangements for the care of her six children and then left to be with her mother. By the time she got to her mother, it was too late. The older woman was dead, and as commonly happens in hot climates, the burial was done quickly, before the daughter arrived.

The woman lost all control of herself. Her sisters tried to reason with her, but to no avail. She began beating her head on the ground until she broke a blood vessel and had a cerebral hemorrhage. She lost consciousness and eventually was brought to our hospital. She never again regained consciousness.

Her youngest child, a happy, gurgling six-month-old, lay at the breast of the unconscious woman in the hospital bed during her last hours of life. Her husband was a fine, intelligent, respected man in town. He saw the folly in the woman's mourning but was powerless to prevent it.

It was difficult to get used to some of the horrible medical cases that came to the hospital. Often my heart would cry out, "How can God's beautiful creation fall so low?" So many of the cases were rather simple in themselves, but illiteracy and ignorance made them deadly.

Many of the mothers would come to the hospital as a last resort. Methods they had used for years before hospitals were established (including superstitious practices) were tried first. When the cases finally came to us, it would take a long time to effect a cure. At other times, we came up against social customs that seemed heartless and cruel. Yet, God's grace was there and there were miraculous healings. Praise God.

During my first spring in Amarah, I assisted in the delivery of twin boys. The young mother, who happened to be from one of the few Catholic families in the town, was unmarried. The pregnancy was looked upon as a disgrace to the family.

The hospital workers kept the whole unpleasant affair quiet. After the mother recovered from the birth, she quietly went back to her family. She was unable to care for the babies, since her delivery would thereby be exposed in the community.

So it was up to the hospital staff to care for the babies. I took care of the babies, whom we named Saliem (meaning "peace") and Sabbah (meaning "morning"). For six weeks the little ones were part of my life. I kept them in a special room in our home. I broke away from my duties at the hospital to feed and check in on the two boys. Khalfan, a helper in the home, also kept his eye on them while he was going about his work. They were good babies, and as the weeks passed they began to recognize me. I grew to love them and hoped that they would have good lives.

On the sixth week, however, little Saliem grew ill. Even our best medical treatment was to no avail, and we could see he was slipping away. The mother asked us to contact the local priest, who would administer last rites. We followed the girl's wishes. The priest performed the Catholic sacrament and then little Saliem passed away. The mother could not attend the funeral; nor was there anyone else in attendance.

I carried the baby to his grave in a barren cemetery behind the town. Although the baby's family had abandoned him in life and death, we missionaries cared and grieved.

Some time later, we were able to place Saliem's twin brother, Sabbah, in a Catholic orphanage in Baghdad.

One night I was called outside of the city to assist in a delivery. It was a dark, moonless night. The father and a young lad came to get me, saying that their village was "further down the river." I did not know them and I had never been to the village, but I threw together my kit and climbed into the horse-drawn buggy that was waiting outside our compound. The driver decided to take a short-cut, and the pathway became very bumpy. I was thrown out of the buggy at one point. Fortunately, the buggy lurched away from me just as I fell out, so I was not injured by the wheels.

We finally arrived at the village. In the dark, I could barely make out rows of date stick huts. Then the buggy stopped. Climbing down with my bag, I went through a low doorway into a hut that was lit by a lamp made of reed wicks stuck in a bottle of kerosene. It took a moment for my eyes to adjust to the dimness and shadows. Then I could see a number of women seated in every conceivable space around the room. The floor was dirt, covered by a mat made from date fronds. A granny midwife was present. She may have been there for some time.

The poor mother, hemmed in by so many women, was on her back on a mat. I sat by her asking her many questions. It seemed

A date stick hut where the poor of Amarah lived.

that her contractions were strong and she was in fairly good shape physically. The fetal heartbeat was good. I went ahead with the prep and enema and made ready the mercury bichloride solution. I didn't open the sterile pack until later, when she neared delivery. Her contractions began to increase after the enema. The fetal heart remained steady and good. I sat on the mat covering the dirt floor and waited, encouraging the mother and talking with the women.

During the process of waiting, someone made tea and served it to me. The patient's mother sat down beside me and offered a steady stream of advice. After a while the patient was in the "pushing" stage. I opened the pack and instructed the women not to come near. I washed my hands and put on sterile gloves. At two o'clock in the morning a healthy boy entered the world, and great excitement filled the hut and spilled out into the village.

When a girl was born, there was little rejoicing, but when a boy was born, there was plenty of noise. The women had a way of making a loud, joyous, shrieking yell with their tongues that carried for miles. The sound filled the hut and echoed around the village.

The Arabic word for this sound corresponds to the word "hallelujah" that we read in the Bible.

The horse and buggy were not available to take me back to Amarah after the delivery, so the only thing to do was to bed down with the women in the hut. They honored me with brand new bridal linens and blankets and fixed a bed for me on top of a low cabinet. As daylight appeared, after an excellent breakfast, they secured transportation for me and I returned to Amarah.

In December, 1947, we admitted a desperately sick young girl who was afflicted with sores such as I had never seen before. She had been getting progressively worse at home for more than a month before she came to us, and her lower back and hips were one ugly, festering, deep-seated sore. In places, the tissue was eaten away to a depth of an inch or more. The odor alone was almost unbearable. The family had given up hope and expected her to die in the hospital.

I vividly remember caring for her when she was first admitted. First I had to clean the girl, then cut away dead tissue. As we worked on her, we found other problems. She was covered with lice and had so many nits in her hair that we simply trimmed her hair down to her scalp. Then we found she had pneumonia. Several times her heart seemed about to give out from all the extra strain on her system, and our doctor gave her cardiac stimulants. For some reason—possibly because she had been lying in one position for a long time, or possibly from malnutrition—one of her arms and both legs were stiff.

We worked day after day, cleaning her sores, changing the dressings, administering medications, moving her limbs, and showing her the love of Jesus.

On Christmas Day, 1947, I wasn't sure that she would live through the day. I remember praying that the Lord would at least let her make it through the day. She did. And slowly she began to recover. How we thanked God when we could see that the girl was going to recover! She stayed with us in the hospital nine weeks, all told, and during the last two weeks we had many good conversations with her. She attended services in our chapel the last two Sundays before she was discharged.

The girl's family could hardly believe what had happened. They immediately recognized the power of Jesus as the healing force that brought their daughter back from the edge of the grave. They freely expressed their gratitude to Jesus Christ. Sadly, however, they did not recognize Jesus as the Lord of their lives. They were not able to see Jesus as more than a prophet on the same level as their own Mohammed. As the girl left us for her village, we could only trust Jesus to carry on the work he had begun in her young heart.

Two people in Amarah wanted to become Christians and receive baptism, but as they went through the steps it became very evident that their desire was not sincere. One woman lived in "habitual adultery" and she had no intention of changing her style of life. Mistakenly, she thought that becoming a Christian put some kind of stamp of approval on her behavior. She thought she would be accepted by the missionaries and somehow get a stable job. Another fellow also fell away, and it was evident that the Lord had not been working in his life. Both were looking for some kind of personal gain from baptism. (I asked my friends in Mt. Greenwood to pray for the two people, in hopes that the Lord would continue to nourish seeds that might have been planted in their lives, even though it seemed to us that there was little hope.)

But then there were people in whom the Spirit *did* move. How wonderful it was to see their conviction and courage!

Ajila, a victim of leprosy, lived in a village in the marshes. She was receiving treatment from us in the mission compound when we received word that her mother had died, back in the marshes. As leprosy victims were not allowed to travel in public conveyances, we put her in a mission car and drove her home. Life was very difficult for Ajila, but we knew she was letting her light shine for the Lord as best she could. Ajila could not work up the courage to travel to Amarah for her treatments, so a relative would come for the medicine and tell us about the girl. We prayed many times that the Lord would be especially close to her in her loneliness.

Two young women, Kereema and Adeeba, came wanting to talk. They were from native Christian families and enjoyed Bible studies on the mission compound. They came one evening and joined the hospital staff for end-of-the-day conversations and devotions. After everyone left they lingered, wanting to talk some more about the Lord. So we continued looking into the Bible. One of the passages was 1 Peter 2, where it says "You are a chosen people...a people belonging to God, that you may declare the praises of him, who called you out of darkness into his wonderful light" (vs.9). The three of us prayed together, and I remember receiving a strong feeling of being blessed and spiritually enriched.

Then each of the young women told me that Jesus had spoken to them through dreams during the previous week. Kereema, who had heard many stories about Jesus while growing up in and around the mission compound, said that her two-year-old child had been sick and she and her husband had been very worried. (They had lost a child a year earlier.) "A man appeared to me in a dream," Kereema said, "and called me by name."

In her dream, Kereema asked, "Who are you?"

"Don't you know me?" the man said. "I am Jesus."

"Don't be concerned about little Casib," the visitor said. "All will be well with him."

Kereema said she woke up shaking with fear, but at the same time her heart was at peace. She described the dream to her husband and he, too, was greatly relieved. They knew that the same Jesus we missionaries spoke about cared for them and their baby.

Adeeba, the other young woman, was progressing very well as an "inquirer" in the mission. She faithfully attended Bible studies and other classes. I was always inspired by her forthright, honest prayers. At that particular time, Adeeba was preparing to enter college. Remember that this was in Iraq in the 1940s—she was a very unique young lady! The week before, she had been studying night and day for her college entrance examinations. As her fears mounted, she grew very anxious. Then one night Jesus spoke in a dream: "Don't fear, Adeeba. You will do well in the examinations."

Like Kereema, Adeeba felt fear mixed with great relief. Adeeba later passed her examinations and went on to college.

Yusef Toma was a young Iraqi man whose parents were Christians. His father, a former school teacher, was a fairly important man in the ration department in Basrah during the war. Young Yusef was brought up by the family to be a Christian, although he attended Muslim schools and was taught by Muslim instructors. When he came of age, Yusef confessed his faith in Jesus Christ and began living a Christian life.

With the help of our missionaries in Basrah, Yusef attended Hope College and later went on to study oil engineering. Several times he was a guest in the home of my parents in Mt. Greenwood. My family learned as much from him as he did from them. In later years, Yusef returned to Iraq and worked for the government in the oil department.

One of the privileges of being a missionary is working with nationals, having contact with patients, and being able to show and tell of the love of our Lord. During an especially busy two days in the hospital, I could feel one of the inpatients watching me. It was a sixteen-year-old girl. Eventually she asked, "Why do you Christians work so hard to serve others?"

I was in a bit of a hurry and answered in haste, "Because this is my work. I enjoy what I'm doing—God has put me here to help you and your people."

Thankfully, the teenager pressed me for a better answer. "But why? Does it have something to do with Jesus Christ—with serving him?"

I realized that I almost missed a wonderful opportunity to tell about my Lord. I stopped for a moment. "Yes," I said. "You are exactly right. That is the real reason."

I was happy that the girl had seen further than my first answer, and also thankful that she had glimpsed Jesus through our work.

A twenty-eight-year-old mother came to us. She and her young husband had two beautiful daughters, but no sons. The husband had divorced her a year earlier, and according to custom he took the girls with him. The young mother had nothing left to live for. We were able to share the love of Jesus with her while she was in contact with us.

A five-year-old boy came to us, badly burned. His dark-eyed sisters came with him. Solemnly, the parents told us that it would have been better for both girls to die, rather than for the son to be afflicted. The girls counted for very little, they believed, while the son was everything. We talked with the family and prayed for them.

A black-covered woman in labor was brought to us on a stretcher one morning. The people who brought her were afraid that she would die, and when I peeled back the cloth I was ready for almost anything. After she had a bath and was prepped for delivery, I could see that the labor was actually going pretty well. She eventually delivered a healthy, nine-pound boy and the frowns of worry became cheers of delight outside her room. The woman spoke with me about the baby and then asked me to name it. I chose the name *Shakir*, which means "one who is thankful." I explained that we were thankful to God for the healthy boy.

There also were times of discouragement. At one point the son of our wonderful Iraqi evangelist and colporteur was arrested and accused of being a Communist. The charge was very serious, particularly in the years immediately following the war, and the government investigated the activities of the boy. It turned out that the boy was living a double life—as a good student in the mission school, but also as a frequenter of clubs and questionable political gatherings. His parents, our good friends, were sick about the charges. The father, who was not well physically, began to walk about as if he had a giant weight on his shoulders. Two years later this fine Christian gentleman passed away. During his last year he underwent operation after operation for cancer. Death, when it came, was a blessing.

About the same time, the son of another Protestant Christian family in Amarah (and at that time there were only four or five Protestant families in the city) was found guilty of squandering a large amount of his employer's money in a gambling escapade. To make matters worse, the young man attempted robbery to regain the missing money. The boy's sister had to leave school and go to work, in order to help support the family after these events.

Meanwhile, in Basrah, Dr. Van Ess's health was taking a turn for the worse (he was to pass away in 1949). We also learned that Dr. Moerdyk was suffering from tuberculosis. Dr. Lewis Scudder, with his wife and family, came to Amarah to replace the Moerdyks. Lew and Dotty had been stationed in Kuwait, a place they had come to love dearly. I remember that they had to work hard to adjust to the different style of Arabic spoken in Amarah. (All of us struggled with variations in the language when we were transferred from one station to another.)

The Scudders, unlike the Moerdyks, had small children in their family. But even though I sometimes felt like an intruder as I boarded in one of their rooms and ate at their table, they were most kind. Lew, the son of missionary parents in India, loved to eat rice and curry twice a week. After a time I learned to love rice and curry as much as he did.

I should mention one other doctor before I go on to other topics, Dr. Maurice Heusinkveld. He was sent to Amarah later, so the Scudders could return to Kuwait. He and Elinor came with two boys (later another son was born). Maurie was another fine doctor. Years later his murder would be a shock to all of us in the RCA.

Political conditions in Iraq grew steadily worse in the waning years of the 1940s. One incident, in December, 1947, remains in my mind. There was a cholera scare in Cairo during the fall of 1947, and government leaders in Iraq feared that cholera would break out in the poor quarters of Amarah. An order came from Baghdad that all the poor people in town, who lived in the date stick huts, were to be moved across the Tigris River. One day the police drove big trucks into the poor areas and told the people that moving day had come. The police then threw the people's possessions on the trucks and dismantled every hut in town. Although some tried to transport reed mats for their huts on the trucks, the effect was to put the poor people out of town with very little shelter and hardly any warning. Some of the poor families came to the mission compound, and we tried to do what we could for them. We built some temporary shelters on land we rented near the hospital.

At about the same time, the situation in Palestine was grave. Arabs and Jews were at each other's throats. As the nation of Israel was about to be established there were terrorist acts, outright fighting, and much bloodshed. Arabs in the Middle East were upset about the role of the United States in the establishment of Israel, and there were anti-American demonstrations in Beirut, Baghdad, Amarah, and other cities. American missionaries were advised to stay indoors during the demonstrations, and the mission compound was given a police guard in front and in back. From the windows of our buildings we could see students marching about in the street. We could not know it at the time, but it was the beginning of the end of our mission work in Amarah.

In May, 1948, 'Ata, one of our dependable workers in the hospital, who had been associated with the mission for six years, was shot to death. He was just twenty-two years old. To the young workers in the hospital, he had been like a brother. It happened during national elections when tempers were high and outside agitators reportedly were in Amarah. Apparently a gunman specifically targeted our young man, who had made some political statements during the course of the election campaigns.

It seemed that half of Amarah turned out for the funeral. The townspeople, young and old, mourned his death and marched to the mission compound to share their grief with us. To keep things under control, we had to lock the gates while the funeral procession was in the area. That afternoon the young man was buried in a Muslim cemetery not far from the hospital.

As a mission staff, we couldn't help but wonder why the Lord allowed 'Ata to be taken. He seemed to have such a bright future! Not only had he worked in Amarah, but he had taken a course in surgery in Bahrain under Dr. Harrison. While in Bahrain, I later learned, he had some good talks with Ed Luidens and had testified to Ed about his faith in Jesus Christ. He faithfully attended church services and partook of communion. The day after the young man's death we closed the hospital to observe a day of mourning.

Three months later I took my first trip to Kodaikanal, India. The trip was meant to be a vacation, and it was a refreshing and welcome respite in the months of hard work. The excursion also gave me a chance to meet many missionaries in Katpadi, Vellore, Raniput, and Palmaner.

Kodai was part of an interdenominational mission center, where children of our Persian Gulf missionaries attended a boarding school. The town was located in beautiful green mountains at an altitude of 7,000 feet. Up there in the cool air it was easy to rest and recharge spiritual batteries. There were trees of all kinds: pine, palm, fir, eucalyptus, and other kinds I didn't recognize. There were beautiful wild flowers, shrubbery, and cactus plants that would reseed themselves and keep spreading.

At Kodai I met Ed Luidens. (Ruth had taken their son Donnie to the States.) Jay and Midge Kapenga were also there from Oman. Their son Peter was born that summer in Kodai. I learned through a letter that my sister Millie also had her first son. (For that matter, the whole Sam Boersma family had grown. Six grandchildren were born while I was in Amarah!)

Little Peter Jay Kapenga, born in August, 1948, was the central figure in quite an adventure when he was about a year old. Jay and Midge were stationed in Muscat. They urgently needed streptomycin for little Peter, who was fighting dysentery and was not responding to treatment. Streptomycin was so new that it was not available in Oman. Dr. Mary Allison told Jay to search out any and all possibilities of obtaining it for Peter.

They sent a telegram to the nearest mission hospital in Bahrain asking for the medication. It was there, but it turned out that boat transportation to Muscat would result in a long delay in receiving the medicine. Little Peter's illness was serious. Time was getting short.

Ed Luidens, who was serving in Bahrain, received the telegram asking for the medicine. Just as he had done for us years before in Lisbon, Ed began making inquiries in Manamah. "Would it be possible to fly the medicine to Muscat?"

"Yes," was the reply, "but it would cost a great deal to do that. Besides, the air field in Muscat is little more than a strip of dirt. A large plane couldn't even land there."

Ed continued to make inquiries and to seek a solution to the problem.

While Ed was at the Bahrain airport a big U.S. Air Force B-17 rescue plane flew in. Ed ran up to it on the tarmac and waved to get the attention of the pilot. Passengers rapidly disembarked, but before Ed could do anything the crew slammed the door shut and prepared for an immediate take-off. There was no hope of yelling over the roar of the four big engines.

Just as Ed was about to give up, the engines revved down, the door reopened, and the pilot appeared at the door. Ed rushed up to him and explained the need for getting the medicine to Muscat.

To make a long story short, the medicine was dropped by parachute into Muscat. A grateful Jay Kapenga had spelled out the words "Thank You" in giant letters made of old flour on the ground. Little Peter Jay Kapenga recovered fully, with the help of the streptomycin that came via special airlift.

Fellowship with brother and sister missionaries and their families was a high point of my service in Arabia. I use the terms "brothers and sisters" because that aptly describes the bonds that developed over the years. We studied, struggled, worshiped, worried, prayed, rejoiced, planned, and dreamed together. We saw each other during high points and low points. We learned to know each other's strengths and weaknesses. We cared deeply about each other.

As the years passed I had opportunities to visit our other mission stations in the Gulf and assist in our other hospitals. Annual Arabian mission meetings in Basrah included representatives from all the stations, and we all got to know each other. There were often hard decisions to make, but the meetings were times of good fellowship and spiritual growth.

The workload in Amarah seemed to increase steadily. Just when we thought we had set an all-time record for seeing the most patients with the fewest hospital workers, we would see even more patients again. Dr. and Mrs. Scudder worked hard as they kept up the heavy medical work, as well as raising their own children. I have nothing but respect for the service above and beyond the call of duty that was performed by this unique couple.

It was after a hard day of work with Dr. and Mrs. Scudder in the Amarah hospital that the Lord put me into a situation that gave me a very specific calling for the rest of my life.

IV
Being Single

*The Lord is my light and my salvation—whom
    shall I fear?*
*The Lord is the stronghold of my life—of whom
    shall I be afraid?*

Psalm 27:1

Often in the hospital in Amarah, patients would ask me: "Do
your parents miss you?" "Why did they let you come?" "Have you
sisters or brothers?"

My reply would be something like, "They miss me very much.
But God gave me to them and they gave me to God. They are
happy to know that I am in God's service, helping you here in
Amarah."

The questioners always seemed to find my answer intriguing. It
was something outside of their experience. One old woman
responded, "I wouldn't let my daughter out of my sight!"

My Arab patients were very sensitive to my status as a member
of a family. Every day someone would bless my family with the
words, "God keep your mother and your father," or "God keep your
sisters and brothers," or "May God lengthen the days of their
lives." It was a delightful custom and I enjoyed telling them about
my family in Illinois. Then I would inquire about their own
families.

(Receiving family blessings such as these helped me understand
better the Old Testament accounts of blessings, such as those
bestowed by Jacob upon his twelve sons. What I encountered in
Amarah was certainly a remnant of a custom that had existed in
the Middle East for thousands of years.)

Sometimes a patient who was not aware that I was single would venture to bless my children. In a good natured way, helpers around me would chuckle and I would have to explain that I was single. The idea that a healthy young woman would choose to be single and therefore childless seemed to be another new concept to many of the people I met. In their culture, the normal thing was for every young girl to be married to the man of her parents' choosing. If a woman did not marry, it indicated some kind of problem in the family. Some people suspected I was abnormal or perhaps even immoral! They could not believe that a healthy girl could remain both unmarried and chaste!

When some of my friends discussed my singleness with me, I tried to explain that I was perfectly normal and that being single was not unusual in other cultures. Celibacy was God's will for me, I would say, and I could do more for God by remaining single. My friends usually accepted my explanation in the same good humor that it was offered.

Being single was an important aspect of life for me in the mission field. It affected my relationships with others, my work, my spiritual life, my time alone, my ability to function in times of stress, my fears, and the way others saw me. In all of these areas I saw God's leading and increased ability to serve him, but I won't pretend there weren't some difficult times. Most of this chapter is about the rich blessings that the Lord gave me as an unmarried woman.

The ability to remain single is a special gift from the Lord. God equips and enables us to fulfill our callings. When I was in Illinois, the Lord gave me a clear call to mission work, and then in Amarah he gave me a very clear call to remain single. In 1947 in Amarah, Dotty Scudder and I were assisting Lew in the operating room when Khalaf, a medical orderly, came in to tell us a desperate mother had brought in a very sick baby. There was no way we could leave the surgery to see the baby. Dr. Scudder told Khalaf to ask the mother to wait, and he would see her as soon as he could. The surgery took much longer than expected. When we finished, the sun was going down. Coming out of the operating room we looked in vain for the mother and baby. They were gone.

We stood there wondering what to do. We were all tired and hungry. What could we do? The woman hadn't even stayed to talk to us, although we had been clear about seeing her as soon as we could. Dr. and Mrs. Scudder had a responsibility to their family. They went home to the three children and supper. Being single I

had fewer demands on my time. I asked Khalaf who had brought
the sick infant. Khalaf informed me that it was Ateeya. I knew
Ateeya and where she lived.

When I got to the hut, I found Ateeya in tears. She thought it
was over for baby Hamood, and she had brought the child home to
die. The child's body was burning with fever; his respirations and
pulse were very rapid. I didn't know how a little one could survive
a fever that was obviously so high, but there was no doubt that he
was still clearly alive. So great was my concern for baby Hamood
that I picked him up and almost ran to the hospital.

The baby's temperature was indeed dangerously high—107°, the
highest I ever saw on a thermometer. We packed the baby in cold,
wet cloths and summoned the doctor.

Dr. Scudder said Hamood could not possibly live, but that I
should start injections of penicillin in crystalline every three hours
(this was before the days of penicillin in procaine).

We clustered around, working hard and fast on the little one, but
I'm afraid we didn't have much hope. Mrs. Pennings came and
offered prayer. Somehow, the baby seemed to hang on. Ateeya
and I remained with Hamood through the night, changing the
moist ice packs continuously, checking his temperature, giving
injections and children's aspirin.

The temperature began to drop, and in the wee morning hours I
went home to get a few hours sleep before the next work day
began. Somehow, by God's grace, Hamood lived through the night.
He kept improving. There were many prayers of gratitude over the
next few days as the child steadily grew stronger.

It was a great day when Hamood could be discharged from the
hospital. Ateeya was most demonstrative and unreserved about
telling everybody that her son had been at death's door and that
Christ had miraculously healed him. How happy and grateful his
parents were, as were the rest of us! It was truly a miracle.
Hamood grew to become a young man and to lead a normal life.
Incredible as it may seem, there was no brain damage. The Lord
had given complete healing.

As I pondered these things, something became clear to me. If I
had been married, or if there had been no single missionary on
duty at the hospital that afternoon, the baby would have died that
night. God spoke to me, telling me that he had a place for single
missionaries in the Arabian mission and I was called to be single.
He would give me the qualities necessary to live that kind of life—
the "gift" of being single.

Jeanette with a baby

I never forgot that lesson. The call to singleness was so important in my life that I could never have been happy if I had stepped into matrimony. Marriage proposals did come and I'll admit that in times of weakness I was tempted to say, "Well, others do it—why shouldn't I?"

One of the first young men in my life was a fellow named Gil, a fine Irish fellow who saw me twice a week when I was finished with nurses training and working at the hospital. I remember driving with him to some of the scenic attractions in the northern Illinois-Indiana area: Swallow Cliff, Starved Rock, the Indiana Dunes, and the beautiful forest preserves. Sometimes Gil would come by the street car at the end of the line, as I sat waiting for it to begin its 10:30 p.m. run into the city. He would honk the horn of his car and I would spring up from my seat, collect the unneeded fare from the conductor, and ride with Gil all the way to Roseland. Had I allowed the friendship to continue, I know marriage would have been a possibility. As weeks went on, I could see that things might get serious, and I suppose I had a feeling that my parents would be against the relationship. I discussed it with my friend and confidante, Grace. She advised me to break off the relationship, which I did. I fear I was too abrupt with Gil, however, and many times since then I have wondered if I hurt him. I think I did the right thing, but in the wrong way.

After Gil, there was another young man we called Red. In Amarah I met a young man we called Finn, who was a driver for a British officer. Finn's interest in me was soon obvious. He made it very clear that he wanted to marry me and would not take "no" for an answer. People at the mission station guessed that I would be one of the next single nurses to leave the service during my first term!

I was in a dither, not knowing how to respond to Finn. At one point I wrote to my family about it. Dad wrote me a fine letter, saying, "Jeanette, don't do it. The Lord has called you in service to him."

I had always respected and obeyed my parents. They were very concerned about me. I decided to listen to dad's advice and continue in my calling.

Finn could not understand why I needed to consult my parents or why I listened to them. He was very upset and tried to convince me to make up my own mind. I knew in my heart that as good and handsome as Finn was, God had other plans for me. It was a real temptation to give in and say yes, and I can well understand how other young nurses felt. But by God's grace, my loyalty remained with the mission.

Then there was an oilman who attended our Sunday evening services. He was a fine young man, in some ways like my father. Not only was he a good Christian, but he was highly respected by his coworkers and was able to witness effectively to people in his company. We immediately hit it off and spent some evenings together. We loved to sing hymns on our dates and to harmonize together. Early in the relationship I felt I had to tell him that I was completely dedicated to missionary work and would never marry. I shared with him my experience in Amarah. He was downcast at first, but he respected my feelings about my calling. I informed him of a new missionary nurse having arrived in another station. They were later married. God blessed their marriage.

Later in Oman I met and enjoyed the company of some of the young men who worked in British firms. Their weekends began on Thursday noon and went through the day on Friday. On Thursday afternoons we would enjoy climbing the thousand-foot mountains outside of town. There we would sit with picnic lunches and watch fishing vessels and steamers. Occasionally we would go to the beach. God kept us on the straight and narrow. I pray that the Lord used me in their lives in influential, constructive ways.

One of them moved away for a time, and when he returned to Oman he wrote that he was anxious to see me again. When I failed to respond he showed up at my door, not a little upset. He didn't take no for an answer and came back whenever he could get transportation. He was a problem to me, to the point that I wished he had never been transferred back to Oman. Satan would have ensnared me, but the Lord kept me safe.

An officer from a Greek freighter gave me even more trouble. He came to our mission hospital accompanying the wife of his ship's captain who was going through a miscarriage. The sailor carried her to the upstairs apartment that night, and I set up a cot for him in the living room.

While the woman slept, the man came close to attacking me. He expected me to be easy prey and when he found out I wasn't available for him, he became very upset—hot and burning. For all intents and purposes, I was alone. I was very scared. I decided my best bet would be to go to the screened-in cage on the roof and hope he wouldn't think to look for me there.

The stairs to the roof were inside the apartment. I was afraid of being heard by him, so I walked ever so quietly up those steps. It took me a while to get to sleep that night. Nothing happened, however, and in the morning I gave thanks to God for his protection.

Before I go on to brighter subjects, I should mention loneliness, one of the more difficult aspects of being single. It is fairly easy for a single missionary, isolated in a foreign culture, to develop acute feelings of loneliness.

Praise to God I never had time to be lonely. The work to which God called me kept me busy from before daybreak to bedtime. There never seemed to be enough hours in the day.

By God's grace I had a good rapport with the girls and women at the hospital. After duty hours in the evening we would sometimes go for long walks and make visits in homes. Should I be home evenings, there were always callers. Muslim women from town would call. I also visited them in their homes.

I enjoyed good fellowship with my missionary colleagues. We were one and we were in the work together. We saw much of each other as we were together in worship services, in meetings, and in social activities.

I had the friendship of the Omanis and I had the fellowship of the missionaries. I was indeed truly blessed. Above these amenities there was the work God called me to do, which kept me busy and gave me joy. When God calls, he equips and provides. As a single person, I experienced fulfillment and joy. There was no room or time for loneliness.

A primary benefit of singlehood, of course, is the freedom to move around without worrying about the effects on a spouse or children. A single person could work all night on a case without neglecting a family. Travel, spur-of-the-moment activities, time-consuming projects, prayer vigils—all these are much, much easier for a single person to accomplish. The Lord only knows how many lives were saved on the mission field by single medical people who had the freedom to change their schedules at the last moment!

It almost goes without saying that women missionaries were the only ones who had access to the sequestered Arab women in their homes. I always felt that being single helped me develop unique friendships among the Arab women. Some of the women I met continued to be good friends for the rest of my days of service. Being a single woman opened new doors of friendship for me.

Single people can perhaps devote more time to such spiritual disciplines as prayer, meditation, and Bible study. Almost all missionaries begin or end their days with devotions, but singles are less apt to be interrupted by family concerns. I loved spending moments alone with my Bible and my God. In later years especially, the Holy Spirit seemed to open the Word every time I came to it, and I filled the margins of my Bible's pages—as well as notebook pages—with many notes on spiritual things. The last two years I have read through the Bible cover-to-cover on a one-year plan. Some of my family and friends read the Bible through in one year on a regular basis. One dear old pastor has done so for sixty years!

Again, let me add that all this is of the Lord, not from me. Being single is a gift and having time to spend in the Word is a gift. "He must increase; I must decrease."

I feel that I have "children" all over the world. Being childless in the physical sense has not been a cross for me to bear. In a spiritual sense, I feel I have hundreds of "offspring." Not a week goes by that I don't receive letters from different parts of the world addressed to "Aunt Jeanette." Babies that I delivered years ago are grown up, and I receive letters from them and from their children. I receive visits, phone calls, letters, and even gifts from people in Canada, India, Bahrain, Oman, and other places. I can't remember how many times I was given the honor of naming a baby.

Acquiring material possessions is certainly not a goal of remaining single, but I should say that the Lord provided for me in wonderful ways. During my years of service, my paychecks were always modest, but every now and then a gift would come from an Arab friend that would be unexpected and breathtaking. At different times I received a gold watch, gold pieces, heavy gold bracelets, gold earrings, a gold pen set, fine coral beads, perfume, beautiful cloth, and pieces of jewelry with diamonds and rubies. I regarded most of these treasures as temporary acquisitions rather than possessions and was able to give many of them to missionary friends who were in need, and to others.

When I considered my retirement from the mission field, I wondered where I would live. The Lord, however, had things all worked out for me. At the proper time he provided a beautiful little house in Mt. Greenwood, not far from the church that had faithfully supported me all my years in Arabia. Not only did the Lord provide a house, but furnishings that were beyond my expectations. (But I fear I'm jumping ahead in my story. I shall write more about this later in the book.)

All these blessings I recount as personal examples of the care of a loving God. The Lord works in each life differently. But I feel I should encourage those who remain single and are trying to serve the Lord. In 1 Corinthians 7, the Apostle Paul says quite frankly that it is good to remain unmarried, and that an unmarried person who is content with that state should not change it.

Following are a few guidelines for the single person. I hope I can encourage some readers who may be single. Some of the preceding paragraphs are very personal and experiential. But the following ideas are intended to be more general in nature and suitable for many people.

1. *Some are called to be single.* As I speak in churches, I sometimes encounter people who say they once felt the call to missions, but instead of answering it they settled down to raise families. These comments always seem to be tinged with regret. Two thoughts come to my mind: First, I wonder if they truly were called. For some people, there's no hiding from God's call. If God fully means for you to go to missions, God will get you there. If you have ignored God's call, it may not have been a true call in the first place. Second, I wonder if God allows some people to step away from his call and follow their own inclinations? God respects our decisions and may let us go our own way. If so, I have a feeling that these people miss an exciting life of service. I wonder if they will find real happiness in their "second best" endeavors?

There may be some unhappiness associated with an ignored or diverted call. Abraham was called to follow the Lord and produce many descendants. He was sidetracked, however, when he listened to Sarah and had children by Hagar. Much pain came into their lives when they ran ahead of God instead of waiting and patiently following his leading.

The basic principle in this is to keep one's eyes focused on the high calling of life in Christ Jesus. If God is fully in control of a person's life, he will let us know whether or not we should be married—and the spiritually sensitive person will wait and follow his guidance.

(Some of the following ideas are adapted from an article by Karen Witte, which appeared in *Christian Life* magazine.)

2. *Singleness is an option.* Perhaps a long-term marriage relationship *is not* best for each person. Although times are changing, many women still think in terms of establishing a career path and then marrying and devoting their lives to a family (or vice versa). That is fine if it is God's will, but I think we should be open to singlehood as another option. Some men, as well, may be able to serve the Lord better as singles and shouldn't be blind to that possibility. It starts with an openness to look at another option besides marriage.

3. *Reject the lies of society.* Our Western culture puts a premium on being in love with a "significant other." Modern movies and books, of course, don't give much attention to marriage. They just emphasize meaningful relationships and love affairs. Teenagers

are not taught to regard abstinence, celibacy, or singlehood as reasonable lifestyles. In fact, sexual continence is laughed at.

The sensitive Christian must be willing to ignore all the media messages that promote fast love, promiscuity, and various kinds of affairs. God's way is different. Teenager, believe it or not, God may want you to remain unattached and self-sufficient.

4. *Count the cost.* Jesus does not tell us that life will be problem free. Being single is not always easy, just as being married is not always easy. Those who follow the Lord's leading should not be surprised to experience difficulties, whether they be doubts, fears, insecurities, anxieties, or rejection. These things are part of the package. Jesus said in Matthew 16:24,25, "If anyone would come after me, he must deny himself and take up his cross and follow me. For whoever wants to save his life will lose it, but whoever loses his life for me will find it."

The cost of discipleship and singlehood is dear, but the results are great and can give us joy. "I tell you the truth," Jesus said to his disciples, "No one who has left home or wife or brothers or parents or children for the sake of the kingdom of God will fail to receive many times as much in this age and, in the age to come, eternal life" (Luke 18:29,30).

5. *Live life to the fullest.* If you are convinced that the Lord has called you to be single, concentrate on the benefits and step forward in faith. Dorothy Watts, in a *HIS* magazine article written years ago, discussed some of the same ideas I have been considering in the last few pages:

> To some women, even at an early stage, there comes a definite call from God to be single. So often the single state is regarded as something negative; it can be something positive. Life in the community would suffer seriously without the devotion and care of single welfare workers, nurses, and teachers. But Paul went a step further when he compared the life of the unmarried woman with that of the married. The unmarried woman concerns herself with the Lord's affairs, and her aim in life is to make herself holy in body and in spirit. But the married woman must concern herself with the things of this world, and her aim will be to please her husband.
>
> It is true that God does call some women to this life of single devotion to him. He may lead them into a work

which is so absorbing that it could permit no marriage obligations. Mary Slessor, after the death of her mother, pioneered among fierce cannibal tribes where death was a possibility. Amy Carmichael was called to devote herself utterly to the children and women of Dohnavur. Mildred Cable rejected an early suitor because marriage would cut across God's call to do pioneer work in China. God has work at home and abroad which only a single woman can do. There is a place for the married and the unmarried in the divine order of things, and the work of one is not more important than that of the other. What is important is finding what he wants us to do and doing it.

God has a calling and work for each of us. I praise and thank God that he called me to singleness. As a single Christian, you will have tremendous freedom to go places and devote time to special activities. You have the ability to focus your attention on important things and change a schedule at a moment's notice to shift attention from one thing to another. You can travel swiftly. You can spend uninterrupted time with the Lord, growing and developing spiritually. You can cultivate many friendships among men and women. You have opportunities to be a blessing to many people. You can stand up and look at the big picture.

God has a place for single people in the world.

V

Changing Assignments

*The Lord is my rock, my fortress and my
deliverer...*

Psalm 18:2

Just before my first term of service was complete, the Lord sent some intense experiences my way. Mrs. Pennings, who became so ill in 1948 that we thought the Lord would take her home, had slowly recovered to the point at which she enjoyed a New Year's Eve dinner with the rest of us at the home of a Christian Iraqi. Dr. Heusinkveld carried her to a waiting automobile, which took her to the Iraqi home. It was the first time since the onset of her illness that this patient, saintly woman had gone anywhere except her house and the church. We were glad to see her make this tiny foray out into the world, and it was fitting that it would be to the home of a Christian Iraqi family.

A month later, one of our inpatients was the wife of a sheikh who lived in a village about fifty miles from Amarah. She had been with us for many weeks, suffering from typhoid. While she was with us her daughter, back in the village, came down with the disease and was brought to us for hospitalization. The mother and daughter stayed together.

One morning we heard that two of the woman's sons, in the same village, also had contracted the disease and died. Somehow the family members had talked themselves out of sending the young men to the hospital. We were told this in confidence, without the mother or daughter's knowledge. The family members wanted to break the news themselves, back in the village, when the mother had fully recovered. Our hearts bled for the woman and her daughter. We hoped and prayed that she would not be severely affected by the shock.

About a month before I left Amarah, we received the exciting news that Dr. and Mrs. Nykerk, Nellie Hekhuis, and Ed Luidens had made a trip bringing medical services into the interior of the Arabian Peninsula, at the request of King Ibn Saud. Every trip to the interior was big news for all of us in the mission as we were anxious to establish a toehold for the mission inside the coastal areas.

As Rose Nykerk described the experience later, it was a difficult expedition. Dr. Nykerk had just returned from a trip to Qatar when the summons came from Emir bin Jaluie. Dr. Nykerk was asked to leave immediately for Hafoof, which was located a day's journey inland. He was eager to go, but not as eager to spend more time away from his family, so he asked permission to take his family along. The Emir assented. Like other mission physicians, Dr. Nykerk also asked permission to take his spiritual advisor, "Padre" Ed Luidens. Again the Emir assented. As quickly as he could, Dr. Nykerk also rounded up other staff members who could join the expedition.

The medical team, as it turned out, was shorthanded. There was a mountain of work to do in Hafoof. The mission staff people worked long hours, but they still felt they weren't satisfying all the needs that came to them. They took enough medicine for a month's work, but the time rolled on to six and then seven weeks. The people still needed help, but the supplies finally ran out and the team went back to Bahrain.

Tired, but happy to have made another trip into the interior, the team returned in March. They wondered if the Lord would give the mission other chances to reach inland, perhaps establishing a permanent base. (As I write this years later, the Lord still has not given the mission an inland site.)

In Rose Nykerk's account of the Hafoof trip, written in 1950, there is a little statement that hinted at future developments in the mission. Referring to the outlying mission stations and the central "home bases" of the mission, Rose wrote, "Our 'branches' seem to be getting too strong for the main stem, and we have had some rather serious discussions as to what is right and the best policy."

In April my first term of service ended and my furlough began. One of the joys of missionary life is the homebound trip after a good term of service. In my letters home, I had been making preparations for months in advance, so everything was ready when the time came. I said farewell to my friends in Amarah and went to Basrah. After taking care of some business there, I was given a send-off at the train station by George and Chris Gosselink, Harry and Bev Almond, Miss Kellien, and Rachel Jackson.

The next morning found us in Baghdad, where we boarded one of the famous Nairn desert buses that had a self-contained, air-conditioned coach. Like a train on tires, the bus traversed the desert and took us to Beirut. There we were met by Ed and Ruth Luidens with their children Don and Carol, who were also beginning a furlough and would be traveling with me. As I enjoyed the company of the little ones, I thought of how things had changed since we first came to the field years before. My own brothers and sisters, too, would introduce me to children who had entered the world since I left the States.

Our trans-Atlantic crossing was aboard the *S.S. Exeter*, the most beautiful ship I had seen until that time. It was known as an "export ship," meaning it carried both freight and passengers (200 in all) and made a number of stops in international ports. During the three-week voyage on the *Exeter*, I saw Alexandria, Athens, Naples, Genoa, and Marseilles.

In Athens we had a little time to see ancient sites. I was struck by the locations that were reflected in the words of the Apostle Paul. We saw a race track that reminded me of his exhortation to "lay aside...the sin which doth so easily beset us, and let us run with patience the race that is set before us" (Heb. 12:1, KJV).

At Mars Hill there was a brass plate with Paul's words inscribed on it: "I see in all things that you are very religious...." The Bible passages about Paul's sermon at that very spot came alive for me that day.

On board the ship, Ed, Ruth, and I had devotions together and directed most of our thoughts toward friends and families in America. We were full of anticipation and high spirits. I remember laughing merrily as we reminisced about my falling off a wooden plank bridge into an irrigation ditch in Basrah. It happened just after a wedding, when I was all dolled up in my finest attire. Harry Almond fished me out of the water and carried me to high ground.

During quiet moments I worried over upcoming public speaking engagements. I had yet to develop any skill as a speaker, and I wrote out the words of every speech and memorized everything beforehand. During the ocean voyage I prepared several speeches for groups that I knew would ask me to tell them about the mission work.

The voyage was clear and brisk, and we arrived in New York three weeks and a day after we embarked. We were met at the dock by Mrs. Gnade, a precious soul who met all of the missionaries coming from the various mission fields. She threw her arms around us and gave us a big welcoming hug. We stopped at the mission offices on Riverside Drive and then made our way to Buck Hills Falls, Pennsylvania, where the Reformed denomination's General Synod was meeting. The mission board wanted us to attend the synod upon arriving in the States, partly to maintain our interest in the issues before the denomination and partly to stimulate mission-mindedness among the delegates. I remember that Simon Teggelaar was the elder delegate from my own church in Mt. Greenwood. It was so good to see him.

Ed, Ruth, and I joined other missionaries from many fields in a time of reflection and fellowship.

The highlight of the synod for me came on the sixth day, when my parents; my sister Harriet; her husband, John Beintum; and their two-year-old child, Shirley, arrived in Buck Hills Falls. It had not been an easy trip for my mother, who was so emotionally overwrought while waiting for my return that she contracted a severe case of shingles. Nevertheless they came. In the beautiful green hills of Pennsylvania we were together again. The Lord had kept us. It was so good to be reunited. How happy we were to meet again after an absence of five and a half years. They all looked a little older, but I knew I had changed too. John was a fine young man. My new niece Shirley was a little beauty. We talked and talked. We said heartfelt prayers of thanksgiving that night.

I recall walking through the lush grass and shrubbery down the trails of this beautiful section of the country. The tall trees and thick brush were in complete contrast to the dusty fields and plants of Iraq. The air was fresh and moist. Clouds drifted in the sky. The blessings of life in America were flooding back to me: cold tap water, cold milk, the lush green countryside, rivers full and flowing, well-fed farm animals, and summer rains.

Back in Worth, our family was not the same. It was much larger! Two children had been born to Ted and Grace, two to John and Millie, and Mel introduced me to his fiancee, Dorothy. The wedding was to take place a few months later and I would be a bridesmaid. What a crew of new nephews and nieces! Davie, Billy, Shirley, Carol Sue, Linda, Janet, and Richie.

How I enjoyed talking to these little ones, giving them gifts and souvenirs, and telling stories. In each little face I could see traces of my brothers and sisters and their spouses. The Boersma family was blessed and prospering.

Ted had put the war experiences behind him. Always practical and down-to-earth, Ted had focused his energies entirely on his family and occupation. He looked strong and hearty, and the wartime captivity seemed little more than a bad dream.

I'll never forget the first Sunday morning back in the Mt. Greenwood Reformed Church, when we could all file into the pew together and worship as a family, as we had done so many years before. My friends in the church greeted me warmly and invited me to their homes. The women's group asked me to talk, and I was happy to tell them how all of the articles in their mission boxes had been distributed to the people in Amarah.

As much as I would have enjoyed spending all my time in my parents' home, there were other duties to attend to.

I was anxious to obtain further medical training. (It was fairly common for missionaries on furlough to pursue advanced training in their field, while they were back in the States, and the mission board was very generous about assisting them.) My nurse's training had given me a general knowledge of obstetrics and gynecology, and my years of experience in Amarah had given me lessons in practical childbirth techniques, but I wanted more training and certification as a midwife.

The Frontier Nursing Service in Kentucky had a good six-month program in midwifery. I originally found out about it from the mission board, and with the board's blessing, I enrolled in the school in the fall of 1950.

The school was located in Wendover County, Kentucky. First-time visitors were immediately impressed by the fact that all the buildings on the Hyden campus (where I did most of my work) were made of logs cut right out of the nearby forests. The health care center at Hyden featured a number of buildings: a hospital, nurses' quarters, midwives' quarters, a doctor's residence, and various sheds and barns.

The service was committed to offering prenatal and obstetrical care to the region's women at little or no cost, through seven prenatal care centers scattered throughout the hills. There were many unsung heroes on the staff—people who made many sacrifices to care for the women of the area. An instructor at the service who made a great impression on me was Miss Fedde. Besides being an excellent teacher, she was a good, upright woman.

The twice-weekly classroom sessions were well organized, but my most vivid memories are of the people in the area, especially the housewives deep in the hills. As we followed up on obstetrical cases and childbirth cases, we often went out to meet these women. I often thought that if anybody deserved special rewards in heaven, it would be these longsuffering mothers.

Their families lived in log cabins or small shacks comprised of two, three, or four rooms. There usually was no wallpaper or paint on the walls. There were chinks between the logs, through which the wind often blew. There were no attics or basements. They heated their homes with logs in fireplaces.

The women were adept at canning sweet potatoes, cabbage, beans, and fruit, which they would store under a loose slab in the floor of the cabin. There was no running water; buckets of water were carried from wells hundreds of feet from the cabins or taken directly from a nearby creek. When we would visit the cabins, invariably we would find the drinking water in buckets with a hand dipper hooked to the side. Kerosene lanterns, always trimmed and ready, were used for light.

I was continually impressed by the self-sufficiency of the hill women. They chopped their own firewood and sometimes dug their own coal out of the hills. They raised their vegetables in little garden plots, after clearing off trees, rocks, and shrubbery. It was the women who did most of the gardening, since the men worked long hours in the coal mines. Twice a day they milked the family cow (or purchased milk from someone else) and churned their own butter. Like their counterparts in Arabia, the mothers in the hospital worried about their milk cows as much as their children!

Near a hill cabin there were always some chickens scrabbling in the gravel and pigs lounging in a pen, living off discarded foodstuffs. A mule or horse was usually at hand, and even in the 1940s these animals were important modes of transportation.

The hill families were early risers. In winter they would be fixing breakfast at four o'clock so the menfolk could leave for the mines by five. Frequently we nurses would be up all night on childbirth cases, and I still remember the hearty breakfasts we would eat as the sun came up: cornbread, salt pork, eggs, and strong coffee.

Daytime work for the women consisted of sewing, childcare, laundry duties, and special food preparation. A family with ten children was not unusual. Older girls would help their hardworking mothers with the young children. Since it was the only way of life they knew, the girls didn't object to the workload—in fact, they always seemed to be cheerful about it. Most of the younger children went to school, although many of them ended their education at the fourth grade level (which was often more education than either of the parents had).

The families were generally healthy. They seemed to hold together well, and they were usually happy. There was a Bible in almost every home and visitors would see plaques with Bible verses hanging on the rough walls. Their faith was simple, and many of them professed to be Baptists. They prayed often. Many of them attended one-room chapels.

I liked the people. Working with these women was a rare experience.

The Frontier Nursing Service covered 700 square miles of hills, mining operations, and woodland containing about 10,000 people. Along with the five other women in the program, I rode horseback to get to many of the cabins. Once a week we would curry the animals in the stalls on the campus. Only two of us, Florence Shade and myself, were able to drive the four-wheel-drive Jeeps that were also available for the nurses. We spent many exciting hours bouncing over deeply rutted roads and fording mountain streams in the vehicles. Little did dad realize when he taught me to drive years before that he was preparing me for service in the Kentucky backwoods (or in the Arabian deserts, for that matter!). How I thanked the Lord for those driving lessons!

During my stay in Kentucky I helped deliver many babies in the cabins, sometimes with logs crackling in the fireplace and children in adjoining rooms or asleep on the floor in the same room. We boiled water in the fireplaces and put kerosene lamps on bedside tables as we worked. Children and other women would pitch in to help with chores around the house during the newly delivered mother's postnatal period.

After completing the necessary courses, attending the required twenty deliveries, and passing state board examinations, I became a certified midwife. During my first term in Amarah, government

Newborn baby delivered by Jeanette in Kentucky during midwifery training.

officials had mentioned that such a certificate was necessary, but none of the officials had taken me to task for not having one. The Lord enabled me to carry on with my work.

Now, however, I was armed with the official-looking document and some excellent training that would answer any future questions.

My health was generally good, but like many missionaries I left America with relatively low immunity and came back fighting a number of "bugs" that I picked up from the environment and from infected patients. While in Iraq I had a few bouts with dysentery and had contracted infectious jaundice or hepatitis twice. Throughout the furlough, under the care of a physician, I took medicine to overcome hookworm and anemia (with a hemoglobin of fifty percent).

My parents tried to help me return to normal by providing nourishing food and taking me out frequently for chocolate milk shakes and sundaes. I tried to explain that the treats wouldn't affect my hemoglobin count, but they would hear none of it. We had fun visiting the soda fountains. When I returned to Oman a year and a half later, an Omani colleague looked at me with concern and said, "Jeanette, you have become fat!"

I traveled extensively on behalf of the mission during the final months of my furlough. I still suffered from shyness when confronted with a group of people, and I memorized my speeches word-for-word. Showing slides seemed to help me overcome my fear of speaking. But I made many, many new friends as I traveled. It would take an extra chapter of this book to list all of the wonderful people who gave me food and lodging during my travels, and all the others whom I met at conferences and mission festivals. Today, as I write these lines, I feel that I have Christian friends in almost every corner of North America. I still correspond with many of these dear people.

While all this was going on, my name and job were being discussed back on the mission field. I learned via letters what was transpiring back in Iraq and Oman. Personnel shortages were causing problems, it turned out. There were two mission hospitals in Oman and not one R.N. to assist the doctors there. The Rev. and Mrs. Dirk Dykstra, evangelists in Oman for almost twenty years, were about to retire and they were desperately seeking a woman to take over some of Mrs. Dykstra's duties. I learned later that some emotional discussions took place at the annual meeting of the mission.

My fellow missionaries decided that I could best serve in Oman after my furlough. A letter came to me, giving me details of the decision. Upon my return to the Middle East, I would stop briefly in Amarah and then proceed to my new assignment in Muscat, Oman.

The exciting, fulfilling days of my first furlough drew to a close. I carefully planned and packed my boxes for a return trip to the Persian Gulf. I went to downtown Chicago to Steven's department store to purchase enough uniforms to last five and a half years. I bought other dresses, shoes, stockings, and personal items that were not available in the Gulf area. I replenished my supply of nurse's caps from the Roseland hospital, taking some extra time to renew acquaintances with people there. From food stores I bought cases of canned fruits and vegetables. Some of my friends on the mission field had asked me to bring back things for them. The hospital needed special items. There were gifts, books, medications, clothing, letters, and tools. A room in my parents' house began filling up with material destined for the Middle East. Box after box was sent east to Keatings Overseas Shipping.

One health problem refused to fade away: anemia. My hemoglobin count was not bouncing back to a normal level. As the departure date approached, it was still too low. There was a delay. As I waited for new test results I became almost panicky, wondering if my health would be permanently impaired. But in the Lord's time, about six weeks, the problem subsided and I was ready to go. As I think back on other furloughs, I would have to say that a fairly serious problem or two cropped up almost every time I was preparing to return to the mission field. I have to conclude that forces of evil were behind many of these problems. But in each case the Lord's power overcame the delaying factor.

The Mt. Greenwood church organized a special farewell service for me on Sunday evening, August 17. The King's Daughters and the Ladies Aid put on a little play called "The Missionary Clinic," the children gave me a corsage, the Men's Society showed a mission film, the Rev. Lambert Olgers brought our joys and concerns before the Lord in prayer, and the Co-Wed Club sang "God Be With You 'Til We Meet Again."

Saying goodbye again to my family was not easy. All of them would be six and a half years older when I saw them next. But the Lord again provided me with a firm sense of being *called* back to Arabia. Not for a moment did I question the need to return to my adopted homeland. In fact, I was anxious to get back and resume my duties in the hospital. We did not shed tears at the final parting—that was not our manner—but there were some personal moments of sadness later, when the good-byes were over.

My ship for the return trip was the *Queen Mary*, which was even more beautiful than the *S.S. Exeter* of a year-and-a-half before. The Atlantic was rough as we sailed for London, and I remember holding on to dinnerware on the table while eating. One night I was afraid I might be tossed out of my bunk. On one of the walls in the lounge was a big map of the North Atlantic, with the water routes between England and the United States marked. There were two slowly moving lights on the routes: one which indicated the progress of our ship, the *Queen Mary*, and another light that indicated the progress of its sister ship, the *Queen Elizabeth*.

In England I saw Buckingham Palace, double-decker buses, and beds of gorgeous flowers. Soon after arriving, I caught a KLM Royal Dutch Airlines plane to the Middle East and en route found myself surrounded by Dutch-speaking passengers. I could understand all of the conversations that were within earshot, but after one or two futile attempts to engage in conversation in Dutch, I had to admit that I could not converse intelligently in the language of my parents. When I tried to talk, the Arabic would have its way and come to the forefront, always pushing back the Dutch of my childhood. I was thankful that most of the people spoke English well.

After a night stop in Munich and breakfast in Cairo, the plane touched down in Basrah on October 14. The city was the same. There were the narrow streets, latticed windows, irrigation ditches, birds, donkeys, white hot sun, and the palm trees above the skyline. It was good to be back.

I was greeted at the airport by a customs man who informed me that Basrah's summer had been the hottest on record. "Hell hot," he said. When I cleared customs I was greeted by the Gosselinks and Miss Kellien. I remember thinking that the summer must have taken its toll on them. They seemed to be tired and a bit thinner than before. On my first night back in Iraq, I had supper with Mrs. Van Ess, the Gosselinks, and Miss Kellien.

I was soon back in Amarah for a brief visit and to pick up personal belongings. I received a goodly welcome from the nationals and Maurice and Elinor Heusinkveld, their children, Christine Vos, and Dr. Donald and Eloise Bosch. The Rev. and Mrs. Pennings had gone home to Orange City, Iowa. Mrs. Pennings had taken the trip well. The Bosches, with their three little ones, were a new addition to the staff. I could see that they would be good for the mission effort.

That afternoon we attended a women's prayer meeting led by Ajeela, a fine Christian woman who had suffered from leprosy.

But the greatest joy was to see Shereefa Moh'd. It was evident that during my year-and-a-half absence she had grown in the faith. There was no doubt about her commitment to Jesus Christ. On my first Sunday back she led the women's Sunday school class. She was waiting for the return of Ed Luidens, at which time she planned to publicly profess her faith in Jesus. I recalled how Shereefa and I used to sit in the sun on my rooftop, studying and discussing the Bible.

Preparations to leave Amarah for Muscat were not easy. I had made many friends there; they had become my family away from home. I would miss them. After one week I was on the move again en route to my new posting, Muscat. On the British India

Steamship Line from Basrah to Oman I met Dr. Wells Thoms and his wife, Beth, for the first time. We would be colleagues and friends working in close proximity for the next twenty years. Wells was the son of Dr. and Mrs. Sharon J. Thoms, who had come to Arabia in 1899. His mother, Mrs. Marion Wells Thoms, a physician, died in 1905 of typhoid fever. His father, Dr. Sharon J. Thoms, one of the first mission doctors, died tragically in 1913 in a fall from a telephone pole near Muscat. Beth was a daughter of the well-known Scudder missionary family of India. They were both "mish kids." As we traveled, Dr. Thoms discussed plans that would involve me.

Wells Thoms dispensing medicine to Omanis with wife Beth

He told me about the debates between the evangelistic and medical divisions of the missionaries, when the problems of under-staffing became acute. He confirmed what the earlier letters had explained—my labors were to be divided between the two divisions: I would work part time in women's evangelism and I would also be in charge of the Women's Hospital in the old part of Muscat. I could see it was going to be a busy life.

The Rev. and Mrs. Dirk Dykstra and Jay and Midge Kapenga would be in Muscat; while Dr. and Mrs. Thoms would be living in Mutrah. The Dykstras and Jay were supervising the evangelistic work, as well as the school (formerly the Freed Slaves School started by Peter Zwemer), while Midge was studying Arabic. The Dykstras would be preparing for retirement.

One's first impression of Oman, in the southwest part of the Persian Gulf area, focuses on the hard, black, barren rocks that rise up out of the sea. Ancient castle-like fortresses rise from

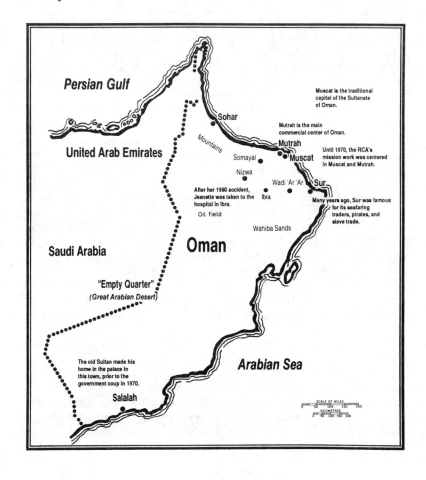

prominent rocks above the coast, giving a fairy-tale appearance to the skyline.

Within the natural harbor at Muscat, the names of ships were painted on the rock surfaces. Some of the names, barely visible, were hundreds of years old. Visitors couldn't help but think of Sindbad the Sailor, the legendary hero of "One Thousand and One Arabian Nights," who supposedly was born in this country, made his fortune in Basrah, and had fantastic adventures throughout Arabia.

Oman was one of the first countries to embrace Islam during the lifetime of the Prophet Mohammed. For centuries the country was a loose federation of Muslim desert tribes. There were many battles between Shi'ite Muslims, who believed that the Islamic world should be ruled by heirs of the Prophet, and Sunni Muslims, who believed in the right of a democratic election of Islamic leaders by representatives of the people. A majority of the Omanis are Sunnis.

For centuries the desert tribes were relatively isolated, self-sufficient, and strong minded. They developed strict codes of behavior based on Islamic law. Even today one encounters these ancient attitudes, almost unchanged in thousands of years, among Bedouins who live in the interior parts of the country.

The modern history of the country began about 1500, when the Portuguese moved in to open up new trade routes to the East. The Duke of Albuquerque was one of the infamous characters associated with Portuguese control of the country. Omanis removed the Portuguese from the capital, Muscat, in 1650. After that they were under the French and British. At one point Napoleon had plans for taking over the country, but the British outmaneuvered him by signing a treaty with the Omanis in 1799. The rulers of Oman at that time, from the Said family, controlled Zanzibar in East Africa, too. They kept up their alliance with the British for many years. Indeed, the British were still active during my terms of service.

The population of Muscat in 1950, when I arrived, was about 3,000. The people lived closely together. Each house had its own wall and seclusion. The bazaar had many shops in close proximity. Muscat's sister city, Mutrah, was located three miles away. While Muscat, the older city, was the seat of power for the government, the younger city, Mutrah, was the commercial center. Mutrah had about 9,000 residents in those days. Our church had activities in both cities.

When we arrived, water was still carried in goatskin bags from wells on the backs of men. Water was a precious commodity. Fresh water was saved for drinking and cooking and salt water was for other domestic uses, such as cleaning, dishes, bathing, etc. At first the mission hired men to bring bags of water to the hospital and mission homes; later donkeys replaced the human carriers.

Housewives also walked miles to the wells to get water— sometimes several times a day during the hot season. A harnessed ox, led by an experienced and adept Omani, walked down an incline toward the well. A bucket would be lowered into the well. When the bucket was full the ox would walk back up the incline. The water would be emptied into a trough that led to a nearby stand

Women returning from well.

of date palms. For a few cents the man at the well would empty the bucket into the women's waiting pitchers.

Each woman would walk with one water pitcher on a hip and another balanced on top of her head. They did not go alone. They were always in groups: talking, visiting, and laughing all the while. They had a good time socializing and passing along the news of the day. I could hear them walking by, under my veranda, discussing their families and friends as they chattered happily.

Obtaining wood for cooking fires was a problem, since there were few trees near the city. The women wood-gatherers would leave the city early in the morning, carrying coffee and dates for their lunch. They spent many hours in search of wood and, after finding the wood, the five-to-six-feet-long branches were put together in bundles. When each woman in the party had assembled a good-sized bundle they would return to the city en masse, balancing the heavy loads on their heads, walking so fast that they almost seemed to run over the path. During a typical day they covered many miles. It was no wonder they had slender, muscular bodies.

Their lives were not easy. Many of them did all their cooking over an open fire. Some had progressed to using primus stoves. The primus stoves could be compared to modern camp stoves. They ran on kerosene and required vigorous pumping to build up fuel pressure. The women did their cooking—by fire or by stove—at ground level, squatting on their haunches for long periods of time while meals were in preparation. During the month of fasting, Muslims did not touch food or drink from sunup to sundown, when temperatures could climb as high as 120 degrees Fahrenheit. Even then the wood had to be gathered, water brought from the well, and the food prepared for the children, as well as for the adults, for they would eat and drink at night.

The Omani women were very clean in their personal habits. Water was a part of their ablutions for personal hygiene; also both men and women washed five times every day before praying. They would have access to salt or brackish water in town, which was used for washing their clothes. There would be the occasional flash-flood, when the *wadis* (dry river beds) would fill with water. After the rain subsided, you would see the women coming from all sides, flocking to the running water with the narrow-rimmed wash tubs on their heads. These metal containers were filled with dirty clothes and some soap powder. They would have an exciting time washing their clothes in the abundance of soft rain water.

Religious practices at the time did not permit birth control. Women of childbearing age were pregnant almost as soon as they stopped breast feeding. Sometimes in the interior, a woman's second or third pregnancy was life threatening, due to a birthing custom that damaged the reproductive organs. (I will write more of this later.) These often pregnant, sometimes malnourished mothers bore a heavy burden as they provided food, wood, and water for large families.

In those days there were no newspapers, radios, or television sets in the country. Information about internal events in the city would travel from person to person very effectively through a well-developed word-of-mouth grapevine. Official government proclamations would appear on the walls near the city gates from time to time. But information about the outside world did not penetrate into the towns and cities. The people were virtually isolated from the world of the twentieth century.

Oman was and is famous for its dates and camels. Twenty-two varieties of dates are grown on the Batina Coast, north of Muscat, and another sixty-two varieties are grown inland. The people also grew sour limes, bananas, mangos, pomegranates, and onions.

Omanis took pride in their fine camels, just as Kentucky horsemen appreciate thoroughbred horses. Omani camels are famous throughout the world for their speed and endurance. Sheikhs from adjoining countries often journeyed to Oman to purchase prize animals. These sheikhs could tell at a glance whether the animal was from good, average, or inferior stock.

Oman now exports oil, but it was one of the last Arabian nations to do so. When I arrived in the country in 1950, exploration was just getting underway in the interior deserts, but nothing promising had been discovered. The Sultan reportedly had given up on finding oil in his domain.

In 1951, the houses on the mission compounds were fairly large. Some held two families. Each house had a large, screened porch that was high enough to catch sea breezes and thereby receive some cooling ventilation at night.

Muscat was considered the hottest country in the Gulf. Because of the heat, when the general rule for RCA missionaries was a leave or vacation away from the field every two years, the ruling for missionaries in Muscat was a field vacation once a year. There were the hot, dry *gharabi* days, when the temperatures would reach 120 degrees in the shade; and there were the days with high humidity, called *ratooba*, when the temperature would be in the lower nineties and the humidity ninety percent. Perspiration would then pour from us and there would not be a dry stitch on our bodies. We would be covered with prickly heat. Like people in the American Southwest, we preferred the *gharabi* days with the higher temperature.

The mission in Muscat contained several compounds. One contained the school and church. The Peter Zwemer Memorial School was a substantial building with a main room about twenty by thirty feet on the ground floor. Above the school was a missionary residence which later housed two families. Jay and Midge Kapenga lived on this compound. The mission's second church had been built south of the school.

The second compound held the old mission house, which had rooms for two families upstairs. I lived in the back apartment during my years in Muscat. The house had originally been purchased by Dr. Cantine, who rebuilt it in 1903. The house and adjoining pieces of land had been upgraded over the years by missionaries who had a talent for remodeling.

The first Christian church in Oman was on the first floor of this home. On the walls were Arabic quotations from the great men of the Old Testament such as Noah, Abraham, Isaac, Ishmael, David, and Solomon. These men are considered prophets in the Koran and thus known to Arabs. The first floor also contained the prayer room and women's *mejlis* or place of meeting. At the back was the pastor's study and several store rooms.

There was a narrow road for donkeys and people to the west of this compound. My bedroom overlapped this roadway, so that people and donkeys actually traversed beneath it. Beyond the animal shelters and another wall was the tennis court built by the British Bank of the Middle East. To the north was the Christian cemetery owned and maintained by the mission. Several local believers and Indian Christians were buried there.

Looming up as the west wall of the two resident compounds was the barren rock escarpment we called the Iron-Clad Mountain. This massive rock took in the heat of the day and held on to it all night, too! It was Rev. Dykstra who said that the temperature in the compounds remained hot both day and night because even though there was no sun, the mountain threw off extra heat at night.

There was also a walkway to the east of our compound, beyond which was a garage, workshop, and storeroom for supplies. And to

Muscat

the east of this section was *Beit Ameena*—property that was purchased by the Dykstras and named after Minnie Dykstra. Up to four poor Omani Christian women were housed there. This compound had its own enclosed toilet and salt-water well. Next to the well was a date stick bathhouse.

To the south of this compound, with another walkway between, was the Women's Obstetrical Hospital.

The mission also owned a piece of property alongside the mountain about a block south. This bit was also purchased by the Dykstras and contained a complete home similar to *Beit Ameena* and large enough for a family. It often housed Omanis who worked for the mission, and sometimes it was rented out, with the proceeds going to the school.

In Mutrah three miles away, there was another set of mission buildings. On two large compounds were homes for missionary families, one of which was a two-family house. Another residence was built on top of a garage and housed a single nurse; still another was built for career and short-term nurses; and two others housed Indian staff people.

One compound contained our large general hospital, most of the residences, and a chapel. A road separated this from another compound which had originally been given to Wells Thoms by Sultan Said bin Taimur to be used for the tuberculosis and leper hospitals. A two-story home for missionaries, as well as beautiful trees, adorned this compound.

The local Christians came to Muscat from Mutrah for Sunday morning worship. After the service we all socialized and drank Arab coffee, with the men and women separated according to the demands of the culture.

I was welcomed by the church group that first Sunday. We ate dates and drank strong, bitter Omani coffee in small glass cups. In Iraq we drank strong, syrupy tea, but in Oman people drank the strong coffee. Most of the people took three cups, but until I could better accept the bitter coffee, I drank only one. When we had had enough, we held the small cups between our thumbs and first fingers and shook them.

It was at this first meeting that I was named *Naeema*, which means "Grace."

After coffee time, the missionaries hastened away to attend a second hospital service in Mutrah. Sunday evening vespers were in the Mutrah chapel. (Our mid-week prayer meetings were held alternately in Muscat and Mutrah; Sunday school for the children was held on Friday.)

At first I lived in the front apartment of the old mission house that had been renovated by the Rev. Cantine. The Dykstras lived in the back apartment. We had our meals together in the dining room at the front of the house.

About a week after I moved into the house, a thief quietly cut a hole in the screen door of the upstairs veranda that led to my bedroom and reached inside to unlock the door. I was sound asleep at the time.

He started going through some of the boxes that I had yet to unpack. He could have been there for some time, because so much had been taken apart and strewn all over. Something awakened me and I saw a man with a flashlight sitting on the floor not far from me. I jumped out of bed, which frightened him. He ran out so fast the same way he had come, he could have been an Olympic sprinter. I ran after him. He jumped from the veranda, two stories down to the roadway below. I screamed as loud as I could. The missionaries didn't hear me, but I learned in the morning that other neighbors had.

I awakened the Dykstras, who thought I had forgotten to lock the screen door. But upon investigation it was noted that the screen had been cut. Mrs. Dykstra also had a box in this bedroom that was ransacked. He took what items he could carry with him as he ran, but the items were not of great importance. Had I not frightened him away, he would have taken much more. The fellow was never brought to justice.

Mr. Dykstra made the door more secure the next day by adding some bars across the screens. I didn't think the thief would dare return again. I knew the door was secure, so I felt safe and slept well! The episode was never repeated.

The Dykstras were busy packing every day in preparation to leave. They had served forty-six years in Arabia and had accumulated much. They gave away many items; others they sold. Their departure was very hard on the people. Everybody loved them. Although childless, they had been the spiritual parents, mother, father, sister, and brother to many in the Christian community and to others as well. Together they had gone through trials, difficulties, births, deaths, and moments of joy. Tears were shed by even the hospital staff while discussing their coming retirement.

Between periods of packing, the Dykstras took me on trips to introduce me to their friends, while they said good-bye to them. Mrs. Dykstra took me to many homes in town. Their hope and prayer was that I would be able to keep contact with these people after they left.

There were many farewell dinners and teas. And then the day of departure came. Their boxes and luggage were taken to shore and put in *hoories* (small canoes) and transported to the British India Steamship Line.

It was very quiet after they had gone.

Jay and Midge Kapenga were my next door neighbors right from the start. It was a blessing for me to be able to join them for tea every afternoon, when Midge often served pastries and baked goods. Jay and Midge and I tried to get away from the heat and work on Saturday afternoons by packing supper and going for a swim in the sea. The Kapengas always thought of me at these times, even in later years when they were raising children.

Another important figure in my life during those first weeks in Muscat was an Indian Christian woman known throughout the region as "Nurse Mary."

Nurse Mary began working for the mission in 1917. During her years of service she worked under Mrs. Van Peursem and Dr. Hosmon in the Women's Hospital, when Dr. Harrison, Dr. Storm, or Dr. Wells Thoms were in Mutrah. She was trained as a nurse in the Madanapalle Hospital in India, where she was associated with the Reformed Church's Arcot Mission. She had a way of winning the confidence of the Omani women as she delivered their babies. At that time women did not yet come to the hospital for deliveries, so Nurse Mary had to go to their homes. She gave years of faithful service at all hours of the day or night.

Nurse Mary was a quiet, self-confident person. At fifty-five years of age, she was a large woman who had the strength and stamina to handle difficult deliveries under many circumstances. She was never married but was a mother figure to many. She had a pleasant laugh and smile. She beamed the love of Christ.

Technically, I was coming into the hospital as Nurse Mary's supervisor. But I knew I could never pull rank on this very special woman. I concentrated on learning from her and putting her skills to the best use. Dr. Thoms wisely advised that this would be a good time to teach the women to come to the hospital for their deliveries. There would be the "special" cases, who would yet insist upon a home delivery, which Nurse Mary accommodated. It took a little time before the women agreed to come to the hospital for their deliveries, but gradually they did make this change. I knew too that changes should be made tactfully and slowly, as Nurse Mary and I worked shoulder to shoulder.

When we had a difficult labor or some other serious situation, we called for the services of Dr. Thoms. Jasim, one of the helpers, went "across the mountain" (up and over the little mountain pass between Muscat and Mutrah) to get the doctor. At night Jasim would awaken the doctor by pounding a pebble on an iron rod leading up to the roof where Wells and Beth slept in a screened-in cage. He would then hitch a ride with the doctor in his vehicle on the return trip.

Later we had a Jeep station wagon that served as an ambulance for transporting a patient from the Women's Hospital to the Mutrah facility. The back seat was removed and we threw a mattress on the floorboards. The driver would proceed slowly and carefully over the mountain.

As the days passed I began to establish a routine. As Dr. Thoms had said, my duties were divided between work that could be called "evangelistic" and work that was "medical"—although in practice the two divisions were often one and the same.

Since I was single, I was able to open my home during "off hours" to women of the town. As months passed, many came to visit me—the lonely, the sick, needy, and even members of the royal family.

Sometimes, in Amarah and then in Oman, young girls would share with me some of their deepest feelings about their marriages. As I got to know them, I realized that a good marriage meant everything to them and a bad marriage could be a disaster. Great importance was attached to a girl's being a virgin before the marriage. If she could not give proof of her virginity, the marriage was off and the bride's father had to give back the dowry.

One time I was both embarrassed and honored to have a young woman's "proof of virginity" shown to me. It was the wedding night's bedsheet, spotted with blood. Such a sheet was not kept hidden by a family—in fact, many people saw it after a wedding night.

Some of my visitors could not go out during the day, but only under the cover of darkness. They would come completely covered in their black *abbas* with faces veiled. As soon as they were inside my apartment, the veils were thrown back over the top of their heads and there was a sense of release for them. They laughed, and their pent-up personalities began to take expression. Some came for medical treatment and I would take them to the hospital.

But most came just to talk. We had good conversations ranging from religion to news of the day to local customs. I always had scripture portions ready to give them to take home. As is the culture and custom of the East, refreshments were served to each group of visitors.

They knew I was available for them. And they felt free to come, because there were no men. Their homes were open to me, and my home was open to them.

Sometimes we planned a three-mile hike to Mutrah. These particular women, of whom I speak, seldom got out. They were inside their homes all day with no exercise. When we went on an outing, they were like children romping, laughing, and free. They felt safe in my presence.

I often thought during special times like that, "God knew what he was doing, when he made me a woman!"

VI
Oman

Not to us, O Lord, not to us but to your name be the glory, because of your love and faithfulness.

Psalm 115:1

As I write these lines, I wear the Sultanate of Oman's coat of arms on a necklace. People often ask me about the meaning of the insignia and my reason for wearing it. Oman was my home for thirty-five years, and my heart still belongs to its people. In many ways, even today, my heart is closer to the Omani people then to my own family and friends in America. My last prayer before going to sleep every night is for them. I still receive letters, cards, and telephone calls from Oman.

This love for Oman might seem like a curious thing to someone from America. Why Oman? Why would a woman of Frisian heritage, who grew up in southwest Chicago, feel this attachment to such a faraway country? I can only say that this love was from the Lord. Just as I was pulled to the Arab world by a divine call, I was given this love for its people. Those whom the Lord calls, he also equips. And love is a necessary part of being fully equipped for missionary service.

This love was not from myself. I must give the Lord all the glory. I could not have served even a year in foreign missions if I had to draw from my own internal supply of love. Jesus Christ is the only source of this kind of powerful love. "What wondrous love is this" that can propel Christians across mountains and seas and labor for decades among people whose ways are completely different from their own!

I want to write honestly about my experiences on the mission field. If there is anything that strikes a reader—particularly a reader from my beloved Oman—as unpleasant or negative, I hope the reader will remember, above all, my love for this country. I believe that the integrity and beauty of the Omanis, whether they be Christians or Muslims, will shine through an honest description of our missionary work in Oman.

We must never forget that the Muslim rulers of Oman were kind enough to welcome into their country strangers and foreigners whose religion was different from their own. If no other facts were written, that alone stands as a testimony to the Omanis' patience and strength of character. They are good people.

The Oman of which I will write in the next couple of chapters is different from the Oman of today. Oman in the 1950s was ruled by a man who maintained strong ties to the past, who had inherited a country deeply in debt. By exercising great caution and frugality, he eventually paid off the entire debt.

Although search teams were looking for oil in the country's interior, there was no sign of it. It seemed very likely that Oman would be the only nation in the Persian Gulf which would not contain oil. Old ways were enforced. Change and progress were looked upon with suspicion. Even the son of the ruler, who was educated at Sandhurst, a fine military school in Great Britain, was kept away from positions of power or influence.

Today that has all changed. I have the highest regard for the current ruler of the country, His Highness Sultan Qaboos bin Said. As I spent many years in Oman, I became personally acquainted with a few members of the current ruling family. They are upright and conscientious; they have a love and concern for their people. There have been incredible changes in the country in recent years, and through it all they have treated our missionaries well.

But in the 1950s it was a different place.

Great changes were sweeping across the world in those days after World War II. Feelings of nationalism were on the rise throughout the Middle East. In Iraq, several revolutions took place during the decade. In 1952, the King of Iraq, Faisal II, was assassinated. The emergence of the new nation of Israel was sparking great unrest throughout the Muslim world. Oil riches were changing the lives of people in Iraq, Iran, Saudi Arabia,

Bahrain, Kuwait, Qatar, the United Arab Emirates, and other nations.

Independence was flowering in India, as Great Britain had relinquished its control of the country.

A number of RCA missionaries in China were forced out of the country as Mao Tse-tung's Red Army marched across the mountains of the north and down into Shanghai.

The old ruler of Oman worried about the changes that were spreading into the Gulf area—perhaps with cause. In some Gulf countries the changes ushered in some of the worst aspects of western culture: lack of interest in religion, immorality, weakened families, and increasing alcohol abuse. Foreigners were looked upon with suspicion, even though they were still allowed in the country.

During this time internal political events in Oman caused us problems on Sunday mornings. A few government soldiers appeared at our doors and around our property, keeping an eye on our worship activities. It was understood that they intended to keep us from proselytizing and Christianizing native Omanis. They often checked to see if any Omani was attending. Only foreigners were allowed to enter the church.

Mrs. Dykstra, in her solid, straightforward manner, walked up to some of the soldiers and explained to them that we missionaries were serving God, not earthly rulers. We were not trying to oppose their government in any way. She went on to say that she realized they were under orders, but in fact they were working against God. The soldiers, armed and uniformed, had sneers and uneasy grins on their faces as they listened to the sturdy missionary lady in her plain cotton dress, but they let her say her piece.

Walking into the door of the church became an act of faith for our friends, some of whom were second generation Christians. Some wouldn't go to services, although we knew they kept the faith. A number of Omani Christians, Noor, Beder, Jameela, and other women, were taken before the *Qadhi*, fingerprinted, and asked why they came to church. Most said they worked for us. They were then told not to attend church. These noble Christians remained strong and grew in their faith. They did not drift away at this time; instead their faith became stronger.

One time the soldiers seemed about to take one of our courageous Omani women away, but some earnest talking by Dr. Thoms quieted the situation. One woman came early to services and would stay inside the church building after the service until the soldiers were gone. One of our trusted male workers had all kinds of trouble getting approval for a trip to Basrah because he was known to be a Christian. About half the children in the mission school did not attend classes for a period of time.

Then there was the Omani Christian gentleman who came every Sunday morning to church with a Bible tucked under his arm. Even during the week, he walked through the streets of Muscat with the Bible plainly visible. I wonder how many of us would have that kind of courage in similar circumstances! The Lord was with him, and somehow he maintained his witness during those difficult times.

Through it all, the work continued. Our task was clear. We were to be faithful in our daily duties. The Thoms, Dykstras, and Kapengas had weathered storms before I had come to Muscat, and they weren't about to be put off by the situation.

When the Dykstras first came to Muscat during the Depression, the mission's budget had been cut sharply. With little money and considerable ingenuity, they kept the work moving along. When Jay and Midge arrived in 1948, the mission school actually had been closed by the Sultan and classes met clandestinely in downstairs rooms of the mission house, in the homes of teachers in the neighborhood, and on the mission house verandas. At that time attendance dropped to just thirteen pupils. Mr. Dykstra and Dr. Thoms asked for and received an audience to discuss the situation with the Sultan. During this audience, the rest of the station and the Christians gathered for prayer. The Sultan knew we taught Bible and had prayers. He considered it good for character building. He told us that he did not feel threatened by a Christian presence in his country. Afterwards, he gave permission for the school to be reopened.

The hospital work was not affected by the government's close scrutiny. The number of patients coming to the Women's Hospital rose steadily—and the total number of deliveries climbed from 156 the first year to 252 the following year, and upward from there. When I first came, the hospital had seven inpatient four-bed rooms. With Jay's help, four more rooms were constructed during my first year, above what was then the outpatient department. One room became a second delivery room and was also used as a special private room for royalty and wealthy patients. These added rooms not only helped our crowded situation, but also helped us financially. Our hospitals had to be self-supporting and produce income. There were no grants or help from other sources.

Nurse Mary, approaching retirement, was very patient as I slowly worked new procedures into the hospital routine. She handled the home deliveries. I stepped in when she was unavailable or out on another call. Though I did not agree with the techniques used by Nurse Mary, I could not change the habits of fifty years. I could, however, introduce new techniques to the staff.

Babies had not been born in the hospital before I came. So, when the women slowly did come to deliver in the hospital, staff had to be taught enemas, post-partem care, bathing of babies, and sterile techniques. I enjoyed teaching the medical orderlies, as they were called (a British term for nurses aids). The Women's Hospital had an all female staff. As work increased, the staff also grew. Nurse Mary covered for me in the afternoons when I devoted myself to evangelistic work.

Three young women helped us in the Muscat hospital: Saalima, Noor, and Khamisa. Saalima, besides being a good worker, was developing into a fine Christian young woman. When she was barely out of her teens, she traveled to her home in the interior and encountered sorcery and devil worship. Boldly, she stood up against some women in the interior and told them about the true God. She took a difficult position, but the women of her town respected her for it. She even read to them from the *Injeel*, the gospel. She returned from her vacation in the interior all excited. God had given her a boldness she had not experienced before.

Noor and Khamisa were Baloochis, citizens of Oman but not of Arab extraction. Baloochis came from Baloochistan in Pakistan and from south Iran. They had their own language, which is unwritten, but I understand that efforts are being made today to put it into writing. I once asked a Baloochi gentleman, "Where did your ancestors come from?" He answered without hesitation, "From Aram in Damascus." In 2 Kings 5:1 we read, "Now Naaman was commander of the army of the king of Aram" (and Damascus, in those days, was the capital city of Syria).

Baloochis had the reputation of being hard working, progressive, clever, and conscientious. Many Baloochis did well in little business ventures, and they were an integral part of life in Muscat.

Noor was a big help to us. She was Nurse Mary's first helper. She was a good worker, capable, strong, and faithful. She was pleasant and conscientious and could laugh. Yet she was a mystery to us. She had been baptized and professed her faith in Jesus Christ. During the Muslim fast days, however, she would observe the Muslim customs of refraining from food and drink during daylight hours. Like many Muslims, she would not even swallow her own saliva during those days.

Khamisa, another Baloochi, came to us just after her husband had divorced her for a younger woman. Still a young woman herself, she had two small children to support and was emotionally devastated by the experience. (Her husband took with him her oldest son.) When she first came to us, she could not speak Arabic, but she learned quickly and became a faithful assistant in the hospital. She was to work with me all my years in Muscat. She remained a Muslim, but she gave the Lord Jesus full credit for working through the missionaries to provide for her family. She, like the others, was a big help to women in labor. Between contractions we shared and talked about many things and came to know and love each other.

I believe the Spirit of Jesus was reflected in Khamisa, too. One time a boat load of poor, jobless people from India was stranded along the coast of Oman by an unscrupulous ship captain. He had cheated them out of an exorbitant fare with the promise of jobs in Oman and then dumped them in the middle of nowhere. The Omani police, of course, rounded them up. Since the people were undocumented aliens, they had to stay in a barbed wire enclosure in the middle of an open field until the Omani government officials decided what to do with them. Faithful, compassionate Khamisa went to those poor boat people twice a day with tea, coffee, and dates.

The time for retirement came for Nurse Mary in 1952 after having worked many years serving her Lord in Oman. Many friends, merchants, and people from the community, plus mission staff people, came to the tea given in her honor. She was remembered by many with lovely gifts. The mission gave her a gift of money. Tears were shed and gratitude expressed as they said good-bye to her. She returned to her home in South India.

About that time we added another helper, twenty-three-year-old Shemsa, from Bahrain. Shemsa's mother died in our Bahrain Mission Hospital just twelve days after her daughter was born and her father refused to take her. After living in our mission's orphanage for two years, Shemsa came under the wing of our Dr. Bertis Tiffany (later Mrs. Haencke). Eventually she received her education and nurse's training in one of the India missions, and she professed her faith in Jesus Christ. It was Shemsa's own desire to return to Arabia to work, even though she had to learn Arabic after she returned to the Persian Gulf. She won the hearts of those around her and was a valuable addition to the staff. She was "bread cast upon the waters" that eventually returned.

I was blessed with close relationships with many staff members. We shared joys, problems, and sorrows. My apartment was open to visits from these women and women in town. Whenever I left on a vacation or a furlough, many friends dropped by to bid me farewell. When I returned, well wishers came up the steps of the old mission house to spend some time with me. I never had time to be lonely, and love ever surrounded me.

I must say that there were times when I felt it would be nice to have an evening to myself. I sometimes resented the intrusions, but tried not to show it. I received the people, served them, and heard them out. They too were considerate, and, except for a few, were thoughtful of my time.

Life on the mission field was busy. Minnie Dykstra set the standard in hard work and fierce dedication. "Indefatigable" was an adjective that Midge used to describe the woman, even when she was well past seventy years of age. Mr. Dykstra and the others were also always busy, too, but Mrs. Dykstra was a pusher for work.

Our ordained ministers provided spiritual leadership, taking the many services on Sunday and during the week. Jay also supervised the school, taught, oversaw the maintenance of the station, and worked at construction projects.

Midge raised three small children in those years. She also had the weekly *mejlis*. After completing the language requirements, she taught full-time in the school and shared supervisory duties with Jay.

The Bosches and Kapengas each had three children of the same ages. When the Bosch and Kapenga children were too young to go to South India to attend school, Eloise taught them in her home in Mutrah, enabling Midge to devote more time to the school. When the children went to school in South India, Eloise joined the teaching force in Muscat.

On a typical day the alarm went off at 5:30 a.m. After breakfast at 6:00 and listening to world news from the British Broadcasting Company (BBC), we met for prayers led by Jay at 6:30. Later, as the number of Christians grew, Jay set up a day for each of us to be responsible for leading morning prayers. We sang two hymns, read responsively, commented on a scripture passage, and closed with prayer.

Kapenga family, Jay with Margaret, Peter, Barbara, and Midge.

I was on duty at the hospital, where we met staff for report, at 7:00. A snack of coffee and cake was delivered to the hospital each morning at 9:30.

If there were outcalls, these were made after clinic hours, during the heat of the day. Outcalls were difficult at that time of the day. Blood sugar was low, and mind and body were tired. A medical orderly would go with me, carrying the doctor's black bag. Sometimes we would trek over the mountain to a place called Kelbu, or Towwiyyan, some blocks behind the hospital, or to the reed huts in Mudebbiga. Occasionally we went to Aiga, a distance of about two miles. We felt a duty to help people in the community, and income from the outcalls also helped the little hospital be self-sustaining financially.

When we came home late, Jay would be in his office below my apartment. At that time of the day, especially when they were in heat, the goats on the mountainside could really be noisy. They would disturb my rest. Jay would then go out and throw stones at them to chase them away, so I would not be disturbed! Friends and colleagues were supportive in a variety of ways.

Late in the afternoon I changed gears. Usually I devoted the late afternoon and early evening hours to my evangelistic duties. On Tuesdays, Midge and I would gather attendants and patients' visitors, along with community women, and bring them to the mission house for the women's *mejlis*. We sang, shared Bible stories, and spent time in prayer. Following the formal part of the *mejlis*, we would "let our hair down" and have fun together. We became acquainted with the women in the neighborhood and those from the interior. We exchanged news. We rejoiced with those who had good news and wept with those who suffered.

On Wednesday and Friday afternoons I conducted women's Bible study classes, which were usually well attended. Again, there was time for all to participate in prayer. Mondays were reserved for getting out into the community and visiting women in their homes. I was usually welcomed and graciously given permission to read from my Bible. I appreciated the hospitality given me by the Omani women.

Every Wednesday afternoon at five o'clock the national Christians and missionaries would come together for prayer and Bible study. One week it would be in the chapel in Mutrah, and the next week we would meet in our prayer room in Muscat. The leadership of these meetings was also set up by Jay.

Before Anne De Young arrived in Mutrah, I assisted Dr. Thoms in surgery one afternoon a week. Until Midge had completed language study, I also taught part-time in the school.

Saturday was a regular work day conducting the clinic, taking deliveries, caring for the inpatients, and going on outcalls. We tried to get away for a swim and supper at the beach on Saturday afternoons. The Kapengas and I would join Beth and Wells at Seh el Malah. Before taking a swim in the sea, we caught oysters and dug the meat from their hard shells. There was always a goodly supply of them available along the shoreline. We came home with fresh oysters to make oyster soup, of which I became very fond.

During the hot months, when missionaries took their vacations, it was not uncommon for those few remaining in the station, holding the fort, to be in charge of all the classes and worship services. This happened to me occasionally, and I found myself playing the organ as well as preaching and teaching. As I read letters I wrote to my parents during those busy times, I see many statements about God's grace providing me with strength to do what had to be done.

"We do keep going, and God gives us strength," I wrote in 1952. "God is pouring forth his grace and Spirit and is present with us. It takes me less time to prepare now, because instead of being frightened and feeling unprepared, I write an outline in my notebook and then let God work through me. Before, I tried to plan and prepare the message perfectly beforehand, writing it all out. I found that the message was staid and without power. But when the Holy Spirit leads and guides, there is blessing and power." I wrote another time, "Sometimes I feel like an Old Testament prophet, warning, exhorting, and preaching. I perhaps am less shy and afraid now, and I find that I have more boldness, which I know is from God."

There were many more joys during those years. It was a great surprise to me when my parents wrote that the Mt. Greenwood Reformed Church of Chicago had collected enough money to purchase a Jeep station wagon and ship it all the way to Muscat. Several months before, I off-handedly wondered if the church might be able to contribute something, earmarked for replacing one of our worn-out vehicles. When I brought up the topic in a letter, I mentioned that the mission also had some funds that could go toward the purchase. The generous people of my church, however, raised the full amount themselves, mainly through a Thanksgiving offering. They also provided an additional thousand dollars to ship the Jeep to Muscat.

A 16mm movie projector from the church also became a tool used to strengthen the faith of our Christians and to share with our Muslim friends. I was able to get some Moody science films, the *King of Kings* dramatic film, plus health films to share with them.

The women of our denomination worked hard at making supplies for medical work in the Gulf and also in China and India. These consisted of sewing materials, thread, cotton cloth, adult and baby blankets, gowns, quilts, dresses for adults, skirts and blouses for school children, school supplies, white gauze squares, and rolled bandages. These supplies were sent to the Women's Division of Foreign Mission of the RCA in New York, as it was then called, and the board did a Herculean task in crating and boxing the enormous amount of supplies and sending them out. They first had to be unpacked and sorted; then repacked into huge wooden boxes that were lined with water-proof paper. I remember how happy we were to receive these boxes, for they contained so many supplies that we could use. Some of the skirts and blouses fit us, too!

A group of women from the Mt. Greenwood Reformed Church, who called themselves the "White Cross," contributed throughout the years to these mission boxes. The women asked the congregation for clean white sheets, which were cut and torn. Then they came together once a month to roll bandages, make the gauze squares, sew baby dresses and blankets, do hand sewing, and make many other supplies. Later, when the Women's Division in New York discontinued the guild boxes, the Mt. Greenwood women continued to sew supplies specifically for our hospital in Muscat.

Years later, when Oman's government was able to supply the needs of our hospital, these women continued to sew for the denomination's work in the hospital of Madanapalle, South India. Nothing stopped them; they would not give up. These women, sitting quietly behind the scenes, did much for the work of mission. Through their work, our babies were attractively dressed and comfortable, and many ulcers and sores were cleansed and bandaged.

As time passed, the number of deliveries climbed to more than fifty per month. The women were learning to come to the hospital for their prenatal care. Every Wednesday was prenatal day, which in time became our heaviest clinic day. By the end of the morning my ears were sore from the stethoscope I used to check blood pressures and fetal heart sounds.

One day in 1954 I was called to a home where a young mother had just given birth to a 2 lb. 12 oz. premature baby boy. This was the third time she had delivered in her seventh month, and she had lost the previous two. She had never been in for prenatal care.

I immediately sent the mother and tiny infant to our hospital. I didn't think the preemie could make it, but we wrapped the baby in flannel blankets (donated by the women of the Mt. Greenwood church) and put two hot water bottles on either side of him. Incubators and oxygen were not available in Oman in those days.

The little thing lost weight steadily as we cared for it, finally reaching 2 lbs. 6 oz. The mother could not produce enough breast milk, so we did the best we could with vitamin K, calcium, cod liver oil drops, and Klim powdered milk formula administered every two hours by medicine dropper. We knew that she desperately wanted the little child to live—for its own sake and for the sake of her marriage. God blessed our feeble, conscientious efforts, and prayers of joy ascended when the little boy rallied and began to gain weight. Eventually he was strong enough to be discharged. Later his mother brought him faithfully to the hospital for check-ups and advice.

Another premature baby, little Behja, was born to one of our Omani teachers in the school. She was born on a very busy night in the hospital, and placed in our improvised incubator.

The hospital's first incubator was an ingenious, homespun invention. The basic design came from Dr. Al Pennings, the son of the Rev. and Mrs. Gerrit Pennings. Working with Nasir, our mission carpenter, Dr. Pennings came up with a wooden box about two by two by three feet, with a slatted shelf half-way to the bottom of the box. Two round holes were cut out of the sides below the shelf, into which light bulbs were inserted. The bulbs provided the right amount of heat to keep babies warm during the cooler months of the year. A bicycle basket (just the right size to hold a baby and blanket) was gently lowered from the top to rest on the slat shelf.

We kept baby Behja warm and pumping mother's breasts. We also fed her by medicine dropper. Again the Lord blessed our efforts. The little girl lost a few ounces at first, but then began to gain steadily. She grew up to become an excellent nurse in a modern government hospital in Oman.

An Omani friend of ours, Raheema, delivered twins prematurely during the heat of the summer before the hospital had air-conditioning. One of the twins died after just a few hours and the second one began running a high temperature. With perspiration dripping down our faces, Raheema and I looked at the surviving twin and realized that it would not live unless we could get it to a cool room. And there just was no room that was cool.

Only two places in town had air conditioning, the British Consulate and the offices of the oil company. The oil company offices were located just inside the city wall three blocks from the mission. I spoke to the manager of the oil company, explaining the situation. He graciously offered us the use of the downstairs dining room of his combined home and office building. We transferred the child immediately to the dining room, taking with us a baby crib, baby supplies, a bed for the mother, and all equipment necessary for their care. The mother and child lived in the dining room for several weeks, and the boy became strong and healthy.

Patients coming to our clinic increased to two, three, four, and even five thousand per month. To say that clinic work kept us busy is an understatement. It kept us *running*. In one of my darker moments, after an especially trying month, I wrote the following: "The clinic is frustrating. The sick crowd and push; they are noisy; they don't like to wait; some expect immediate attention. The staff people have a difficult time keeping order. The women and children are sick and their needs are great. Infant mortality is high and there is so much malaria causing anemia and weakness. And malaria can cause abortion and miscarriage in pregnancies. So many come to us with fever. And so many children come with diarrhea. We are grateful that we are here to help them. We look to our God, who is our ever present help and he is faithful." I knew that after I wrote such a letter, I would receive special prayer support from family and friends at home.

Malaria was the most common disease we encountered in those days. Malaria is caused by a parasite called plasmodia, which is transmitted by the bite of an infected anopheles mosquito. The plasmodia invade the liver, then the red blood cells, where they multiply. Symptoms include headache, chills, vomiting, and fever with a temperature that may reach 105 degrees. The chills and fever testify to an invasion of an enemy in the body. The plasmodia are identified by the laboratory technician taking a blood smear.

The parasites can enter the brain, too, leading to coma, convulsions, a high fever, and death if untreated. Unfortunately, convulsions are associated by many in Oman with demon possession. The patient is not taken to the hospital, but a religious leader or exorcist is called. If untreated, death comes soon. If a feverish child began convulsing, the parents would insist upon taking him home to call the "teacher." How often I pleaded with the parents to leave a victim with us. I would explain the cause of the convulsion, but to no avail. We groaned within, knowing the end result, when we could have helped them. There was a good and specific treatment for malaria and the response was quick.

Malaria has a way of lying dormant in a person's body and popping out when something unusual happens. Malaria attacks occurred when penicillin was administered for an infection or when smallpox vaccinations were given to children. A child who was unaccustomed to swimming or some other strenuous activity could come down with a flare-up of malaria. Following the delivery of a baby, malaria would pop out in many women. We gave malarial drugs routinely along with the vitamins and analgesic for after-pains the first three days postpartum, so women would not be faced with fever and malaria when returning to the interior.

The government, with the help of World Health Organization (WHO), worked to eradicate malaria by spraying with DDT. This helped for a time. Eventually, however, the mosquito became immune to the DDT and the malaria problem continued.

Like everyone else, I, too, fell victim to malaria. One time I got a severe headache and fever. I gave myself an injection of quinine in the thigh and the result was amazing. The headache and fever left. In the morning I started my own course of nivaquine and was able to go to work. I never had malaria as badly as Midge. We all took the preventative, but malaria had a way of popping out in Midge. She had to fight it constantly, even though she took the required daraprim once a week or nivaquine twice a week. Having Midge down with malaria affected all of us, for when there was sickness in our midst, it affected the rest of us, too.

Because malaria was so prevalent, I once wrote a paper on its effects on pregnant women and presented it to a women's group in Muscat. They were not aware of its harmful effects and thanked me for it.

Trachoma, too, was rampant, as it had been in Amarah. Dr. Thoms and his staff in Mutrah spent many hours on their feet in surgery repairing deformed eyelids, to bring the lashes up and out of the eye. He did as many as twenty-four in one afternoon.

Jay and Midge wisely had me come to the school to treat the school children for trachoma. I believe we saved many a child from blindness. In fact, one student whose father, brothers, and sisters all had trachoma, later said to me, "The time you treated us in the school, it was very painful. We hated the two days you and Noor appeared on the veranda all set up to scrape the eyelids, but I know that I would be blind today had you not done it." Jay and Midge maintained good discipline and good order in the school. We had no problem treating the eyes amidst squealing and squirming children. It was painful, but it had to be done.

During my first years in Muscat I was called into town to see a man who was supposed to have died and come to life again. I was taken to a large open courtyard, and as I entered I encountered rows of women sitting in absolute silence. Looking about, I saw someone near a litter beckoning to me. The blanket-covered litter rested in front of rows of motionless men. I knew it was the dead/alive man, and they wanted me to see the body.

I felt all eyes upon me as I walked before the men with my doctor's bag, knelt down at the litter and lifted the blanket. There was no movement in the body. No breath. I listened carefully with my stethoscope but could not detect a glimmer of a heartbeat. I looked up at the person near the litter and quietly offered my opinion that the man was dead. It was as if a switch was thrown in the assembly. Immediately the rows of motionless people began to weep and to wail.

My theory was that the man had died of a heart attack in his sleep, and as the attendants were preparing his body for burial they saw movement in the muscles of his limbs.

Some of our patients received a new lease on life—at least in strictly medical terms—because of blood donations from missionaries and hospital workers.

It was not uncommon to have a woman brought to the hospital after days in labor in shock, sometimes with a ruptured uterus, and gray from loss of blood. If these women came to our obstetrical hospital in Muscat we would immediately start them on intravenous fluids, throw a mattress in the back of the Jeep station wagon, load them in the vehicle, and proceed rapidly to the surgical facilities in our other hospital. Malallah, a laboratory technician in Mutrah, would frantically type the blood of the patient and put out the call for a blood donor.

Omanis did not realize in the early days that giving of blood was relatively easy to do. They feared that if they gave blood they would lose health and strength. I spent many an hour trying to convince relatives that a patient would benefit from a donation of whole blood. When they would not respond, in desperation I called other sources. Europeans, Americans, Indians, and missionaries came to the rescue, donated their blood, and saved many Omani lives. The blood types of foreigners in town and the missionaries were on our records. Dr. Thoms, in an emergency, would stop midway through surgery to have his blood drawn for the patient on the operating table. Later in Sur, British navel officers and young men from the Omani army training camp gave their blood. The British and Omani officers were very cooperative any time, day or night, bringing young trainees to the hospital for blood grouping.

During this time, as women from the interior began appearing in our hospital, I encountered the terrible effects of rock salt treatment after childbirth. Women in interior areas learned that

when salt was placed into the vagina following delivery, the
mother would live; when not used, she sometimes died from
infection.

The rock salt packing was also supposed to aid the healing
process and to restore tissues that had been stretched in the
delivery. Midwives would mold damp rock salt into a banana-like
shape and insert it in the vagina. This was to be kept in place for
seven to ten days and replaced as necessary. Salt was used as an
antiseptic, but it did untold damage to the vaginal tissue.

The salt tended to shrink the delicate tissues of the vagina and
cervix in a condition known as atresia. Many times women would
come to us with partially or wholly closed vaginas. The fortunate
ones were having difficulties with the flow of blood during their
menstrual periods, and we could correct the problem with a D & C.
Sometimes women would come after the flow had been blocked
for several months, in great discomfort, and were relieved by
surgical intervention.

If a woman did become pregnant, the atresia often prevented the
normal birth of a baby. Too many times we would take in women
who had been in labor for days, unable to deliver. Before the latter
1960s when taxis became common, women with ruptured uteri due
to atresia came to us on the backs of camels and donkeys.
Amazingly, these women did not hemorrhage to death. Blood
from relatives, friends of the mission, or missionaries themselves
would be given immediately; a hysterectomy with removal of
uterus and fetus was performed; and by God's grace a good
recovery was often made. We will never know how many women
started out for our hospital and died en route.

I shudder to think how many times women in the interior had
died in labor over the centuries because of the custom of using
rock salt.

Having a fruitful wife was very important to a man. Should an
emergency hysterectomy be performed, the woman would be in
danger of divorce. There was the occasional Omani man who
loved his wife so much that he would not divorce her but instead
would take another wife to give him children.

It was hard to see women suffer this kind of abuse simply
because "it has always been done this way." We patiently taught
our patients to abandon the rock salt procedure. We sometimes
confronted the husbands, too. Change was long overdue.

We had a female doctor from India with us for a time. She had
us send flyers or leaflets in Arabic into the interior with every

patient telling of the danger of using salt. This was highly effective. Various campaigns like this one over the years decreased atresia of the cervix until it became a thing of the past.

In the 1950s there were a few old, destitute women in the area who needed a home. I took over an unused area located behind our mission compound. A wall was built around this area. We had people repair some existing huts, and then we moved the women in. A mission worker was hired to care for them. She brought them their water, cooked for them, served them, and helped them in all their needs. Women from churches that supported me—Mt. Greenwood, the Wohelos from First Reformed Church of Roseland in Chicago, the DeBruins of Zeeland, Michigan, and others—sent me gifts of money at Christmas and birthdays. I used this money to help these women.

About this time, I began to experience a slow spiritual decline. There were the morning prayers, the weekly meetings including the mid-week prayer service, a full schedule of services every Sunday, and women's Bible study groups. But this was not enough. There must be the *personal devotions* and a *personal* relationship with the Lord, which is what I let slide. I was busy; the workload continued and there were other interests. I was tired at night. And I began to neglect my time alone with the Lord.

When Christians neglect their personal walk with the Lord, the Lord doesn't punish them; nor does he leave them. In love, the Lord keeps on bestowing blessings and sends many reminders that he is still waiting with arms outstretched. He waited a long time for the prodigal son to return, as we read in Luke 15. His love *never* fails.

But being busy in one's career—even church or mission work—is not a substitute for a close personal relationship with Jesus. And when Satan sees a Christian slipping, he is waiting to take over. Even if he cannot win a believer's soul, Satan seems to delight in throwing unhappiness and chaos into a life that is meant to be glorifying to God.

Young missionaries often experience attacks as they become more and more involved in the work and in serving their Lord. As I write these lines I have the advantage of years of hindsight, and I would advise any new missionary to remain in close fellowship with the Lord, and in the Word and prayer. I would advise them to put on the full armor of God, even as we are told to do in Ephesians 6:12-18, to withstand the tactics and snares set by Satan.

In the mid-1950s, a story began circulating in the States that charged the missionaries with laxity in theology and attendance at inappropriate social events such as receptions at the British Consulate at which cocktails were served. This created a difficult situation for us. We answered the charges to everyone's satisfaction, but the incident drained us of much-needed energy and could have created serious misunderstandings in our supporting churches. Thankfully, our mission board gave us a strong vote of confidence. And our churches never wavered in their support.

Also in the mid-1950s, at the urging of the mission board, each missionary was assigned more than one supporting church. My home church, who had been carrying my full support, wasn't too happy about the new ruling, but the Mt. Greenwood people realized the wisdom of sharing the responsibility for the effort. Half of my support began to come from the Union Reformed Church of Paterson, New Jersey, whose pastor, the Rev. Allen Dykstra, came from my home church and was a friend of my brother Mel. In later years, other churches contributed to my support (see list at the back of this book). Even more encouraging than the financial help over the years was the knowledge that people in these churches were *praying* regularly for the people in Oman, for people in our mission churches, and for the missionaries themselves. Every time I received a check or a box of items for the hospital, I knew that it was accompanied by many prayers from loving people in the States.

How we needed those prayers!

We needed prayer against attacks by the forces of evil. These attacks could be very cruel. They always were designed to break down our ministry, and they always seemed to hit us when we were weak or unprepared. I know that a dark, superhuman presence was the driving force behind these events.

When I first moved into the old mission house I smiled when I heard that it was "haunted." But as the years went by I began to realize that the "powers of darkness" did indeed occupy the house in a peculiar way. A remarkable old Omani woman, who stayed with us for a period of time (and of whom I will write later), once remarked that demons lived in the house. "People sometimes see them on the roof of your house at night," she said matter-of-factly.

Another time Jasim, our helper in the Women's Hospital, had an encounter that was baffling to medical science but easily explained by our Omani friends. It was the task of Jasim, you may remember from a previous chapter, to walk across the mountain from Muscat to Mutrah to summon help from Dr. Thoms in the days before the telephone line was installed.

One day he came to our doctor in much discomfort. "It is like boiling hot water being poured into my head and flowing down my body," he said. "When it goes all the way down to my feet, the pain becomes like cold water going back up to my head. Then it happens all over again."

We examined Jasim. The problem was discussed between ourselves, Dr. Thoms was consulted, and we tried to diagnose the pain from a traditional medical perspective. We ran many tests. No stone was left unturned, because Jasim was dear to us. Everybody loved him. But neither Dr. Thoms nor Dr. Alice could find anything wrong.

"It is an evil spirit," the Omanis said quietly. "Jasim was attacked in Towwiyyan, not far from his home."

A Muslim friend even offered to send for a Mullah who would read from the Koran and had a reputation for freeing people troubled by demons.

"No," Jasim said. "I want *Khatune Naeema* to come" (I was called by this name in Muscat.) If you bring a Mullah, I will only ask him to leave."

The Christian Omanis and Indians, too, believed it was a case of an evil spirit. We began to approach the problem on a spiritual level. Noor and I visited Jasim, read to him from God's Word, and prayed with him that Jesus Christ would release him from the pain and suffering.

After three of these visits the terrible sensations left him. It was power of the Word, prayer, and the name of Jesus that gave Jasim healing. We rejoiced in Jasim's healing and gave God thanks.

Another time evil took on a very definite shape that I could see and hear. It happened to me shortly after the Muslim's month of fasting, Ramadhan. I was concerned about being at a low ebb spiritually and decided to use some free time for rest, prayer, and Bible study.

After spending the entire day with the Lord, I went to bed at nine o'clock, which was unusually early for me, and expected to get a good night's sleep. I was not asleep long when I was awakened by a swishing noise. I opened my eyes, and in the shadows I saw the form of a tall, dark man. On his head was a turban and he wore a dark lumber jacket and baggy trousers. He was holding a long black whip, flicking it first along one side of my bed than the other. He didn't say a word; he just stood there silently. I knew I was awake. My brain immediately tried to make sense of the situation.

The house was locked tight. There was no way a man could be standing there. It could not be a human being.

Calmly, I decided that I was seeing some kind of manifestation of evil. I had spent the day in communion with God. I had made confession of my laxity and sin; and I was back in fellowship with my Savior, Jesus.

I knew, too, that Jesus was more powerful than the forces of darkness. There was no need to fear. Satan was angry that I was forgiven and back in good fellowship with God. He thought he almost had me. And he was showing his anger.

I got out of bed, walked to the light switch, turned on the light, and went to the bathroom that adjoined my bedroom. Upon returning to the bedroom a few moments later, I saw that my visitor had disappeared. I crawled back in bed, offered a prayer of thanksgiving and commitment, and immediately went back to sleep.

I never forgot that incident. From that time forward, the Lord created in me a new sensitivity to evil. God was making me more sensitive to the spiritual warfare that goes on all around us every day. He was leading me down a particular road of his choosing. I simply followed.

VII
Spiritual Warfare

The Battle

> *And there was war in heaven. Michael and his
> angels fought against the dragon, and the
> dragon and his angels fought back. But he was
> not strong enough, and they lost their place in
> heaven. The great dragon was hurled down—
> that ancient serpent called the devil or Satan,
> who leads the whole world astray. He was
> hurled to earth, and his angels with him.*
>
> Revelation 12:7-9

The Leader of the Forces of Darkness

> *He [Satan] was a murderer from the beginning,
> not holding to the truth, for there is no truth
> in him.*
>
> John 8:44

> *[Jesus said] I saw Satan fall like lightning from
> heaven.*
>
> Luke 10:18

The Struggle

> *Then from his mouth the serpent [Satan] spewed
> water like a river, to overtake the woman
> [Christ's Church] and sweep her away with the
> torrent. But the earth helped the woman by
> opening its mouth and swallowing the river
> that the serpent spewed out of his mouth.*

*Then the dragon was enraged at the woman
and went off to make war against the rest of
her offspring—those who obey God's
commandments and hold to the testimony of
Jesus.*

Revelation 12:15-17

*Just then a man...who was possessed by an evil
spirit cried out, "What do you want with us,
Jesus of Nazareth? Have you come to destroy
us? I know who you are—the Holy One of
God!"*
*"Be quiet," said Jesus sternly. "Come out of him!"
The evil spirit shook the man violently and
came out of him with a shriek.*
*The people were all so amazed that they asked
each other, "What is this? ...[Jesus] even gives
orders to the evil spirits and they obey him."*

Mark 1:23-27

Human Beings Participate in the Battle

*When Jesus called the Twelve together, he gave
them power and authority to drive out all
demons and to cure diseases, and he sent
them out to preach the kingdom of God and to
heal the sick.*

Luke 9:1,2

*The seventy-two returned with joy and said, "Lord,
even the demons submit to us in your name."*

Luke 10:17

The Victory is the Lord's

*That evening after sunset the people brought to
Jesus all the sick and demon-possessed. The
whole town gathered at the door, and Jesus
healed many who had various diseases. He
also drove out many demons, but he would not
let the demons speak because they knew who
he was.*

Mark 1:32-34

There are no neutral zones in spiritual warfare. We are on one side or the other. There are no noncombatants. Whether or not we recognize the manifestations of the Evil One, we either work actively in the Lord's service or we are weak spiritually and our ability to serve is compromised.

Christians and Muslims have many things in common. We share a common heritage in Abraham. We believe that God created heaven and earth, and that God is all-seeing and everywhere present. We are both "people of a book"—we believe that principles for life, justice, and salvation can be found in special divine revelation.

Another thing we have in common is an understanding of the forces of evil. We believe that evil has existed since Satan was driven from the presence of God and that Satan has at his command legions of spirits (fallen angels) that are personally active in the affairs of humankind. Even today, many Muslims hold a view of Satan and demons that comes right out of the pages of the Bible. They speak often out of personal experience with the kind of demons and demon possession that are described in the gospels.

I, too, encountered the specific work of evil forces on the mission field. My fellow missionaries held various views: some of my good friends had little time for the topic, and others felt that they, too, could see Satan's evil spirits at work in very identifiable ways. Among us there was plenty of room for differing opinion, and I don't want to downgrade the excellent work of those who didn't see things the way I did. The Lord used all of us in various ways, no matter how we viewed the spiritual realm.

From my first months in Iraq I came into contact with Muslim beliefs about evil spirits. Muslims are very sensitive to spiritual matters. The name of God is always on their lips and they believe (as we do) that God watches daily activities. Likewise, the forces of evil are also very close to the daily lives of men and women.

The verses at the beginning of this chapter outline briefly some of the important aspects of spiritual warfare. Satan was banished from heaven at some point in the past, he has immense power and cunning, he has the support of an army of fallen angels, and he has the capacity to lead "the whole world astray." God has limited Satan's days, and Satan knows it is just a matter of time until he will be cast into hell. Satan's helpers have the ability to enter human beings or animals, to cause illness and pain, to weaken or even kill people, to lead people astray from a productive life, to bring chaos and death to many, and to disrupt the lives of God's chosen people. All these characteristics of Satan and his helpers are described throughout the Bible. Many of these characteristics are also known and understood by our Muslim friends.

Christians, however, are blessed with a Savior who has conquered Satan and his evil spirits. Jesus Christ, God's Son, has the power to rule over Satan. Jesus encountered Satan immediately after his baptism, just after the three persons of the Trinity were revealed to witnesses: Jesus, the Son, stood in the River Jordan; the Holy Spirit was visible in the form of a dove; and the voice of the Father was heard saying, "You are my Son, whom I love; with you I am well pleased" (Luke 3:22). The identity of Jesus was made plain at that time—the same Jesus who strikes fear into Satan and his helpers.

Satan came to Jesus to tempt him in the wilderness and was defeated (Matt. 4:10,11). Over and over Jesus demonstrated authority over the forces of evil, exposed Satan's helpers, and had the power to remove them against their will (Mark 1:25,26). Jesus cast out many demons at one time and made them inhabit animals (Luke 8:33). He cast out a kind of demon that was different from others (Luke 9:39). He gave power to cast out evil spirits to his disciples (Luke 9:1). Jesus protected his followers from Satanic attacks (Luke 22:31,32). It is clear throughout the Bible that the forces of darkness are very real, that Jesus has complete power over them, and that he allows them to exist on earth.

Our Muslim friends understood Satan well and the ways he could destroy people, but they lacked a knowledge of Jesus Christ, the Son of God, who has all power over the Evil One.

Year by year, as I worked in Iraq and Oman, I began to experience spiritual confrontations that were similar to the kinds of events recorded in the Bible. As an R.N., I approached problems from a scientific, medical perspective. I would pray for general guidance and for the general health and spiritual condition of my patients. I was also prepared to share God's love with a kindly deed, a word about Jesus, prayer, or a reading from the gospel. Occasionally, however, a person would come in with problems that we couldn't diagnose. We would test and retest, but results didn't fit the problems. Further, the symptoms didn't even seem to be in the physical realm—something else was going on. Sometimes the mere mention of the name of Jesus would create additional turmoil in a patient.

Suaad was a poor, illiterate widow who worked as a nurse's aid in our Women's Hospital. She lived with a grown daughter, son-in-law, and five grandchildren in a date stick hut. They made a living as best they could by raising chickens and selling milk from their cow. (Milk was an important part of the diet for the Hindus in Muscat, and they had steady customers among the Hindu merchants.) There was no grass for grazing in Muscat, so the family members made frequent trips to the marketplace for alfalfa. They also sold vegetables in the bazaar.

Suaad was an able worker. She was a Muslim, and like most Muslims she respected Jesus as a great prophet, second to Mohammed. In the Koran, Jesus is referred to as the "Spirit of God," or the "Word of God," so Muslims do not discount his importance. Suaad had watched us, day after day, as we worked and prayed for the sick, calling upon Jesus for healing. She did not accept Jesus as the Son of God who had shed his blood to redeem humanity, but she knew of him and our dependence on him.

I had observed that Suaad at times would go into spasms while at work. I spoke to her of this and she told me that these attacks were caused by demons living in her. I said to her, "Suaad, Jesus Christ can give you healing."

"I know," she said. She had heard the gospel message many times in the clinic of our hospital and had witnessed the healing power of Christ.

I believed Suaad's self-diagnosis of evil spirits. Like many Omanis, she was very sensitive to spiritual matters. She was thoughtful and very religious according to Muslim tradition. The problem went on. I began praying for Suaad in my quiet times. I would often see her grandchildren come down the mountain behind my home at night, searching for food for the cow or chickens. I felt close to this family.

I occasionally visited Suaad in her home and read scripture with her. She respected the Christian Holy Book and she appreciated having someone read to her. One evening, while I was reading, a severe seizure came upon her. Her muscles tensed and jerked convulsively. I knew immediately that her problem was not something for the emergency room; the forces of evil were attacking her. My first reaction was *anger*. What right had Satan to disrupt our quiet time together? I cried out in the name of Jesus, asking for relief for the poor woman.

Suaad came out of her seizure tired, spent, and upset that I should have witnessed her problem. She was concerned for me and asked if I had been frightened. I assured her that I was not frightened, only angry. Before I left we prayed again, asking for Christ's healing touch and presence and asking God for a good night's sleep. We committed each other to go "in the faith of God" (an Arabic expression for "good-bye").

The next day Suaad was back at work, feeling well. She told me that after I left she had not been able to milk her cow. Each time she went near it, the animal would kick viciously. "It was as if the cow had lost its mind," Suaad said. The next morning the cow was full of milk but again she would not let anyone near her. The cow was sold the same day.

We then knew that the evil forces in Suaad had gone into the cow. They needed a body to inhabit. It was a striking reminder of the story in Luke 8, when Jesus cast demons out of a man. When the demons were commanded to go out of the man they asked Jesus to allow them to go to a nearby herd of pigs. The pigs then rushed headlong over a cliff and drowned themselves. There is another reference in Matthew 12:43,44 that speaks of an evil spirit's need for a body to occupy. "When an evil spirit comes out of a man, it goes through arid places seeking rest and does not find it. Then it says, 'I will return to the house I left.'"

Experiences such as the one with Suaad made me realize that the spiritual struggles mentioned in the gospels and other parts of the Bible were *still* going on in a very literal sense. I began to observe the "special cases" that came to us, and I talked to Christians whose judgment I trusted.

In a cage in my room were a pair of beautiful blue and green budgie birds. They were noisy and active during the day and at night they would sleep. I enjoyed watching the birds and they were good company. But there were times in the middle of the night when they would flutter about in sheer terror. I recognized the disturbance to be caused by spiritual forces of evil (Eph. 6:12) sent to disturb my sleep. One time I saw these evil forces come in the form of a dog to a home in the States, where I was a visitor. This home had no dog, not even a cat. Since I knew the source, I ignored the manifestations and quietly returned to my sleep. We don't ever have to fear "the powers of this dark world" because "the one [the Holy Spirit] who is in [us] is greater than the one who is in the world" (1 John 4:4).

The forces of evil may afflict people in cruel, painful ways or they may be gentle and seductive, appearing as an "angel of light" (2 Cor. 11:14).

Jasim, as I mentioned in the previous chapter, was afflicted with severe pain like boiling water pouring through his body.

Satan and his helpers don't always depend on brute strength and cruelty. They have great intelligence. They are capable of understanding human plans and disrupting them in many ways. Some attacks can be so well conceived that a person doesn't even realize what is happening.

The disciple Peter once became an unwitting instrument in the hands of Satan. In an emotional moment, Peter drew Jesus aside from the disciples and "rebuked him" for speaking about dying and being raised on the third day. "This shall never happen to you!" Peter said.

"Out of my sight, Satan!" Jesus responded (Matt. 16:23). Jesus saw through the "noble" emotion to the clever prompting of Satan.

Each time I returned from Arabia to the States on a furlough or vacation, something would happen to delay or possibly even cancel my return to Arabia. Several times I had medical problems that needed to be cleared up before departure. During my first furlough I had hemoglobin difficulties. Another time I had passport problems. At the time I did not recognize these events for what they were, but now as I look back, I believe that clever forces were at work to upset my plans.

These kinds of things happen to other missionaries, too. I think young missionaries are often singled out for special attacks. When I first arrived on the mission field, I found my faith was weaker than I thought it was. I also knew of other "first timers" who felt the same way and older missionaries who spoke of the difficulty of their first months. Even on the mission field it is easy to go along with the world and not take time for scripture reading and prayer.

Young missionaries who came out of Iran in the 1940s spoke of the power of Satan and their struggles against evil. My RBC friends Cornelia De Witt and Mary Kuik wrote to me about struggling with the powers of evil in New Mexico. Satan tries anything to uproot the work of new missionaries.

In the late 1950s I mentioned to a person of the mission board my strange experience of seeing the man holding the whip at the foot of my bed. Concerned people then asked me to go in for a battery of tests with a Christian psychiatrist in Chicago when I returned on my next furlough. I wasn't too happy about it, but I did as they asked. After answering hundreds of questions within a certain time limit I had to enter a room with four psychiatrists sitting in a panel. During a period of consultation, I heard the remark, "This is the lowest mark I have ever seen on such an exam."

My heart sank. I immediately assumed I had failed miserably and my further service was in jeopardy. On the way home I said to my sister, "I fear I failed the exam."

I did not hear the results of the examination for the remainder of the furlough, and I did not ask for them because I was afraid I had not passed. I continued to speak in the churches as well as to complete a course of study in a nearby college. When the mission board later called and told me to prepare to go back to Oman, I was so happy that I still didn't ask for details of the tests. I just got my immunizations, packed, and left.

It was some years later that one of the same Christian psychiatrists who had interviewed me came to Oman. He was a friend of the mission and often traveled, at his own expense, to encourage missionaries on various mission fields. He devoted an hour to each missionary in a private setting. When he saw me, he asked if I knew who he was. At first I didn't recognize him. Then he said he was on the panel of men who interviewed me in Chicago years before. I finally had enough courage to ask about the tests.

"You did extremely well," he said. "Low scores were exactly what we were looking for! In fact, your scores were among the best."

He was indignant to hear that I had not been told the results of the tests and promised to speak to responsible parties when he returned to New York. I was relieved to hear the news. As I look back I can see that God sent this man to Oman to put the matter to rest. But for a long time Satan used the manifestation in my bedroom to harass me and take some of the joy out of my work.

I have also experienced strange noises in the homes in which I have lived. There would be knockings in different places and creaking noises on stairways. In Muscat I sometimes heard booming noises above the roof of my room which were not audible to anyone else. When I identified these noises as coming from the forces of the evil one, I knew it was an attempt to frighten me and make me lose sleep. After a while I lost my fears. "In the name of Jesus, I command you to go away," I would call out. And the noises would cease.

Some of my Omani friends would tell me about evil spirits in wells of water. One woman told me she heard noises in the well in our mission compound. A professional British soldier named Ranulph Fiennes wrote a book about military action in southern

Oman in the 1960s. He admitted in one chapter that his squad of hard-bitten soldiers was attacked one night by strange, unseen forces near an old well in the interior desert.

Evil spirits seem to be attracted to both water and fire. The New Testament tells about a particular spirit that would not respond to the disciples and threw a boy into fire or water, in an attempt to kill him (Mark 9:22).

I encountered this same affinity for fire and water in my work, as I treated a woman named Fatima and came to know her husband Shafeeq. Fatima and Shafeeq usually rose before dawn. Fatima would say her prayers at home and then begin to prepare breakfast while her husband walked down the street to a nearby mosque to pray with other men. Then he would return for breakfast and the day's work would begin.

One morning, as she usually did, Fatima lit the primus stove on the floor of their home and then put a large container of water on it. Soon the water was boiling. Then, in Shafeeq's words, evil spirits threw her into the boiling water. A skeptic, of course, would say that the woman merely tripped and fell into the water, but a later incident with Shafeeq led me to believe that the accident was indeed caused by the forces of evil.

Shafeeq returned from his prayers to find his wife writhing in pain on the ground, with severe burns all over her body. He called a taxi and transported her twenty miles to the hospital. The first week in a severe burn case is always critical, and we did everything possible to prevent complications of shock, dehydration, and infection. Several pints of blood were needed, along with constant intravenous fluids. Sterile techniques were used daily in the changing of her dressings; sterile linens were used on the bed. Sterile supplies were prepared in the operating room daily by the surgical staff. It takes a large team to care for a burn case. We put Fatima in an isolation room and permitted only one family member at a time to visit her. The week passed and Fatima began the slow process of recovery.

Then for months we treated Fatima and went through a skin grafting program. She responded well, but it was a difficult time for Shafeeq and the children. I can imagine that Satan, the "murderer from the beginning," had intended to take Fatima away from her husband and children permanently, but with proper medical care she was recovering and they could look forward to her return.

But the evil forces were not done. One day while I was talking to Shafeeq on the open veranda of the hospital, the man suddenly went into a severe seizure, such as I had never witnessed before. His whole body quivered and shook violently. I was at first taken by surprise, but then I realized evil spirits were at work. I was terribly perturbed; in fact, I was furious. I cried out in the name of Jesus and in the power of Jesus' shed blood on the cross that they should come out of the poor man.

This was happening in a government hospital, at a time when public prayer or calling out to Jesus in public would not be accepted. But by God's grace we were alone. Normally there are many folk who would gather like gapers to gawk, but on that day there was no one nearby.

Shafeeq continued to convulse, thrash violently, and foam at the mouth as he lay on the cement. I was very upset and continued to call out and command the unclean spirit to come out of him "in Jesus' name." I remembered Mark 9:17,18,28,29: "Whenever it [the evil spirit] seizes him, it throws him to the ground. He foams at the mouth, gnashes his teeth and becomes rigid. [The father] asked [Jesus'] disciples to drive out the spirit but they could not." I knew, too, from experience, that it sometimes took many encounters before the spirits would release their grip.

The severe thrashing with rapid contortions and twisting of the entire body continued for what seemed to be minutes. Then Shafeeq was quiet. He sat up and spoke quietly. He told me that the seizures came frequently upon him and that he had been possessed for a long time. He took it all with the attitude that everything was the will of God. I told him that there was salvation and release in the name of Jesus. I further explained this to him, emphasizing the power and healing in Jesus' name. Shafeeq listened, then stood up and we went back to our duties.

Fatima recovered and went back home. I never saw Shafeeq again. I hope and pray that Jesus will enter their lives, but what remains with me is a memory of the murderous power of Satan and his spirits.

Sometimes pleasant aromas or foul odors would appear in my room, and there was no logical reason for the smell. There would be the sudden smell of costly perfume or a most terrible, putrid, rotten stench. I would again recognize Satan's helpers at work and ask them to leave me alone, in the name of Jesus.

The forces of evil also afflict people with problems that are related to legitimate medical or psychiatric conditions. One who reads accounts of the early days of the Arabian mission is struck by the number of deaths that occurred among pioneer missionaries and their families. Bishop Thomas Valpy French, Ian Keith Falconer, George Stone, and Peter Zwemer succumbed to what were diagnosed as standard medical conditions. Some of the children of the early missionaries died. Some of our medical missionaries in Basrah died of typhoid when they treated infected soldiers. Very serious cases of clinical depression also hit some missionaries.

When you add up the sum of all these events, I think you can see Satan's hand in the medical problems. He was using subtle, deadly forms of illness and disease to strike down the early missionaries.

Spiritual warfare can also be manifested in other ways. I already mentioned major and minor medical problems. One of my friend's sisters constantly suffered from a series of vague complaints that were not attributable to standard medical problems. Young, unmarried women in prominent Omani families sometimes lived alone in apartments, and they told me of attacks of a sexual nature. One young woman had trouble sleeping through the night because of the persistence of the attacks. Then there are quiet impulses and promptings that come from evil sources: impure or fearful thoughts, dishonesty or thievery, the urge to take unnecessary risks, even suicidal thoughts. We need to pray and seek the Lord when we feel such promptings.

I have a deep appreciation for Martin Luther's hymn, "A Mighty Fortress is Our God." Luther was a struggling monk who felt little peace in his life. Through much prayer and the study of God's Word, Luther's mind and heart were illumined: he understood that salvation comes from faith, not from works.

There are two things that Satan hates and fights against, and if any Christian is active in these areas he or she can expect opposition: prayer and Bible study. When Luther studied the Bible, God's Word, with great intensity, Satan was angered. He opposed and attacked him unrelentingly. On one occasion, Luther even threw an inkwell at a manifestation of Satan!

Keep that in mind (as well as the other things in this chapter) as you read the words to "A Mighty Fortress":

A mighty fortress is our God, a bulwark never failing;
Our helper, he, amid the flood of mortal ills prevailing.
For still our ancient foe doth seek to work us woe—

His craft and power are great, and armed with cruel hate,
On earth is not his equal.

Did we in our own strength confide,
Our striving would be losing,
Were not the right man on our side,
The man of God's own choosing.
Dost ask who that may be? Christ Jesus, it is he—
Lord Sabaoth his name, From age to age the same,
And he must win the battle.

And tho' this world with devils filled,
Should threaten to undo us, We will not fear,
For God hath willed his Truth to triumph through us.
The prince of darkness grim, we tremble not for him—
His rage we can endure, for lo! his doom is sure:
One little word shall fell him.

There are times when Satan and his helpers are behind
catastrophes that affect many people. "He [Satan] was a murderer
from the beginning, not holding to the truth, for there is no truth
in him." The Bible is very clear that Satan sometimes causes great
bodily injury and death.

As I mentioned before, there have been various problems on all
of my furloughs and trips back to the States. Any one or two
problems could probably be dismissed as "happenstance," but as I
look back over forty years of service I have to conclude that there
was a consistent pattern of opposition to my work.

In 1969 I was eagerly preparing to fly to Amsterdam to meet my
family and spend time with them in the Netherlands. We had
been saving and planning for this vacation for months. Just before
I left for the trip I needed to pay a visit to good friends who lived a
boat-ride away from Kuwait, on the island of Failaka. I was packed
and ready to embark on my journey—I intended to spend the
midday with my friends and then ride back to Kuwait on board one
of several ships that stopped at Failaka en route to Kuwait. My
plane was scheduled to fly from Kuwait to Amsterdam at midnight.

Just as it was time to catch a boat to the mainland a furious
squall came up. A number of people gathered on the shore with
me, but we could not find a captain who was willing to launch into
the storm. Finally one captain told us that he would make the trip

for an extra fee. We all boarded and went to a small, enclosed cabin.

The trip to the mainland was much worse than we expected. Water sprang high from the sea and crashed against the cabin windows. The boat tossed to and fro like a child's toy in a whirlpool. I'll admit that I was frightened. I prayed quietly, and deep inside the Lord gave me a sense of peace. By God's grace, we reached the shore of Kuwait and I caught my plane.

I felt the powers of evil in that storm. It is interesting that several respected Bible commentators view the storm mentioned in Mark 4 as "devilish" in origin. After a busy day, Jesus got into a boat with his disciples and fell fast asleep. Then "a furious squall came up," and waves broke over the boat while Jesus slept in the stern. The disciples awakened him saying, "Don't you care that we perish?" According to the Bible commentators, Jesus' words, "Peace, be still," were directed to the evil forces behind the storm. I feel that even today Satan is able to stir up the elements.

That night I relaxed in the KLM plane to Amsterdam. I leaned back, stretched my legs, and went to sleep. The plane was scheduled to land in Amsterdam early the following morning.

Just before we landed, without knowing a thing about it, we almost lost our lives.

I disembarked with all the other passengers in Amsterdam. We had no knowledge that anything was out of the ordinary. I met my sister Harriet and her husband Ben. (Harriet's first husband, John Beintum, died suddenly in 1953 and she remarried in 1955.) We immediately proceeded to catch up on family news. We retrieved my baggage and went on to Roodeschool.

Then we learned what had happened. Dutch radio, television, and newspapers began headlining a near crash of two airliners coming into the Amsterdam airport early that morning. One airliner was my flight from Kuwait. The other was Ben and Harriet's flight from the United States to Amsterdam. It had been a near disaster, with the two planes coming very close to each other.

I again recognized Satan's hand in the events. He was at work, seeking to destroy lives. He was a murderer from the beginning. I'm sure I was not his sole target, but I felt as if the attack had been personally directed at me and the Lord had intervened with his protection. "Then the Lord opened the servant's eyes, and he looked and saw the hills full of horses and chariots of fire all around Elisha" (2 Kings 6:17).

Fallen angels seem to inhabit certain locations. They are not omnipresent like our Lord. Every now and then we encountered evil forces which seemed to plague certain locations such as wells and houses. A Muslim couple I knew in Sur lived in a district close to the seashore. The location did not seem healthy. There was always sickness in the family, and the couple had lost five children at young ages. Only two of their children were strong enough to reach maturity. We discussed the situation at length, and as years passed we wondered if there were special evil forces lurking in the area of their home. I began to feel as they did, that Satan's power was behind the problems in their home. They were very poor, and it was impossible for them to relocate.

I wrote to friends in the States, asking for financial help for the couple. They responded with more than enough money to help move the couple to a different area. I watched the family closely after they obtained a new house. What a blessing! They had six more healthy children! The move to a good home was like the dawn of a new day for that family.

Another location, too, was the source of severe problems. The house in which I lived, the old mission house, seemed to be a focal point for the forces of darkness. My Omani friend Tahira was the first person to set me thinking about this when she said, "All the people in town know about it. Sometimes they see the spirits on the roof at night."

As I wrote before, the house had the reputation of being haunted long before I came to Oman. In the nineteenth century, when the old house was first purchased by our missionaries, the local Omanis already were refusing to live in it. From what we know, the Omani owner was more than happy to sell the house to foreigners who didn't know or didn't care about the situation. Our pioneer missionaries, of course, were very brave. They may or may not have realized what they faced. We read in Ephesians 6:12 (Living Bible) that "we are not fighting against people made of flesh and blood, but against persons without bodies—the evil rulers of the unseen world, those mighty satanic beings and great evil princes of darkness who rule this world; and against huge numbers of wicked spirits in the spirit world."

A number of our missionaries had lived in the old mission house. I arrived on the mission field in 1944. It was in 1945 that the Rev. and Mrs. Gerrit Van Puersem arrived in Basrah to bid farewell to all of us—they were retiring prematurely due to ill health. At the time I remember feeling sad because these good

people were not able to complete their term of service. Later I
learned that the Van Puersems, who had worked in Muscat, had
lived in the old mission house. Before their time, the home had
usually been occupied by our clergymen and their families. The
Rev. and Mrs. Dirk Dykstra left Oman just after I came, and I
remember, too, that Mrs. Dykstra was subject to illness. While
living in the house my own spiritual life in the 1950s reached a low
point, culminating in the appearance of the dark man with the
whips.

I wrote letters regularly to my friends and supporting churches.
In one of these letters I wrote that the local people in Muscat
considered the mission house to be haunted or occupied by evil
spirits. In the nineteenth century, when the Omanis came to that
conclusion, they probably saw recurrent cases of illness and death
and probably noises and movements at night.

This letter made the rounds and fell into the hands of Vivienne
Stacy, a missionary in Pakistan. Many of our Arabian
missionaries knew her and respected her work.

Vivienne was immediately struck by the statements I had written
about the house. She was appalled, first of all, to think that
missionaries were living in a what seemed to be a house infested
by evil activity and, second, to think that we might not fully
recognize the seriousness of the problem while our Omani
neighbors did. "This must not be," she said. She began to pray and
ask the Lord's guidance in this matter.

Then Vivienne had an opportunity to visit Muscat to make
contact with Pakistani Christians who worked in the city's labor
force. Without giving details of her burden for us, she wrote and
asked to stay in the mission house with me. She had spent much
time in prayer before her trip. She was worried about what she
would find, but she also felt strongly that the Lord had
commissioned her to go to the source of the evil and try to cast it
out in his strength and power.

Vivienne wrote about her experience in the mission house in a
book called *Christ Supreme Over Satan, (Spiritual Warfare, Folk
Religion, and the Occult)*. Vivienne gave me permission to quote
from her book and thereby help readers understand her anger,
fear, and determination. The following, then, is Vivienne Stacy's
story. The "American nurse" or "hostess" she refers to is myself.
The two of us were the principals in the following events.

Sometimes a building is so invaded and infested by evil powers that a radical exorcism is needed. My most outstanding experience in this area was in connection with a house in Muscat in the Sultanate of Oman. The house was purchased by Samuel Zwemer in 1897 for a very small sum as the local Arabs thought it was haunted and did not want to live in it. Through the years some of those who lived in the house had troubles which might have had Satanic origins. Peter Zwemer, brother of Samuel, died at the early age of 29. One missionary died under strange circumstances, perhaps having committed suicide. Another was mentally ill and had to leave. Another couple departed greatly discouraged. The Arabs until recently still considered the house haunted, saying that evil spirits frequented the main staircase and the roof in particular. When I heard that Muslim Omanis reckoned that a house occupied by Christian workers was haunted, I was full of indignation. Some months later when I was flying into Muscat on my second visit, the Lord clearly commissioned me to deal in his name with this situation.

How does one set about fulfilling such a commission? My visit was to last eight days and I would be staying in the "haunted" house with an American nurse. At supper the first evening I broached the subject. I asked my hostess to tell me more about her house and why the Arabs considered it to be possessed. She was surprised that I raised this subject as she herself was planning to ask my advice about some demon-possessed patients. I said I would pray for her and with her about the patients but that I had no commission to deal with people but only with the house. I explained that I could only proceed if we were in complete agreement and on condition that if either of us needed the other's help we would call each other by day or night. Also when we were free from our other work we would take all possible opportunities for prayer and Bible study together. We generally managed to spend two or three hours each day praising God, praying and reading the Bible. We read through the whole of Isaiah.

Muscat is surrounded on three sides by mountains and on the fourth side by the sea. One evening my companion and I were praying on the roof when suddenly she called out: "Look at that rock. It is illuminated." I could see nothing except the black outline of the rock. Three times she saw it illuminated. The third time I also saw the rock illuminated by a heavenly light. Immediately I said: "Yes, despite the presence and power of evil, these mountains are full of the hosts of the Lord."

My first task had been to find out what was really wrong with the house. Diagnosis is all-important. I asked the Lord to show me and I took practical steps to find out where evil particularly dwelt. I meditated and prayed in various parts of the house—in the kitchen, the sitting room, on the stairs. Several nights I was driven out of my bedroom by Satanic forces. Even kneeling by my bed, I found it too terrifying to stay. One night I called my companion. We prayed together and I spent the rest of the night sleeping on the floor of her room. Throughout the eight days I rarely slept for more than an hour at a time and never for more than five out of twenty-four hours. The Lord gave me extra strength and I was able to pray and meditate and carry out my normal program of Bible teaching and evangelistic meetings with Pakistanis in the areas around.

One night all hell seemed to be let loose and I decided that I would read in the sitting room Isaiah's servant song about the death and victory of the Lord Jesus Christ (Isa. 52:13-53:12) and praise God whatever happened. I knew that the local people claimed that sometimes they "saw" spirits on the roof and so another day I set out to watch and pray on the roof.

At that time the Lord clearly warned me that if I went on the roof I would be killed. Then the words of the communion service came to my mind: "Preserve thy body and soul unto everlasting life" and I knew I was safe, provided I did not go on the roof at that time. For some days I had prayed specifically that I might know what spirits inhabited the house and its environs (it had a small garden). The answer was clear—spirits of suicide, depression and fear. I commanded them in Jesus Christ's name that they should go. There was no clear proof that the spirits had gone and there were still other manifestations of demonic activities.

One night I found my companion nearly choking. I asked her permission to put my hands on her throat and neck and to pray in Jesus' name. Immediately she was all right. She had heard a strange noise between her bedroom and the sitting room. The next day I dusted all the objects in the wall cupboard in the sitting room, some of which were souvenirs from Africa. She inquired what I was doing and I explained that I was praying over each object that it would be cleansed through the blood of the Lord Jesus Christ. Some weeks later she wrote that she had found one object that was probably the cause of some of the trouble in her room—a curved Omani dagger which had been used to ward off evil spirits from a mother and baby.

Before I left Muscat I was able to tell her that the house was cleansed through the power and blood of the Lord Jesus Christ and that any subsequent evidences of evil would be attacks from outside and could be repudiated and repulsed in the name of Jesus Christ. No longer would the Arabs have reason to note that a Christian home was the dwelling place of evil spirits.

On return to Pakistan I wrote confirming this and quoting Isaiah 60:18 in regard to her house: "You shall call your walls Salvation and your gates Praised." The Lord also had his therapy for me after this long struggle. I had the opportunity to go weekly for six weeks in a row to a communion service. The Lord ministered to my body, soul, and spirit as I heard again the words when I took the bread; "the body of the Lord Jesus Christ which was given for you preserve your body and soul unto everlasting life." Truly Jesus Christ protects and cleanses.

The house was delivered from demonic attacks. There were no further manifestations of the evil that had plagued the house for hundreds of years. (See note at the end of this chapter for principles Vivienne Stacey follows in her ministry.)

For many years I have been reluctant to speak of these things. Years ago some of my friends were offended by statements I made about spiritual warfare. I felt bad about that and have no interest in telling this story for the sake of excitement or intrigue. I simply want to tell what the Lord has done in my life. As I write this, our North American culture is filled with stories about the occult, witchcraft, Satan worship, ritual murders, Satanic music, and the like. I believe that people will no longer be shocked by my experiences. I hope and pray that this will help strengthen the spiritual lives of others.

Satan throws up smoke screens to prevent us from seeing his activity. Even among his own followers and evil spirits, he can create the illusion of casting out demons. He does this to confuse us as to the only real power to cast out demons, which is in Jesus Christ alone. Wilfred Thesiger, a well known British traveler, has written highly respected books and appeared on television specials. He says little, if anything, about personal religious beliefs in his writings. But in one of his books, *Arabian Sands*, he describes an incident that took place deep in the desert of the Arabian Peninsula.

Thesiger was traveling on camels with Bedouins. He recalls being awakened one night by one of his companions rocking to and fro and howling like an animal. His friends said the fellow was possessed by a spirit called a *zar*. They formed a ring around him and chanted in an old dialect called Mahra (which was originally a language of Abyssinia). Eventually the afflicted fellow sobbed, groaned bitterly, and then slept. In the morning, Thesiger relates, the problem was over.

I encountered cases of false exorcism. Often the afflicted persons had to pay large sums of money to others who claimed to have powers over demons. Some people I knew sold off their valuable possessions to find a cure for their daughter apart from Christ. Not only does Satan thereby confuse the issue and keep the glory away from Jesus, but he can bankrupt suffering people.

We all have heard stories about Christians who have prayed and fasted on behalf of someone they believed to be demon possessed, but who in reality had a psychological or physical problem that responds well to medication and therapy. Identifying Satan's attacks is not for amateurs or misguided Christians. In Oman, for example, people sometimes suffered convulsions due to high fever, epilepsy, or attacks of malaria.

Just as some people are too quick to blame evil spirits, others are too slow. There is a myth in many of our churches that Satan and his helpers are less active in North America than in other parts of the world. This myth is fading as we read about Satanic cult murders in the United States and as we hear the words to some of the Satanic rock music. (Today we are also being deceived by the New Age Movement.) I think Satan is just as active in this country, but our eyes have been closed. Science and humanism have been our guides, and neither has room for spiritual things.

All this leads to the question: "How can a Christian recognize and resist the attacks of the Evil One?" Or perhaps for some readers, a more basic question is, "How does one become a Christian and receive this divine help?"

How to Resist Satan's Attacks

Be Sure of Salvation

The primary need we all have is a saving relationship with Jesus Christ. This comes first with forgiveness of sin. Let us remember that God required the sacrifices of the blood of goats, lambs, bulls, and other animals in the Old Testament for the forgiveness of sin. We read in Hebrews 9:19 that "When Moses had proclaimed every commandment of the law to all the people, he took the blood of calves, together with water, scarlet wool and branches of hyssop, and sprinkled the scroll and all the people." In Hebrews 9:21, we read, "In the same way, he sprinkled with the blood both the tabernacle and everything used in its ceremonies." In fact, we can say that under the old agreement almost everything was cleansed by sprinkling it with blood, and "without the shedding of blood there is no forgiveness of sins." In this same chapter (Heb. 9:26b-28) we read,

> But now [Jesus] has appeared once for all at the end of the ages to do away with sin by the sacrifice of himself. Just as man is destined to die once, and after that to face judgment, so Christ was sacrificed once to take away the sins of many people; and he will appear a second time, not to bear sin, but to bring salvation to those who are waiting for him.

In Revelation 12:11 we are told that Satan was hurled down to earth from heaven "by the blood of the Lamb." Jesus Christ became the sacrifice and the lamb of God when he made the sacrifice of his body on the cross for our sins and the sins of the world. It is only through Christ's shed blood on the cross that we have remission and forgiveness of sin and salvation in his name. (The story of the cross is recorded in Luke 22 and 23.)

The cross and faith in Jesus Christ were a barrier almost impossible to overcome for my Muslim friends. The cross of Christ separated us. God knows how often we quoted John 3:16, 17, "For God so loved the world that he gave his one and only Son, that whoever believes in him shall not perish but have eternal life. For God did not send his Son into the world to condemn the world, but to save the world through him."

The phrase, "God gave his only Son," was not accepted by our Muslim friends. It was a stumbling block that prevented them from listening to us. So I began to tell them, "For God so loved the world (and God so loved us) that he gave us Jesus, so that whoever believes in him has everlasting life. Jesus, or *Nebi 'Esa*, is highly respected and is accepted by the Muslims. So when I would paraphrase John 3:16 and tell them that "God gave Jesus," I could continue to have their attention to further explain God's gift of salvation for us.

First John 5:1-4 in the *Living Bible* speaks beautifully of Jesus as God's Son. "If you believe that Jesus is the Christ—that he is God's Son and your Savior—then you are a child of God....Loving God means doing what he tells us to do, and really, that isn't hard at all; for every child of God can obey him, defeating sin and evil pleasure by trusting Christ to help him."

Who could possibly dare to be in spiritual warfare except on the side of Jesus, God's Son? It is the power of his blood shed on Calvary's cross, in the power and authority of his name, in prayer, and in the power of the Word of God that evil is conquered.

Be Much in Prayer

Another important way for a Christian to resist Satan is through prayer. Prayer may be offered by an individual who suffers or by other Christians. In 1965, in Muscat, we saw the power of prayer in a vivid way. Dr. Alice van der Zwaag came to my apartment one afternoon and told me that a woman named Ayisha had come to the hospital screaming and writhing in pain. Alice said, "I ordered an injection of largactil for her and it did nothing to calm her." (Normally largactil would put a person to sleep immediately.)

I had a feeling that the root of Ayisha's problem was spiritual rather than physical. "I'll go and see her," I told Dr. Alice.

I found Ayisha prostrate and tossing and turning in pain. Several of the ladies from my Bible class were there. They surrounded the suffering woman and looked worriedly at one another. I had never been involved in casting out evil spirits before, but I felt strongly that that was what the Lord wanted us to do. "Could this be evil spirits?" I asked the women.

I knew they were thinking the same thing, but they were reluctant to answer. I said again, "Do you think evil spirits are behind this?"

The women nodded. They had known it all along. How often people in other cultures are quick to recognize Satan at work!

I stepped into the circle of women and said, "Join me in prayer." With boldness that came from the Lord, I prayed and invoked the name of Jesus to cast out the evil spirit from Ayisha. Some of the other women joined me, praying audibly for Ayisha, whom they knew and loved.

Before long we noticed a calmness coming over Ayisha. She sat up quietly and smiled at us.

Each of us asked gently, "Ayisha, are you all right?"

"Yes," she replied. "Thanks be to God and you, I am fine now."

Selwa and I offered to walk her home, which was about a mile from the hospital. During the walk, Ayisha told us that when she had been young her mother had cast evil spirits into her. "While I was sweeping this afternoon," she continued, "demons had come seeking a body to lodge in. The demons living in me fought them off. This gave me much pain." In this instance Ayisha's demons were protecting "their territory." Even though she was a grown woman, the mother of several children, she felt that the childhood evil still affected her. What a terrible recollection of her mother and her childhood!

The injection of largactil did not help poor Ayisha. The prayers of God's people, calling upon the power and name of Jesus, resulted in her deliverance.

Prayer for God's help can be a simple, anguished plea, or it can go through several stages. Bill Gothard, in his "Basic Youth Conflicts" seminar, described a beautiful way of praying that goes through several stages. First is a drawing near to God and confession of sin. Then is a purification of the heart and cleansing of motives. God knows deep down in our hearts if we have secret desires (Jer. 17), motives, longings, plans, and goals that may be contrary to God's will. Then ask the Lord to search your heart and try the "reins." Then, when we are close to the Lord and he is in control, we can pray fervently that his will be done in the matter at hand.

Miss Johanna Timmer, our esteemed teacher at the Reformed Bible College, wrote to me in her Christmas letter of 1966, "Satan is loathe to give up his victims, but at Christ's command he must give them up. Satan cannot defeat God's purpose. Believing prayer availeth much. Not that prayer itself changes things, but God changes things in answer to prayer."

Andrew Murray, in his book, *Daily Thoughts on Holiness*, talks about prayer. He goes so far as to say that when Jesus was baptized in the river Jordan, the heavens would not have opened and the Holy Spirit would not have descended were it not for Jesus' prayer (Luke 3:21). Mr. Murray stresses the need for prayer and its great power in Jesus' earthly ministry. Again, when Jesus faced death, he prayed (Matt. 17:2-9).

I had been in prayer the day I was confronted by the man with whips, and I knew that other missionaries, as well as my family and friends in the States, were praying for me, that "Satan would not sift me as wheat." I feel that these prayers helped me get through the experience. How important it is for believers to pray for missionaries, others in the church, and their pastor!

Be in God's Word

Just as important as prayer is the daily reading of God's Word. When Jesus was tempted by Satan in the wilderness, he countered every move of Satan's by quoting scripture (Matt. 4). We, too, must stay close to scripture. Vivienne Stacy and I read through the whole book of Isaiah as we asked the Lord to remove evil from the mission house. I read scripture many times to demon troubled people in the privacy of an empty room in the hospital. As we watched, the Lord freed them from the clutches of Satan. A particular verse in scripture, which Martin Luther had been studying (Rom. 1:17), was instrumental in illumining his heart and mind: "This Good News tells us that God makes us ready for heaven—makes us right in God's sight—when we put our faith and trust in Christ to save us" (*Living Bible*).

Ask God to Rebuke Satan

When we are caught up in spiritual warfare, we can ask God to rebuke Satan. In Jude verse 9, we read: "But even the archangel Michael, when he was disputing with the devil about the body of Moses, did not dare to bring a slanderous accusation against him, but said, 'The Lord rebuke you!'"

A prayer of rebuke might go something like this, "Heavenly Father, I ask you in the name and through the blood of Jesus Christ to rebuke Satan for tempting me to (be impure, to steal, to have self-destructive thoughts, etc.). Quoting a particular passage of scripture, as Jesus did when he was tempted in the wilderness, is also important.

Draw Near to God

Generally speaking, we should draw near to God when we are struggling with Satan. This happens when we go through the process of confessing our sin (1 John 1:9), asking God to purify our motives (Jer. 17:10), asking God to search us for secret sins (Psalm 139:23), and, after self-examination, partaking of the Lord's Supper (1 Cor. 11:17-32).

Recognize and Resist Satan

The Bible commands us to *resist* Satan, his attacks, and his quiet promptings. "Submit yourselves, then, to God. Resist the devil, and he will flee from you. Come near to God and he will come near to you" (James 4:7,8). To resist the devil, we must recognize him. Satan can come quietly to us and attack our minds. Personally, I often feel these attacks as I am ready for sleep, sitting quietly, about to end my day talking to my Lord. Then fearful, distracting thoughts will come to my mind. I know the origin of these attacks and counter them by praying for Jesus' help. Then I can get on with my devotions.

Put on God's Armor

I did not fear Satan and to this day I do not fear him. Satan knows this and this angers him; consequently I face much opposition from him. But I have learned to "put on the full armor of God" daily. These verses, about God's armor, have become very important to me:

> Finally, be strong in the Lord and in his mighty power. Put on the full armor of God so that you can take your stand against the devil's schemes. For our struggle is not against flesh and blood, but against the rulers, against the authorities, against the powers of this dark world and against the spiritual forces of evil in the heavenly realms. Therefore put on the full armor of God, so that when the day of evil comes, you may be able to stand your ground, and after you have done everything, to stand. Stand firm then, with the belt of truth buckled around your waist, with the breastplate of righteousness in place, and with your feet fitted with the readiness that comes from the gospel of peace. In addition to all this, take up the shield of faith, with which you can extinguish all the flaming arrows of the evil one. Take the helmet of salvation and the sword of the Spirit, which is the word of God. And pray in the Spirit on all occasions with all kinds of prayers and requests. With this in mind, be alert and always keep on praying for all the saints (Eph. 6:10-18).

From my Indian friends, I learned a method of bringing these verses to mind in a picturesque way. Every morning, as these women were getting dressed, they would go through the motions of putting on a piece of armor while reciting the corresponding verse from Ephesians.

I began following that custom every morning. I also now go through the motions and think about these verses at bedtime, too. I began doing this after many restless, tossing nights in my sleep. And thanks be to God, since I literally put on his armor not only in the morning in the shower, but at night, too, after I say my prayers, my sleep is quieter and more restful.

Expect Opposition

Satan's harassment has increased with the writing of this book. People in my church who are assisting me have also faced special attacks. All of God's children who are walking in close, intimate fellowship with God experience Satanic opposition. The Bible clearly informs and warns us of this.

Be Persistent

We must be persistent as we resist Satan. In one of my letters home I wrote, "Satan will try anything to uproot the work of the Lord. As long as we live we will have that continuous struggle with Satan. But we know that we will be victorious and conquerors through Christ." Some Christians have waited years for answers to their prayers. Ultimately, of course, time is on our side. When Christ comes again, Satan and his hosts will be thrown into the abyss, where there will be weeping and gnashing of teeth.

Listen to God's Messages

God speaks to us in many ways: primarily through the Bible, but also through the preaching of the Word and through the "still small voice" during quiet times of prayer and meditation. As I mentioned before, there is no substitute for daily, faithful reading of the Bible. I would recommend a disciplined plan whereby a person reads an entire book, the entire New Testament, or the entire Bible in a given period of time. A number of Bible organizations can furnish such a plan.

Also, one of the values of assembling with God's people in worship is to hear his words throughout the service—especially in the message brought by the pastor. Again, this is such an important way to listen to God's messages that I want to stress regular, weekly attendance at worship services. Many churches still conduct a service on Sunday morning and one at night, and I would encourage the reader to attend both, if that is a possibility.

God also speaks in the quiet moments. Sometimes people tell me they actually hear God's voice or see something in a kind of vision. There is plenty of precedent for that in the Bible. I often have strong "feelings" about something, or ideas that suddenly appear in my mind. I test these ideas by comparing them to scripture, discussing them with a pastor or Christian friends whom I trust, and by comparing them to things I have learned in my spiritual walk with the Lord over the years. If these ideas persist, I believe they are from the Lord.

Sometimes God gives one person a specific message for another person. Vivienne Stacey, of whom I wrote earlier, was given a particular commission when she came to the mission house. In later chapters I will speak of Jerome the mechanic, who had a gift for prophecy and bore special messages from the Lord. I sometimes was given burdens for some people and was being directed to share with them.

God also speaks through circumstances. I think that circumstances, when combined with the other things mentioned in the previous paragraphs give a person an indication of God's will. Nothing happens by pure chance. Striking events, highly unusual meetings with people, change of weather, or amazing coincidences are all under God's control. God can and does use such things as he works out his plan in a person's life. Be sensitive to God's leading in these things.

One morning I was very tired and debating with myself whether or not to include some information about prayer and fasting in this book. I had passed the deadline for it and had slept poorly the night before. While I was in bed I prayed, "Lord, if you want me to write this, please give me a message through the woman I listen to on the radio each morning (Gloria Copeland). If she mentions the words 'prayer' and 'fasting' during her talk, I will know you want me to do it, no matter how tired I feel."

The message on the radio program was on the Holy Spirit coming upon Jesus. I guessed the word "prayer" would be included in the message, and it was. But it didn't look like the speaker would mention "fasting." I thought God might let me off the hook. But next came the story of Jesus' baptism and, sure enough, a reference to Luke 4:1,2, in which Jesus was led into the desert for forty days, during which he fasted. It was time for me to get busy and write.

Another way that God brings messages is through nature. We all understand the beauty and majesty of God when we look upon some of nature's awesome displays. We understand God's power when we feel a storm or hear the thunder. But God also uses other aspects of creation to communicate with some people.

God speaks to me through birds. I know when I hear the birds singing in my garden that God has a message for me or is encouraging me. Just after the radio speaker mentioned prayer and fasting, I opened the door of my house and was greeted by a cardinal singing lustily. I knew God was confirming the message on the radio.

My friends and I have on many occasions heard the cardinal singing and sparrows chatting loudly as we prayed. I felt that God was confirming our prayer. Ours is a very personal God, and as we take time to talk to him, God cares and offers encouragement. To me, there is nothing "strange" in seeking God in the little things of life—even the activities of the tiny animals. St. Francis of Assisi also experienced this kind of divine, personal contact through creation.

Often, while driving long hours over lonely stretches of the road in Oman, birds would fly in front of the vehicle. For me, it was the Lord saying, "I am with you. Do not fear." This sometimes happens as I walk down the street in Mt. Greenwood. Once when I was being driven to New Brunswick Seminary where I had to speak, in a snowstorm, the Lord sent a flock of birds ahead of the car in the snow, confirming my ministry and encouraging me in the midst of a storm.

Avoid Satan's Traps

We must also avoid obvious pitfalls. People sometimes walk too close to Satan's traps and become ensnared. Some of these traps are easy to see: relationships with the wrong people, alcohol, drugs, cigarettes, ouiji board use, Satanic music, astrology, and (Deut. 18:10) "divination, soothsaying [predicting the future from omens], sorcery, charms, mediums, wizardry, or necromancy [conjuring up the spirits of the dead to predict the future]."

Be Not Afraid

Fear can also hinder us from resisting Satan and doing God's work. So many times during my last decade of work I had to fight against fear and trepidation. At times I had to throw myself in the arms of my Savior just to get from one day to another. Some people hated me for my work and witness and wanted me out. Satan wanted nothing more than to destroy our mission work. In the midst of opposition God always protected me. Christ is victor over Satan and I was victor with him. It was tempting to forget my calling and just be a health worker and nothing more. Progress was made in the Lord's name when we resisted the Devil, stayed in the battle, and marched forward without fear.

I hope and pray that some of these things will help you in your own spiritual struggle. As I said earlier, there are no neutral corners in this life. Even if Satan cannot rob you of your salvation, he will try to make your Christian life ineffective and nominal. Don't give up. Take up the banner of Jesus and enter into the warfare with courage and high hope.

NOTE

Vivienne Stacey believes ten principles emerge clearly from the exorcism incident at the mission house. I agree with these ten points, having experienced them and used them in my own ministry. They are as follows:

1. The Lord's commissioning is needed for each episode of such a ministry.

2. The ministry is a team ministry and is built on the Lord's commissioning, prayer, praise, Bible study, and obedience.

3. The Lord gives discernment and guidance when he sees it is needed.

4. The deliberate challenge to Satan and his demons brings a backlash and fiercer conflict for a while.

5. The victory is Christ's and rests on his Word, his authority, and faith in who he is.

6. The Lord sometimes gives visions to encourage and strengthen his servants.

7. The glory is the Lord's alone. God alone will be exalted. His glory he will not give to another (Isa. 48:11).

8. It is not wise to talk unnecessarily about such happenings. Only now after more than eleven years have I shared this experience (apart from a few occasions when I was especially constrained to speak).

9. Obedience to Jesus Christ's command, and the cleansing which followed, proved to be the basis for future fruitfulness and blessing in Oman. A year later I returned to Oman for a Bible teaching ministry and stayed with my friend in the same house. There was great peace and serenity and much freedom to expound the scriptures.

10. The Lord strengthens us physically and spiritually for what he commands.

VIII
Friendship, Death, and Revolution

I have set the Lord always before me. Because he is at my right hand, I will not be shaken. Therefore my heart is glad and my tongue rejoices; my body also will rest secure.

Psalm 16:8,9

For a long time we had been praying for a woman doctor to work in the Muscat Women's Hospital. By God's leading, the mission board in New York learned of Dr. Alice Vander Zwaag, who was working in Jordan with the Mennonite mission. It was a happy day when we learned she would join our forces in Oman.

Dr. Alice grew up in Groningen, the Netherlands. Her two-and-a-half years of service in Jordan gave her an ability to converse in Arabic—though the language spoken in Jordan was quite different from that spoken in Oman. Dr. Alice was a committed Christian and a well qualified obstetrician and gynecologist.

Dr. Alice stepped into a busy hospital. Outpatient clinics were heavy and there were not enough rooms for the increase of inpatients. As the work continued to expand, the number of cesarean sections did also. Dr. Alice now accompanied patients from Muscat to Mutrah, where she performed the "C" sections; then brought mother and baby back with her to Muscat for post operative care. She was blessed with special skills in treating vaginal fistulas and cervical atresia.

Dr. Alice lightened the work load of the doctors in Mutrah and eased my responsibility in Muscat. There was no longer any need for Jasim to walk over the mountain nor for Dr. Thoms' sleep to be interrupted by our calls. Besides this, our first Christian nurses from India, Elizabeth Yohannan and Punnamma Mathews, had arrived the year before and were a great help, and the Omani staff were proving to be faithful workers. We now had a complete staff.

As happy as I was to have a doctor on the premises, it was an adjustment for me to relinquish ten years of authority, during which I took most of the deliveries, saw a large outpatient clinic every morning, and made outcalls. Suddenly all the responsibility no longer rested on me. It was a difficult transition.

Over the years the number of patients in our Muscat hospital grew steadily:

- In 1951 there were seventy-five baby deliveries, most of which were accomplished in homes.

- In 1958 there were 478 deliveries, all of them delivered in the Muscat Women's Hospital.

- In 1961 we had 815 deliveries.

- In 1965 there were 1,202 deliveries.

Meanwhile, Mutrah was blessed with the coming of Anne De Young and later Jeannette Veldman. They had been working in China and had been forced out of the country by Mao Tse-tung, along with other RCA missionaries. After a furlough and much needed rest, they transferred to the Arabian mission and came to Bahrain in 1952. Anne joined us in Oman early in 1954, when she was sent to work in Mutrah. "J.V.," as we called Jeannette Veldman, joined Anne in Mutrah later, coming from Amarah. Both came with teaching skills in nursing. They started a nursing school in Mutrah.

Many people on the staffs from both hospitals had been educated in our mission school; now they were being taught nursing in our mission hospital. Anne asked me to teach a class in ethics one afternoon a week. A comprehensive course in nursing principles and procedures was also set up.

Unrest continued to afflict the Arab world in those days, though we in Oman were blessed with relative peace. From missionaries further north we received reports of revolutions and evacuations. In 1958 there was growing tension in Iraq. Our missionaries remember an American anthropologist coming from the back country and stopping at our compound in Amarah. "Be prepared to leave at a moment's notice," he said. "Things are deteriorating rapidly."

In 1958 there was a revolution in Baghdad. King Faisal II, who had been a friend of the missionaries, was killed, along with his prime minister. The new leader, Abdul Kereem Qasim, was not as favorably inclined toward mission work. The new rulers became suspicious and mistakenly thought that the missionaries were spies or Western agents.

In 1959 the Amarah mission station was closed, with much of its medical equipment going to our hospitals in the Gulf. George Gosselink and Harvey Staal were among the last of our missionaries to leave Iraq. They made several attempts to retain the property in Amarah, traveling to Baghdad to talk with the new ruler, but to no avail.

In 1959 the Iraqi government took over the hospital and the mission as we knew it was closed, never to open again. We felt bad about it, and our thoughts were with the nationals left behind. Were they given jobs in the government hospital? Did they remain true to their faith? We could only commit our sixty years of work and our friends to a faithful God. It never was easy to visit the country of Iraq after that. I lost all contact with friends in that country.

Back in Oman, in the early 1960s, we had opportunities to tour the interior to set up temporary clinics in a number of locations. One tour took us to the town of Sohar, about 140 miles up the Batinah coast from Muscat. One of our hosts provided us with the very best house in the town—the only one with electricity (from a generator) and a refrigerator. Dr. Thoms was ingenious at removing doors, placing them on heavy boxes that carried our supplies, and using the door as an operating table! We did much scrubbing down and washing to make the areas clean. Patients lay on the improvised "table" while Dr. Thoms performed many eye operations and other procedures. Patients were seen daily and medicines were dispensed.

In another place, Mazaara', we toured and set up a temporary hospital on top of a mountain. Donkeys transported our patients and supplies up the mountain. The area was lush and beautiful.

We usually stayed about two weeks in a place and left gospel portions behind. I will never forget the amazing hospitality shown to us by the people of these villages. The medical needs were appalling, but the people were warm and friendly. When it came time to leave, the people begged us to stay longer. But we were always under pressure to get back to our work in the hospitals.

A side benefit of these tours for me was no night call. I could go to sleep knowing I wouldn't be roused for a delivery. Although the Lord always gave me strength sufficient to the job at hand, I admit that there were times when three or four full nights of sleep in a row seemed like a wonderful luxury.

In the 1960s I was invited by the minister of interior's adopted family to spend a few days with them in the interior, in a place called Hazam. In those days there was little freedom to travel inland. My hosts got the permission to take me from the Omani minister of interior, but they did not ask for or receive permission from British authorities. For this reason it was all very hush hush. We held our breath at the customs barrier in Ruwi, hoping they would not see me sitting in the cab up front. A white person sitting between Omanis is very obvious, but God kept their eyes perhaps on the soldiers and guns in the back of our vehicle. The Omanis were in awe of the minister of the interior, who, for them, could do no wrong. Once past the customs post, we had clear sailing. The town of Hazam was memorable. Prominent in it was a huge fortress built by the Portuguese in the fifteenth century, which was still used as a military post. Guards were on duty around the clock. The fortress was tall and imposing—a wonder of the world. How it could have been built without modern construction machines was a mystery to me. From the top of the walls we could see for miles in every direction.

The daughter, Saleema, enjoyed showing me the many fruit gardens. We walked distances to see the flourishing date gardens, mango, lime, and banana trees.

There were four big irrigation ditches running through the town, carrying clear, sweet water that came from springs some distance away. The constant, rapid flow of water through the cement-lined ditches (built by the Persians years before) was another marvel. The people bathed twice a day in these ditches, with women and men going to separate locations. No sooner had we arrived in the town than we were taken to the women's bathing spot in an isolated, enclosed area under the open sky. Tiny fish tickled our feet. These fish ate the mosquito larvae and kept the town free of mosquitos and malaria. We immersed ourselves in the warm, flowing water and lost the cares of the day. Following local custom, we dressed and slept in the same clothing that we had worn all day. At sunrise the next morning we bathed again, changed clothing, and went to work dispensing medicine.

One time Dr. and Mrs. Thoms, with Omani staff from Mutrah, went on a tour to Sur. They wore Arab dress and traveled by camel.

In the sixties Dr. Alice and I were called out one evening by a husband whose wife had delivered a baby boy a few days earlier in Somayil, a village about twenty-four miles inland from Muscat. As he described her symptoms, we knew she had contracted tetanus following her delivery. We left in haste, carrying the tetanus vaccine with us, and injected her immediately upon our arrival. Then we brought patient and baby back with us for admission to our hospital. Thanks to God, she recovered. She and baby both did well. The complication was not the trip or the disease, but in our haste we had neglected to get permission from the authorities to go into the interior. We were called on the carpet the next day and duly reprimanded. We explained our situation and apologized, but the government officials were not happy that we had traveled inland without a permit.

Another event of those times was the first Gulf Youth Conference organized by our missionaries in Bahrain in 1961. Fourteen young delegates came from our mission stations in several countries. Midge Kapenga went from Muscat with four of our young people and served as a counselor at the event. In a 1962 edition of *Arabia Calling*, Jeannette Veldman wrote about the conference: "The Muscat delegates with their native dress, their profound grasp of the meaning of their faith, and their ability to break spontaneously into song, held the admiration and attention of all the other delegates."

But while all this was going on outside Muscat, work at home continued. The Kapengas continued to labor faithfully in the mission school. In the mid-1960s the number of students climbed to seventy girls and ten boys. As the school grew, the Kapengas divided the students into eight grades, including a kindergarten class and *temhidi* (pre-first grade). Some girls left to be married before they got past the fourth grade.

Several of the missionary wives worked full- and part-time in the Arabic and English departments, and Eloise Bosch taught a second kindergarten and *temhidi* in Mutrah to relieve pressure on the lower grade levels. In the sixties Joyce Dunham, the wife of the Mutrah hospital's chaplain, the Rev. James Dunham (and the daughter of the Rev. Cornelius De Bruin, missionary to India) joined the school staff, along with Neva Vogelaar, wife of the Rev. Harold Vogelaar. The Vogelaars filled in when the Dunhams went on furlough.

The mission family in Oman in the early 1960s.
Jeanette is in the lower left.

Eventually the school had four Omani teachers, all of whom had graduated from the school itself. For years our school was virtually the only place in Oman in which girls could obtain a standard education. Two of the teachers were married women with their own children in the school. Two younger teachers, daughters of Christian Omanis, had received advanced training in our mission school in Bahrain. Several other older girls, ex-students, taught a few years as well.

Generally, Jay and Midge taught subjects in which we couldn't find qualified national teachers. Jay taught arithmetic and Bible. Midge prepared Arabic reading and arithmetic materials for the lower grade teachers to use, tutored some students, and taught some English.

When Jay and Midge went on furlough in 1957, the long-time missionary-teacher Rachel Jackson came from Basrah to be principal. She remained in that position until her retirement in 1960. Gradually a higher percentage of girls came to the school, as there was a government school for boys in Muscat and a private school for boys in Mutrah. Since the school received more applications than could be accepted, the Kapengas developed a testing program to screen children for visual perception, pre-reading skills, and motor technique.

Sultan Said bin Taimur and his successor, Sultan Qaboos bin Said, allowed our students to study the Bible and have school prayers. In the two older classes, in which most of the students were teenagers, Midge taught a course in comparative religion (Hinduism, Judaism, Islam, and Christianity) and a course called "Development of the Idea of God." All students memorized passages of scripture.

The big event of the school year, and for the mission in general, was the school's Christmas program. There were no movie theaters or television programs in Muscat, so our dramatic presentation attracted parents, other family members, the entire mission staff, young men from the city who wanted to see our girls perform, and so many other uninvited guests that policemen came to maintain order.

The Kapengas had each class stand up to recite Christmas scripture passages and sing an Arabic carol. (Midge translated a number of carols into Arabic.) Older girls sometimes sang carols in English. The Assaada Hospital (obstetrical) staff people and I sang a carol in Arabic at Jay and Midge's programs each year. The annual program outgrew the church and then was staged on the side of the Iron Clad Mountain back of my house. A date stick hut served as the Bethlehem stable and a star was usually mounted up high on the rocks. I occasionally invited acquaintances from the royal family to join me on the veranda of my apartment, which had an excellent view of the proceedings.

Jay's talents extended beyond the pulpit and the classroom. One time Jay and I drove some visitors into the interior on very rough, rocky roads. I piloted the green Willys jeep donated by my home church in Mt. Greenwood. On a stretch of road some loose rocks shot up against the underside of the vehicle. One of the rocks hit my gas tank from below, creating a good-sized leak. In just a minute or two most of the gasoline was gone. There were no gas stations or repair shops, so we had to rely on materials at hand. Jay and the men put their heads together and assessed the situation for a few minutes. Then Jay had an idea. He asked for chewing gum. One of the women had chewing gum in her bag, which we began to chew! Meanwhile, the men gathered some twigs, leaves, and string, and presto!—we had a little repair kit. Jay crawled under the car to insert the gob into the hole in the gas tank. The leak stopped, we poured in some extra gas from a spare can and proceeded on our way. When we got back, Jay built a wooden framework to protect the bottom of the gas tank. And I began to carry a pack of chewing gum in the glove compartment!

Jay was instrumental in redesigning and enlarging the church on the mission compound in Muscat in the 1960s. The little church was a marvel of engineering and design, considering the fact that our budget and building materials were limited. Jay was especially proud of its roof, which featured four, twenty-five-foot load-bearing beams, reinforced with steel, that he and his helpers made from scratch. The roof was built with special wood beams from Africa that were covered with bamboo stripping, matting, mud, and a pitch of lime, gravel, and ash, finally cemented with lime.

The mason and other workman were very conscious of the fact that the church was the house of God, and during the construction process they refused to allow donkeys to go in or out of the sanctuary area with their loads of supplies and equipment. Jay and his son Peter also put the electrical wires in conduit pipe inside the poured concrete floor. This was one of the first buildings in Muscat to have its power lines buried in a concrete floor.

Jay and Peter, with daughters Margaret and Barbara, picked out beautiful rose-colored rock from a location five miles west of Muscat, loaded them into our station wagon, and mounted them as facing in the church. Later an oil company in Muscat used similar rock to decorate its dining club.

Benches in the church were made from old shipping crates and any other wood that could be found. In those days wood was not easy to find in Muscat. Jay also took a table that the Rev. Dirk Dykstra had used for a pulpit, surrounded it with teak wood, and turned it into an altar which was usually used to display a Bible.

At a time when the hospital was bursting at the seams, Jay was able to purchase land adjacent to the hospital from an Omani woman. With our enlarged tract, Jay tore down the old structure and built a new, larger hospital. Starting with a strong foundation, he and his helpers built an admittance room, recovery room, two delivery rooms, supply and sterilizing room, a room in which to bathe babies, and a resident apartment above the obstetrical unit. They added a large veranda downstairs and upstairs out front. Cement benches were built along the walls of the veranda. Staff people would sit on the benches during quiet times to cut gauze squares and roll cotton balls. (Later on, the veranda was enclosed to make recovery rooms.) Jay's hospital building is still being used, as I write this, by Oman's Ministry of Health.

Since I was in charge of the women's evangelistic work on a half-time basis, I was always deeply interested in the growth of our little church. Many of my memories focus on individuals I came to know. Permit me to introduce some of these remarkable people.

Before I came to Oman, Juwaid and his wife made a decision to follow Jesus. They never swerved from that commitment, even through persecution, discouragement, and exposure to all the weaknesses and frailties of the missionaries. Juwaid, a gentleman in his forties when I first came to know him in the 1950s, lived on the mission compound and had a number of responsibilities with the mission. Juwaid worked closely with Jay in the Christian bookstore in Muscat.

Not only was Juwaid a good colporteur, but he was a brave witness for Christ. During the time of government interference in the early 1950s, Juwaid was fearless. He was also good-natured, warm, and inoffensive; he was Jay's right hand man. Juwaid was dependable for the mission; and because he was respected by all in town, he was a big help for each of us. Our staunch Muslim friends did not feel threatened by his presence.

It was Juwaid who first introduced us to Zainab. In fact, he had heard of her through his contacts about town. She was a poor woman whose husband had left her after the death of a child. Near starvation and inactivity had atrophied the muscles in her legs, and by the time we learned of her plight she could no longer walk.

Zainab was carried to the back of Jay's car and transferred to the hospital for vitamin B injections, nourishing food, and loving care. She stayed with us in the hospital in an improvised date stick hut for nearly six months, after which she was transferred to the area of the mission compound we called the "poor farm." Later she lived with Emel, Saalima, and Ruth in *Beit Ameena*. As she recovered, Jay built her a room with a little veranda and an enclosed bathroom.

When she first came to us she had lost hope of ever walking again, but at Dr. Wells Thoms' urging she began to struggle along with a sturdy stick in each hand. Faithfully, she would attend morning prayers, women's classes, and church services.

Another great helper to Jay and the rest of us in Muscat was Beder, a man who didn't learn to read until he was well past forty years old. Beder memorized long portions of scripture and could quote them eloquently when he led a Bible study group. He could also discuss the contents of other books in detail.

Werdi, our cook, served on our mission compound for thirty years. He began working for the Dykstras, and when they left he went to work for me. I paid his salary out of my wages and also put some money away for him each month in a pension. Werdi's meals were excellent and always on time, and he kept Dr. Alice and me in good health all of our years in Muscat. Even when crowds of people would come to our homes, he would prepare group meals without complaint and always with great skill. At the end of his career Werdi retired to a room on the school compound.

Werdi

Emel was an old woman who also lived in *Beit Ameena*. She had originally come to the capital city from the interior. Her mother had died when she was a baby. At age seven, Emel was engaged, and at age twelve she was married to a man from her town. Several of her children died as infants, and at age twenty-six she was struck by near blindness. Turned out by her husband, she was virtually homeless for many years before she came to Muscat and eventually found shelter with us.

Through her association with us, Emel became interested in the Christian faith. She attended worship services, morning prayers, and midweek meetings. She made profession of her faith before God's people and was baptized during an Easter worship service.

I should mention one other Omani woman before I continue with my story: Mahfooda. Mahfooda was a Baloochi girl who could not read or write. Still she had a marvelous way of listening to Bible stories and then repeating them to others in her own way. One of the memorable moments of my life occurred in a devotional meeting when I heard Mahfooda retell the New Testament story of the Samaritan woman who met Jesus at the well. The basic facts of the story didn't come out exactly right, but the depth of emotion displayed by Mahfooda had a profound effect on all the women who heard it. All of the women in the room knew the plight of a woman married five times, and all of the women knew exactly what it would be like to meet a stranger at a town well. In their culture it was not appropriate for a strange man to be talking to a woman at a town well. These and many other details of the story came alive for us through Mahfooda's retelling.

Mahfooda struggled with a hot temper, but as time passed I could see that the Lord was dealing with her and helping her to control this area of her life.

Just as we worried about Mahfooda's temper and prayed for her, we also shared the joys and sorrows of other young Omani women associated with the mission. In the Omani culture there was great pressure on girls to be engaged or even married before they were teenagers. There were no Christian young men for our girls to marry. Some of our girls waited until they were in their twenties to marry, but each of them eventually married a Muslim young man. On the whole, they have been good marriages. There have been no divorces. And God blessed their homes with fine children, who grew up disciplined and did well in school.

Another woman, Zenoob, was Dr. Hosmon's special assistant for many years and was constantly exposed to the teachings of Jesus. At times she seemed to consider herself a believer, but at other times she reverted to Muslim ways. Then, as she grew older, she had to decide whether or not she was going to make a pilgrimage to Mecca. The pilgrimage, of course, is one of the five basic points of Islam, and a Muslim is expected to follow through with it unless there are important reasons why it cannot be done. Zenoob's brother forced her to participate in the pilgrimage, and when she returned it was evident that she no longer considered herself among the believers. She was afraid to associate with us.

There are many happy stories associated with mission work, and I shall tell more of them in later chapters, but there were times of disappointment, as well.

But God is gracious. In May, 1961, my parents gave me a round trip airline ticket to Chicago. Through their gift I was able to use my regular vacation break to spend six weeks with my family. At the time I saw the trip as a welcome change of pace; I didn't realize that it was the last time I would see my father.

My thirty-eight-hour flight from Bahrain to O'Hare, via Damascus, London, Scotland, Montreal, and Detroit, was uneventful. High winds kept our BOAC plane from touching down in Damascus, and at Scotland's Prestwick airport there wasn't enough time to disembark and visit old friends there. Through the door of the plane I saw my old friend Mrs. Nairn and was able to scratch a note and blow kisses to her.

When I emerged from the plane in Chicago, I saw my parents waiting and waving to me. It was a happy reunion; it had been four years since I had seen them. The weather was in the forties—a far cry from the heat of the Gulf. Putting on a coat and sweater, I joined them in their car and we drove to St. Louis Ave. in Mt. Greenwood. Then there was a happy gathering of family. The sixteen children of Harriet, Ted, Millie, and Mel were growing rapidly. The oldest ones among the nephews and nieces were now fifteen years old. As usual, I brought forth from my luggage gift items for members of the family.

Ted and Mel had pooled their resources and gone into business together in a cement block hauling service. My parents seemed to be enjoying good health as they watched their family expand. They were proud of their grandchildren.

After a couple of relaxing weeks with them, I traveled to the General Synod in Buck Hills Falls, Pennsylvania. Eight members of the Arabian mission were there, including several who were retiring. One afternoon nine retirees from the various mission fields in Japan, Taiwan, India, and Arabia were honored, seven of whom were women. I was thrilled when twenty young people were commissioned to full-time service in foreign and domestic fields.

I flew back from Buck Hills Falls to Chicago on June 6 to celebrate my birthday among family and the women of the church. Camp Manitoqua, a retreat center in Frankfort, Illinois, had just been built by the Chicagoland Reformed churches. Dad, mom, and I attended nightly meetings at a Bible conference there. The Rev. Bernard Brunsting of California was the speaker for the week. I had some profitable discussions with him. I renewed the acquaintance of many old friends and made new friends.

On July 4, again at Camp Manitoqua, the Chicagoland Reformed churches celebrated their fiftieth Missionary Field Day. Tena Holkeboer and Dr. John Piet were the speakers. The facilities were filled to overflowing. A week later I attended a meeting in the Loop, at which 4,000 people heard Billy Graham speak. What a contrast to the struggling Christian endeavors in the Arab World!

The six-week respite was over all too soon. Mom, dad, and I had some good fellowship and discussions together concerning the church, our denomination, and the mission work. They were interested in hearing news of my friends on the mission field.

On July 17, I left Chicago to spend a few days with my supporting churches in the New York/New Jersey area. By that time I enjoyed the financial support of six other Reformed congregations in addition to Mt. Greenwood. I showed slides at two of the churches, Clifton's Hope Reformed and Paterson's Union Reformed Church. Following the services both congregations held receptions for me. Increasingly, I was getting to know and love the people in these churches. I stayed with one particular family, Jake and Hermina Warnet and their two sons. One time they served celery with their Sunday dinner. I remarked how good the celery tasted and that celery was not available in Oman. From that time onward, each time I came to speak in their church, they insisted that I stay with them *and* partake of celery with them.

En route home I was able to stop over in London, where the Wynne family met me and took me to their home seventeen miles from the airport. What a beautiful country! The Wynnes lived in an area that had once been the home of the pilgrims who came to America. One morning we visited an old pilgrim church. Another afternoon we attended evensong at the great Canterbury Cathedral. Words fail to describe the majesty of this edifice, where people from all over the world experience the power and beauty of holiness. We also visited St. Martin's in Canterbury, a church built about the time that Islam was spreading throughout the Arab world.

A few days later, at midnight, I was back in Bahrain. Dr. Maurie and Elie Heusinkveld, Bill Dekker, and Nancy Nienhuis were at the airport to greet me. Even at midnight, the Gulf air was hot and humid. I spent a day in Bahrain before flying the 500 miles to Oman. It had been a good summer, a welcome interlude, and a gift from the Lord.

Less than six months later I received a telegram from my mother stating that dad had passed away. He had been taken unexpectedly by a myocardial infarction, a heart attack. Even in the last hour of dad's life, I learned, he had been working on behalf of the church.

On January 8, 1962, dad ate breakfast with my mother, then drove her to her weekly White Cross meeting at the church, where she and other women of the church would prepare supplies to send to overseas missionaries. Our new pastor, the Rev. Harris Verkaik, pulled him aside to talk to him in the church yard. As dad proceeded to do some business in town he felt ill and tried to sit down to compose himself. He fell on the sidewalk and was gone. It was very sudden. We were thankful the attack did not come while he was driving.

I received the telegram in the mission school, where I was busy scraping the eyelids of the children with my copper stick. I remember working on the eyes of the little ones even as my own eyes filled with tears. My friend Noor was with me that day, and she helped me through a difficult time.

God, who knows the end from the beginning, in love made it possible for me to spend my six-week vacation with my parents in the States just before this event.

A few months later, the *Church Herald* published this sympathy resolution from the consistory of the Mt. Greenwood church:

> Elder Samuel Boersma, a devout Christian, who loved his Lord and Christ's Church, was indeed a pillar of spiritual strength. His counsel and guidance will be greatly missed. It was always his joy to serve gladly and willingly in the Kingdom work. Often, he was found in the sick room and in places of need, giving help and exemplifying a Christian witness. He was a faithful father giving one of his daughters as a missionary to the church.

It is the custom of the East, when there has been a death in the immediate family, that friends come to visit and express sympathy the first three days following the death. I, being an American, did not expect this same treatment, but the wonderful women of Muscat poured into my home in the evenings to sit and express their sympathy to me even beyond the three days. In many of their own homes there would have been weeping and wailing, but there was none of this when they came to me. The custom was that coffee and a sweet be served. Helpers from the hospital made the Arab coffee and helped serve the *helwa* (sweet) and coffee in the small cups. In a very natural way I had the opportunity to witness to our joy in the Lord and confidence in the salvation of my father.

Two weeks later it was my turn to lead the midweek prayer meeting. I spoke on the meaning of death for a Christian. Noor, who had helped me so much the day my father died, was in the meeting. Her husband died of a heart attack three days later. He had asked for Christian literature a number of times during previous years, but we were not sure of his heart's commitment. Noor said that he was a believer and that words from a conversation I had with him were in his dying breath. Dr. Van Ess once said, "We who find work difficult among the Muslims will never know how many secret believers there are in Christ until we get to heaven."

My family sent me a cassette of dad's funeral service which spoke to me about those days of shock and sorrow. It was good for me to be able to receive and share in this. The prayers and cards of the good people of my church, relatives, and friends sustained our family and me; and God's grace was there. I could actually *feel* the prayers being offered for us. And the work of a busy hospital was a blessing.

Not only were there prayers, but the ladies continued to send items for the hospital. During one three-month period, I received the following from the church's White Cross group: 906 bandages, seventy-five gauze squares, thirteen crib covers, 134 baby diapers, and sixty-one baby dresses. The King's Daughters also sent 239 bandages during that time. In addition, the Mt. Greenwood church supplied me during those years with another movie projector, gifts of money at birthdays and Christmases, and many cards and letters of encouragement.

In the winter of 1962 some specific prayers of the Mt. Greenwood people were answered in a mighty way. The previous year and a half there had been no rain in Oman. The wells began to run dry in the summer. There would be fighting, impatience, and harsh words among the people who trudged to the well every day. Some of the brash ones would push ahead of others in line, with the result that the old, young, and weak water carriers had extra problems. By the time autumn came, we were desperate for a good rain, which normally would fall in December or January. The months passed without a drop. I mentioned our problem in letters, and at various times the people in my home church prayed for rain in Muscat. One evening my mother sought out pastor Verkaik and asked him if he would offer a special prayer in one of the worship services. Pastor Verkaik was glad to assent and in the Sunday evening service on January 21, 1963, the people of Mt. Greenwood raised their hearts and voices and asked the Lord for rain in Muscat. Since many of them were truck farmers, they knew only too well how dependent people can be upon rain. I wrote in my journal on January 22, 1963, that we had pleaded in our prayer groups in Oman for rain. On Thursday the 24th, at sunrise, we awakened to a downpour that lasted for two hours straight. There were two good-sized reservoirs built by the British in the mountains above Muscat, and both were filled to the top rim—no more, no less. How thankful we were for the water! It meant that we could get through the hot summer without serious water shortages. God spoke to us that day in the rain. God had heard the cries of his people.

The hospital work continued to expand. Jay and his helper, Saleem, built a hospital kitchen in 1967. We began to discourage patients from bringing a retinue of friends and relatives with them. Before we prepared hospital food, people brought with them their cooking utensils and supplies, in order to cook food for the patient and themselves. There simply wasn't room for all the relatives and visitors, pots and pans. Sometimes a goat was brought and tied to a tree for a supply of milk! They bought fish, rice, fruits, and vegetables daily from the market. The discarded fish heads attracted stray cats.

Periodically we would have to call a friend who was a crack shot with a rifle to exterminate cats around the hospital. He would kill as many as fifty in an afternoon. A good time to shoot them, we found, was at noon, when they were asleep on the house tops. (They, too, took siestas during the noon day heat!) He shot from the second floor verandas. This friend never missed—he killed one cat every time he fired.

Jay was also able to build a new outpatient department, which would completely separate the outpatients from the inpatients. We now had a new laboratory, drug room, treatment room, chit room, and payment office built around an open covered courtyard, where benches were placed for patients to sit in the shade. Across the complex of new rooms, adjoining this area, was a large doctor's office.

A cook and helpers were hired for our kitchen. This eliminated the need for family to supply food. Thus we could reduce the number of family attendants to one, and we could now control the number of visitors. Guards were placed at the back door twenty-fours hours a day. All other doors were kept locked.

Income from the patients continued to pay for the hospital's supplies and for the materials used in the expansion. The growth of work in both the Mutrah and Muscat hospitals presented problems. There was some talk of unifying the two hospitals, making them one on the large compound in Mutrah. I was not in favor of consolidation. I felt that the women's work should be kept as a separate identity and would be more effective in its location in the old capital city.

A colorful personality in our mission compound during those days was Tahira, the crippled woman I mentioned briefly in chapter 7, who hobbled from village to village with all of her earthly possessions in a parcel, looking for a place to live. Children seemed to take cruel delight in tormenting her wherever she went, making fun of her and calling her a witch. It was easy to provoke her, and she would lash out at whoever was within reach of her stick.

As Tahira wandered from place to place she would erect shelters made from old rags and reeds, with oil cans for walls. There were always good Muslims who would give her food. (If it were not for their help, she probably would have perished before she came to our mission compound.) We first noticed the old woman when she put up her little shelter against the back wall of our cemetery. I could see from my bedroom window that the neighborhood children were tormenting her, and several times I ran to her rescue. When it became evident that she had nowhere to go (and that I did not have time to chase away all the neighborhood children), we invited her inside our walled compound. With us she could enjoy peace and quiet.

Three times a day Tahira hobbled over to the hospital kitchen, where our cook would fill her dish with rice and fish from the hospital supply. Cook Sulaimon was always cooperative and helpful in any situation. There was plenty of water for bathing, and Zainab filled Tahira's clay pitcher with drinking water each day.

Tahira visited me at night. When she came, she quietly listened to readings from the Bible. We prayed together. She also attended morning prayers. She was bright. Her mind was perceptive. She comprehended what was said.

One night with tears in her eyes she told me how her only daughter had died during childbirth in the interior. Pregnant with her first child, the daughter said, "Mother, bring me to the mission hospital in Muscat."

"No," Tahira had told her. "You will have your baby just like all the women of our town, with the help of one of our town midwives. I had all my children on my own, and you can, too."

Looking back, Tahira realized that the girl was apprehensive and fearful from the start of her pregnancy. She may have sensed there would be complications.

Both daughter and baby had died in childbirth.

The fact that Tahira had not consented to send her only daughter to Muscat preyed on her mind. She blamed herself. She felt so bad. Satan took advantage of her condition to possess her. She became confused and restless and began to wander. And because she was a bit strange, people taunted her. Tahira didn't tell me about her husband, but I suspected that he may have divorced her during this time.

It helped her to be able to talk to someone. She listened and found comfort in the Word. I continued to read to her during these visits. We brought her problems to our heavenly Father, who loved, understood, and cared. As the days passed she grew quieter, and she began to laugh.

It was Tahira who said she heard demons running up and down the stairs of my home at night.

There were times when I would be awakened at night by her blood curdling screams. Mary Markley, who had already given a good part of her life to the work in Egypt under the Presbyterian USA Mission and was now helping us in the school, lived in the front apartment of the mission house, when I lived at the back. She, too, heard Tahira and would run down to her aid. We would find her lying on her cot in great distress and fear.

"What is wrong, Tahira?" we asked her.

"They are attacking me," she would cry. "Demons." And pointing to them she said, "Some are sitting on top the wall over there. Don't you see them?"

We would have to say that we didn't. At this point righteous anger boiled up inside me. I cried out to the demons, "In the name of Jesus I take authority over you Satan and demonic powers; I bind you and command you to get out and leave Tahira alone. You have no right to her and no right to be here. Get out of here."

Tahira would become quiet and we could return to our sleep.

Tahira sometimes felt as if someone were squeezing the breath out of her. Sometimes she was so frightened that she couldn't even call for me. Twice she said that an evil force took the shape of an ugly, fat wolf, which sat on our fence and looked at her. Each time I would exercise the authority over demons that Jesus gives Christians, and they fled.

Tahira stayed long with us, but there came a time when she felt she had to leave. I tried to convince her to stay. I knew that constant torment would be her lot again, but I could not change her mind. She was so steeped in what she had been taught from childhood that for all her insights and common sense, she would not commit herself to the Lord Jesus Christ. She was still restless; the devil had blinded her eyes of understanding, as he had so many and still does today. She was healthier and quieter when she was with us, but she never lost her restless personality. I last saw her hobbling over the mountain toward Mutrah. I grieved for her. My only comfort was to commit her to God, who loved her and would be even more concerned than me.

During a furlough of Jay and Midge's, the Rev. and Mrs. Gary De Jong came from Kuwait to Muscat to temporarily replace the Kapengas. Gary would go out to the British India Steamship, when it came into the harbor every two weeks, to buy food that was not available in Muscat. One time the captain gave Gary a small black kitten. The captain's cat had given birth to a litter of kittens and the captain was looking for homes for them. Gary and Everdene were not interested in cats, but they knew that Cornelia Dalenberg loved cats. Cornelia was living in my apartment and had taken over the work at the hospital in my absence. When I returned to Muscat, I inherited the kitten that was now a mature female cat. I became fond of Pussy, as we called her. She was a good ratter, effectively ridding our area of rats and mice. She also gave birth to kittens three to four times a year!

There were women of the royal family, friends of mine, who were single because of a lack of royal bachelors with whom they could arrange suitable marriages. The government gave them salaries and homes. They were well provided for but very lonely. These women were some of my evening visitors. They became my friends. I also visited them in their homes; when they were sick they would send for me. When my cat had kittens I would give each of them a cuddly kitten. These kittens grew up to clear their new homes of rats and mice, just like the mother cat. They also had affectionate personalities and were good pets. One of Pussy's kittens cleared the royal palace of rats and mice! I often said, "If there is a cat heaven, Pussy will be there." One summer when I was away on vacation, Pussy died of cancer of the breast.

As the years passed, there was one "inadequacy" in me that continued to be a sore spot. I was uncomfortable about the fact that I didn't have a regular college degree like the other missionaries. My father once asked a pastor in Chicago, the Rev. Henry Harmeling, about my feelings. The good pastor replied, "More important than a college diploma is a good knowledge of the Bible."

He was right, of course. I would encourage our young people to study and become well-grounded in the Word. But still, I longed for that college degree.

In 1965, when I was starting a fifteen-month furlough after a six and one-half year term on the field, I met Esther Petter, a young lady from India. She mentioned that she was attending Barrington College in Rhode Island. Barrington, she said, would accept credits from the Reformed Bible Institute and perhaps nursing credits as well. This conversation took place on Tuesday, September 1. I wrote the college the following day and the same week received a telephone call saying they would allow me three years credit toward a B.S. degree. By Friday night the way was clear for me to enroll.

That weekend I spent with Margaret Dykstra, my friend from the RBI, who was on furlough while serving the Christian Reformed denomination in Nigeria. We spent time in prayer, asking God's leading about my attending Barrington or possibly working at a Chicago-area hospital to update my nursing skills. Margaret gave me the verse found in Jeremiah 33:3, "Call upon me and I will answer you and show you great and hidden things which you have not known."

I "put out a fleece," like Gideon, as I prayed for God's guidance. I needed the approval of the mission board to take college courses. They would be expecting me to do deputation work.

I also felt strongly that I should not leave mom alone at this time. If I attended Barrington College, mom would have to go with me. If the mission board *and* my mother said yes, I would go. The following Tuesday the board approved my request and my mother also said she would go with me to Barrington. I now felt God was leading me to college.

Within two days we were packed. Mel and Dorothy gave us a car to use, and by Saturday afternoon we were in Rhode Island.

While we were driving on the freeway, I remember mom asking me why I was passing all the cars in my path. I stayed within the speed limit, but I guess I liked the open spaces rather than an object in front of me. On the busy Route I-90 a man pulled us off the road to tell us our tire was peeling off rubber. He said he had been trying to catch up with us for some time! We thanked him profusely for his concern and help. He said he would put in a call for us at the next telephone for a new tire. The road repair crew came in time and changed the tire. By God's grace and help we arrived safely. All praise to God.

The registrar at the college told us to spend the night in a motel in Seekonk, Massachusetts, about three miles from the college and recommended a worship service in a nearby Baptist church the following morning.

We worshiped with our Baptist brothers and sisters and listened to a sermon about God's calling of Amos. "God calls the unlikeliest people to the unlikeliest places," was the gist of the message. How true that was for my mother and me! My mother was an instant hit with the people of the church, and it wasn't long before she felt right at home. The pastor and his wife became our friends.

Following the service, we were introduced to Matthew and Jo Cellemme, who invited us for supper. They knew we needed an apartment for the next twelve months. As it turned out, Mr. Cellemme had set up a shower and toilet for himself in the basement, plus a comfortable chair, where he could get away from everyday pressures. During supper, Mrs. Cellemme encouraged him to make it into an apartment for us, but he said he was loathe to give up his place of quiet.

The next day they gave us the answer that we could rent it for that year. It had never been rented out before. They added what was necessary to make it comfortable for mom and me and charged a very reasonable price. Our one-room apartment covered most of the basement and contained two single beds, a dining room table with chairs, a stove, and a bathroom with a wash tub—most sufficient for the two of us. I felt that the Lord confirmed the decision to attend Barrington and provided for our needs beyond my expectations.

Mom enjoyed living in the apartment. Our landlords became fast friends, and we visited back and forth. Mom threw herself into the role of a "support person" for me. She knew my forty-seven-year-old brain would have to function at top capacity to make it through the courses. Mom cooked, cleaned, ironed, packed sack lunches, and did the dishes, allowing me to put all my time into study. I would pore over the schoolbooks and study late into the night. Sometimes mom would awaken, see me studying, and call out, "Jeanette, go to sleep."

It was in this apartment that I first saw mom kneel by her bed and pray. Suddenly I realized that she and my father had followed that custom for years. She prayed faithfully every night on her knees before going to bed. One time she shared how she always prayed for every one of her children and grandchildren.

I found that I hadn't lost my ability to study. I took sixteen credit hours per semester in courses such as English, anthropology, Jeremiah, Ezekiel (Bible courses), philosophy, missions, and gym. My report card showed mostly Bs, two As, and a D in philosophy! I found the course in philosophy very difficult and was just glad to have passed it at all.

At first I ate my lunch in my car between classes while listening to the radio. It wasn't long before the college girls invited me to join them. There didn't seem to be an age gap. We enjoyed good Christian fellowship.

While studying I did deputation work locally in different churches. Calls would come to the school office for missionary speakers and I would be sent. I remember one young man coming to me one evening after such a meeting, when I had told them what God was doing in Oman (and so few people in my audiences had even heard of Oman!). He said, "I appreciated what you said. I could understand you. So many speakers talk above our heads!"

I thought about his comment later. My words and manner of speaking have always been simple because God did not give me the gift of a good command of words. In speaking in churches or in conversing with friends, the free flow of words is not there. God uses both highly intelligent, fluent speakers, and he also uses those who have a slower grasp of words.

One weekend the RCA mission board in New York asked me to speak in a Reformed church in Kingston, New York. Mom and I drove through new, beautiful, unfamiliar country. Unfortunately I had broken a finger the week before playing volley ball during gym class. The doctor diagnosed it to be sprained, when it was actually broken, so it wasn't set correctly and was painful as I drove. The people at the church were friendly, interested in mission, and interested in mom! After speaking at the morning service and in Sunday school, we prepared to return after lunch. Then it began to snow! It was a blinding snow that soon began to pile up. The snow plows and salt trucks came out. We got back to Seekonk in the wee hours of the morning, safe and tired. The good Lord brought us safely home. I was able to catch a few hours of sleep before attending classes that Monday morning.

In June, 1965, by God's grace, I received the coveted diploma, and the B.S. degree. It was more than a credential to me. The whole experience was a healthy, refreshing time of renewing my walk with the Lord. I enjoyed attending college, appreciated the teachers, loved my friends, and was blessed through our worship at the Barrington Baptist Church. I grew spiritually and made wonderful friends.

On November 6 a group of relatives and friends gathered at O'Hare to read a brief passage of scripture, sing a hymn, and bid me farewell. I had peace inside as the plane took off. In Akron, New York, near Buffalo, I spent three days with my friend Anne De Young and her father (Anne was home on furlough). After I went on to New York City, I learned that my passport had been sent to Akron instead of New York City by mistake. Anne's brother, a mail carrier in Akron, was able to retrieve it that night from the post office and ship it via air express to my hotel in New York City.

Flying through the time zones, it seemed like only sixteen hours from New York to Bahrain. The following day at sunset, Jake and Louise Holler met me at the Bahrain airport, from where I flew to Muscat. My arrival in Muscat was an event to remember. The space astronauts had nothing on me! My Omani friends threw popcorn and candy all over me in front of the mission house! Children had fun scampering about at my feet finding goodies on the ground. A flag bearing the words "Welcome Home" flapped merrily in the breeze above my house, and even the hospital was specially decorated. What a reception!

Again it seemed as if I had never been away. I knew again in my heart that this was my place—my joy, my love, and my home. This is the place where the Lord would have me work. In the days and weeks that followed, many said to me, "How long you stayed away! We thought you'd never come back!"

The work load at the hospital had increased during my absence. On a daily basis we carried thirty-five to forty patients in our twenty beds. This was not counting the babies. Out of 151 inpatients in the first month back, there were 126 deliveries. During one twelve-hour period we had ten deliveries. One morning we had thirteen delivered mothers and their babies in the recovery room waiting for beds to clear so we could transfer them across the way to the inpatient side. Some of the inpatients had to be discharged early to make room for those waiting in the recovery room. More and more patients came from the interior.

Evangelistically, I saw greater response to God's Word in the first five weeks back in Muscat than in my twenty years of work in Arabia. People listened to the scripture message, they were attentive to the lessons taught in women's groups, and they asked questions. It was apparent that the Holy Spirit was working in their hearts. The power of the Lord was stirring among them.

Soon after I returned to Oman in the autumn of 1965, mom entered the Holland Home for the Aged in Roseland.

A year later the Lord took her home.

Mom's hearing had deteriorated, and she reached the point at which she could no longer be alone. I still have a diary that she kept faithfully up to the day of her death, on Thanksgiving, 1966. The entries, written in her delightful Friese-English style, tell of happiness in little things, a beautiful day, a comfortable room, visits to and from friends, visits from her children and grandchildren, attendance at worship services, and good meals. She was happy there. She died quietly one night after a week-long illness. Dr. De Pree had been in attendance.

She had been a faithful, hard-working, godly woman. I thank the Lord for her and for the time in Barrington, when we were together in close fellowship. Our God is so good. I give God thanks for the pleasant memories I have of mom.

When my Omani friends heard of her death they all grieved with me. Many Omani women came to my home and sat with me to express their sorrow and condolences. We talked. Coffee and sweets were served. Again there was no weeping or wailing, and I could tell them my mother loved her Lord and was in heaven above with him. I had the assurance of one day meeting her again.

The year 1967 was a time that we would never forget. First came reports of the discovery of oil in the interior. Several oil companies had been drilling for years, but until 1967 they brought up nothing but sand. Then, in the town of Fahud, the first well struck oil—black gold. More wells were drilled and the oil began to flow. Word about the oil spread rapidly by word of mouth. People knew about the amazing results in Saudi Arabia, Bahrain, Kuwait, and Qatar; they knew this would bring great change to our country. Many Omani men knew exactly what was about to happen because they had worked in other oil fields in the Gulf and Saudi Arabia.

There was great excitement in the air. The months passed and people watched a pipeline being built between Fahud and Seh El Malah. Huge storage tanks went up, new office buildings came into existence, a city was built on a hill off Seh El Malah for European families, and then oil freighters began to come into the harbor and anchor off Seh El Malah. There was great activity everywhere throughout the land. Like other rulers in the Arab world, Sultan Said bin Taimur kept tight control over the drilling rights and royalties. Oil riches poured in. In 1968 the Sultan started building the first government hospital outside of Muscat, and he talked about making improvements in education and other areas.

Meanwhile, Communists from Yemen (south of Oman) were coming up from the mountain areas and creating havoc for the government in Dhofar, a province in western Oman. Guerilla fighting was reported along the Oman-Yemen border. British commandos were assigned to desert patrols to help keep order.

The Sultan's son, Qaboos bin Said, had been under house arrest for several years, since returning to Oman from Great Britain. He had studied at Sandhurst, an excellent military academy in England, and had become acquainted with western ideas and families. He was progressive, intelligent, far-sighted, and practical. Unknown to everyone, he was also gathering power and preparing to take over the government.

Just at this time the conflict between Israel and Egypt exploded into the famous Six-Day War. Arabs throughout the Middle East felt that Israel was an alien power that had no business taking over the land of the Palestinians. Israel was perceived to be closely linked to the United States, and that relationship created ill will toward America throughout the Arab world. Iraq declared war on Israel, closed off oil to all western nations, and cut ties with the United States. Russia tried to gain influence among the Arab nations.

As you may recall, Egypt was soundly defeated during the war. Arabs were shaken, but their feelings of nationalism did not die. Throughout the Gulf there were demonstrations against Israel, America, and Britain.

Violence seemed to be all around us, even though our hospital work was uninterrupted and I never felt personally threatened.

As nationalism and anti-western feelings grew, bombs were planted aboard British ships in the Gulf. Two of our missionaries, Dr. Jerry and Rose Nykerk, were aboard a ship called the *Dara* when a bomb went off and killed many people. Rose had a harrowing experience and almost did not make it as she clung to a rope ladder during evacuation of the ship. When she got to the bottom, she learned there was absolutely no more room in the rescue boat below, and she had to climb the swaying rope ladder back up to the top. She cried she couldn't do it, but her husband standing at the top of the ladder continued to encourage her saying she could do it and must. She finally did reach the top with God's help. Jerry and Rose reached Muscat safely, but friends of theirs from Dhahran did not make it.

Also during this time of unrest the minister of the interior, Seyyed Ahmed Ibrahim, was himself injured in a bombing. Having boarded the British India ship *Dwarka* at Muscat at noon, he was settling down in his cabin for a short rest. He thought he would be more comfortable if he would change positions on his couch. No sooner had he done so then a bomb intended for his head went off and injured his feet. His ship turned back to Muscat, where the minister was lifted into a *houri*, transported to a vehicle on shore, and taken immediately to our hospital in Mutrah. There Dr. Thoms, who already was a good friend of the minister, cared for him. The minister, by the way, was considered third in command in the country.

Meanwhile, in Muscat and Mutrah, we were busy. I hardly paid attention to the unrest outside our country. Our work and staff continued to increase.

On September 12, 1967, Dr. Maurice Heusinkveld (our doctor in the Mutrah hospital) attended a mission station meeting in my house. The following day was very busy, and that night Dr. Heusinkveld had to come back to Muscat to continue discussions about the MEC agenda. He and his wife came to Jay and Midge's home after supper and stayed until about ten o'clock.

Maurie and Elie, upon arriving at their compound in Mutrah in the dark of the night, opened the gate to their compound and drove the car inside. Elie went into the house while Maurie went back to close the door.

It was then (as we understand it) that a hand holding a .25-caliber revolver slipped through a small doorway built into the larger gate. Maurie evidently had stooped over to close the gate and had just turned around to go back to the house when he was shot at close range. He was hit three or four times in the left arm, left side, and back.

He was able to walk upstairs to tell his wife he had been shot. Elie immediately called Dr. Fred Richards, who lived downstairs in their home. Dr. Richards and the hospital staff carried him on a stretcher to the hospital. Less than an hour later, in the operating room, he died.

Just before Maurie's death, Dr. Richards attempted to revive him with heart massage. Massive bleeding in his abdomen led Dr. Richards to think that an aorta had been hit by one of the slugs. On the operating table, before anesthesia was given, Dr. Richards heard Maurie pray, "Father forgive them, for they know not what they do."

Authorities conducted an investigation. Footprints had been found outside the gate of the compound. The police could determine from reading the footprints in the sand that the culprit had gone to the shore and escaped by boat.

The British did trace the ownership of the gun, but they could not prove anything. It was not expedient to release any information to the public. The murderer was never brought to justice for the crime.

From the time he arrived on the mission field in 1946, Dr. Heusinkveld stood firm on principles of truth and honesty. Gentle but firm, his convictions carried over into his work. Maurie loved the Lord and loved the Arabs. He hated paternalism and strove to teach right from wrong. He operated the hospital in a business like, efficient manner in all areas, including the order in which patients were seen by doctors. He made no distinction between rich or poor; he always saw patients according to the order in which they arrived at the hospital. Thus, at times, a poor person would be seen before a person of prestige or nobility, but this did not daunt Maurie. While most Omanis understood and appreciated this stand, some did not and unfortunately would not accept it. I admired Maurie for taking this stand.

As a doctor, Maurie worked thoroughly and efficiently. As a Christian leader, he was always ready to lead in prayer or even take over a worship service. As the secretary of the mission, he was very conscientious. In Bahrain he had organized the mission's first language school, an institution that was of great benefit to many missionaries. He had been preparing to teach a course in Baloochi (which had no written language) in Mutrah, which I had been looking forward to taking.

Maurie had begun a good work in Mutrah, and we were shocked by his death. It seemed that we were losing a man in the prime of life who could have done much more for the Lord. But Maurie had prayed and asked God to forgive his killers. Hard as it was, we too had to forgive them. We thought of the death of Dr. Paul Carlson in the Congo, in Africa. The answers to the questions of our hearts were with the Lord. We could only continue to trust and obey.

Dr. Wells Thoms and his wife, Beth, were in their last years of service in Oman as the 1960s drew to a close. Wells, who had grown up in Muscat, knew the country better than any of us. The Omanis fondly called him their "father." Wells and Beth were looking forward so much to retirement after thirty years of strenuous work in Oman.

There were many celebrations, parties, dinners, and teas given in honor of the Thoms during their final months. Many tears were shed. When Dr. Thoms crossed the compound to go from his home to hospital, people would come out from everywhere to greet him. They crowded round him, wanting to talk and touch him at the same time! When I saw this, I was reminded of Jesus with the crowds of people surrounding him and crowding him, too. Long after the Thoms left, people in the interior and throughout Oman asked about them.

A year after his retirement, Wells was taken home to be with his Lord.

Meanwhile, tension in Oman's government grew steadily. Other Arab countries gave free medical care to their citizens. Schools and universities were opening in Bahrain, Saudi Arabia, Kuwait, and other countries. But Oman's Sultan was a bit slow in sharing the wealth with his subjects.

The Sultan did not travel from Salala to Muscat any more. He ran his government and all transactions of business via telephone with his regent and confidant, the Seyyed Shihab bin Faisal, in

Muscat. He held close rein on all details of government including No Objection Certificates (NOC's)—visas in or out of the country. Few men or women could go out of the country for study. It was also rumored that the ruler wasn't well physically.

On July 23, 1970, the rule of the old Sultan came to an end. On that day three men appeared at the door of the Sultan's palace. The men told the guards at the gate there was no need to frisk them, for they were well known. They entered the palace after lunch when all was quiet and folk were taking their noontime rest. They approached the ruler in his chambers.

After the usual lengthy salutations, the three advised the old man that it would be wise to step down quietly and give the government over to his son. I understand that they gave him every opportunity to turn over the reins of power peacefully. His reply was for them to come into his office, where he could sign over the throne.

But the Sultan instead took a gun out of his drawer and began to shoot, killing one man and wounding another. The men had orders not to assassinate the Sultan. The next shot hit the Sultan's right arm, causing his gun to fall and go off, which injured his foot.

The coup was over. A waiting British plane immediately flew the wounded Sultan and the other man to a Bahrain hospital for surgery, where their conditions stabilized and then improved. Later they were taken to London by the British.

At the center of government, power had changed hands. Young Qaboos bin Said took control of a country that was about to leap from the old to the new, from centuries-old patterns of life to the new and sometimes chaotic life of the modern world. To this day the people of Oman speak of "Oman before 1970" and "Oman after 1970." The date is a dividing line between two different eras.

The people of Oman knew this meant a release and change from the old. There would be a great and significant change for them and their country. They rejoiced. There was dancing in the streets. They and the missionaries anticipated the change would be for the better. We hoped and prayed that the bloodshed would be over.

IX
A New Oman

*I will tell of the kindness of the Lord, the deeds
for which he is to be praised, according to all
the Lord has done for us—yes, the many good
things he has done....*

Isaiah 63:7

I had been on furlough the year before the coup. During the
winter of 1969-70, I had completed a refresher course for nurses at
the Silver Cross Hospital in Joliet. This was an eighty-mile round-
trip each day from Chicago on Route 80, during sunshine, rain, or
snow. There were times during snowstorms when the expressway
was cleared by the snow-plow, but the side streets in Joliet were
slick and difficult to manipulate. I was a long way from the hot
Persian Gulf!

A certificate was given us signifying the completion of ninety-
six hours of classroom theory and eighty-four hours of clinical
experience. All these hours helped me keep abreast of new
developments in my field: research, equipment, technology, and
procedures. I noticed that as technology advanced, the need for
skilled (highly trained) technicians also rose, and I could see why
hospital costs in the United States were skyrocketing.

Coming back to the West after some years away, I recognized
that hospitals were putting a healthy emphasis on caring for the
whole person. There seemed to be more attention paid to the
spiritual side, reaching simultaneously both the physical and
spiritual, with a greater dependence on the chaplain. More use was
being made of the hospital chapel and prayer rooms. The Muslims,
being very God-conscious, had always combined the two. This

made nursing and care of them easier for us. Our mission hospitals in Kuwait, Bahrain, and Oman had always treated the "whole person" from their inception.

I enjoyed close fellowship with my home church, family, friends, and relatives. There were also opportunities to speak in churches, schools, private homes, youth meetings, and nurses groups in the Chicago area, New Jersey, New York, Iowa, Arizona, Indiana, and Michigan. I remember speaking to Baptists as well as the customary groups of Reformed and Christian Reformed people.

As the furlough drew to a close I took a number of medical tests which I thought would be routine. However, there were some problems with the results, and as late as three months before I was scheduled to return to Oman, I worried that I might not be allowed to continue my overseas career.

But the Lord had more for me to do in Muscat, the problems cleared up, and in June I was on the plane. I was about to enter a period in which sweeping changes would take place around the mission and within the work itself.

Two months after I landed in Oman, the virtually bloodless coup took place. When one considers the destruction that has taken place in the Middle East as factions fight for power, it is amazing that Oman's transition was done so quietly. Sultan Qaboos bin Said deserves much credit for doing what had to be done in an organized, humane manner.

The transition of power marked the beginning of rapid changes that were to reach into every home in the country. The coup was truly a *renaissance* in the sense that nothing in the country was the same afterwards and almost everything changed for the better.

Word of the coup spread quickly among the people.

Soon after the young Sultan ascended the throne, there was a downpour of five inches of rain. Few people could remember such a deluge. The windows of heaven were opened. Dry reservoirs were filled to overflowing and the *wadis* ran. People interpreted this as an indication of God's blessing on the new government.

You could see the joy on the peoples' faces as you walked about Muscat. Never before had we seen such happiness in Oman; it was as if years of frustration and tension had been lifted. There were songs and dances in the streets; drums, trumpets, and bagpipes were sounded. It was hard to believe that just a few weeks before, even the playing of musical instruments in public had been outlawed!

His Highness Qaboos bin Saeed, Sultan,
Sultanate of Oman.

We were reminded of the Bible passage in which King David
brings the Ark to Jerusalem accompanied by joyful music and
fanfare. In later years we would see the pictures of the festivities
in Berlin when the hated wall was broken down, and we were

reminded of the mirth in Oman. The streets were decorated; there was so much joy. People danced and the music continued for days.

Prisoners who had been held for up to thirty-one years were released, and we began to meet them on the streets. One elderly man said he had been locked in a dark cell for years and had lost his eyesight. Another former prisoner was mentally disturbed due to his confinement. Another had been married seventeen years before and had been imprisoned for political reasons. His wife faithfully waited for him, though her family had put pressure on her to marry another.

Radio Station Oman came into existence the first week of the new regime. An attractive, capable young woman named Muna, who had finished the sixth class at our mission school and had been an aid at our hospital, became the station's first female announcer. She later became a newscaster on Oman television with Dhiyyaab Sukhar, who had been a medical orderly trained by Anne De Young in our Mutrah Hospital.

The doors began to open for boys and girls to go out of the country for further education. I recall all the applications, forms, visas, and requirements that we struggled through, years before the coup, to try to get a promising young student into a medical program in a foreign country. Many times the work would be for naught. Now the doors were literally flung open for education, conferences, and travel.

Barely two months after the coup, three Palestinian female teachers flew into Oman. The following day the government's first girls' school opened in Muscat. No longer was the mission school the only institution in the country that would educate girls! Almost immediately, hundreds of families sought to register their children in the new government schools. They required a birth certificate for admission. These families came to us at the hospital to look up birth records, and for the next year a good deal of staff time was spent looking up old records and rewriting lost birth certificates. A birth certificate was a whole new concept for many people.

Some of the teachers at our girls' school transferred into government work for higher salaries. Educated Omanis, who had left the country years before, were coming back for government teaching jobs. The government declared that education would be free for all, and almost immediately the mission school's enrollment dropped. One hundred fifty students dwindled to about thirty.

A community women's club started in Muscat, the first in the Sultanate of Oman. The first president and vice-president were former teachers in our own mission school who had left for government jobs. The attitude of these women was wholesome and good. They were progressive in thought and dress; they wanted to help the handicapped and poor.

Nationalism and patriotism began surging forward as the once isolated and unknown country prepared to take its place on the world's stage. Omanis began to look with new pride at their country and its possibilities, and at the same time they were not interested in accepting foreign ideas and influence. They were Muslim and they were Arab. They would progress but keep their distinctiveness and identity.

The gate in the old city wall now remained open at night. Men were not required to wear beards, though many kept them. Women kept their *abbas* and *laisoos* as coverings when outside, but their modern western type dresses were seen in women's gatherings, when *abbas* were removed. Students at our girls' school began to come with their heads uncovered and their long, beautiful dark hair shone in the sunlight. (Later heads were again covered and a white cloth headpiece became law.)

Motorcycles suddenly appeared everywhere, roaring through the narrow streets. The husband of one of our nurses was given a good position on the new police force, and one of his first jobs was to teach other officers to drive motorcycles. In August, 1970, I received a driver's license from the government. I may have been the first woman in Oman to be granted a driver's license.

One of the first acts of the government was to remove the customs charges on material coming into the country for our work. What a blessing and relief this was! Over the years we had paid the government thousands of dollars in fees for medicines, supplies, and equipment coming into the country. It was a great relief to be free of these charges. I thought of Dr. Wells Thoms and his frustrations and pain over these payments. We didn't have this kind of money to spend.

We now had many salaries to pay; and as the work increased our needs became greater, too. The hospital operating budget received no money from the mission board or any help from the outside. We still had to be self-supporting, through the fees we collected from patients.

Though each of us felt responsible for the overall work, the financial burden fell heavily upon the mission doctor in charge.

There was one pot for the two hospitals. We in Muscat received our supplies and needs from Mutrah. Anne was responsible for organizing the finances until Yohannan from India was hired. He ordered the supplies, kept us in stock, kept a careful record, and distributed the medicines, supplies, etc., according to our needs. Mr. Cooper, our faithful Indian driver, was kept busy transporting school children and supplies.

A busy clinic at Muscat mission hospital.

Strikes, previously unknown in Oman, suddenly erupted here and there as workers felt a new freedom to express themselves. One company responded by firing the striking employees. Even some of the young men in our Mutrah hospital sent a list of demands to the chief medical officer. (The demands were reviewed and some were granted.)

In October, 1970, I received a phone call from the new national radio station, asking for an interview regarding the history and purpose of the Women's Hospital. The broadcast was aired the night after the interview, throughout the capitol area. We could hardly believe all this was happening!

Immediately after taking the throne, the Sultan Qaboos started an ambitious program of development and reform in health, education, agriculture, industry, and mineral resources. He established various ministries to take charge of the different areas and appointed capable Omanis as ministers. A Ministry of Health was established, of which Dr. Assam Jamali became the minister. We found him to be appreciative of the work of the mission.

Al Nahda (meaning "renaissance") Hospital, started by the old Sultan, was rapidly completed. It was large and modern, built alongside the mountain near the old custom's post in Ruwi. An Omani doctor became director of the new hospital in Ruwi. Foreign medical personnel, both doctors and nurses, were brought in for staff positions. The hospital focused on the eye, ear, nose, throat, pediatric, and dental work.

The new minister of health visited our two mission hospitals and described his plans for rapidly expanding health care throughout Oman. He indicated that he wanted us to continue in surgery, medicine, obstetrics, nurses training, and our tuberculosis and leper work.

Omanis who had left for advanced education, men who were employed in oil fields in the Gulf, overseas Omani families, and many others now returned. The various ministries also needed the help of Europeans, Indians, Pakistanis, Sri Lankans; and later Filipinos and Koreans to help develop their country. Muslim, Hindu, Buddhist, and Christian peoples from Eastern countries and Europe began to enter Oman.

Sultan Qaboos began to give free plots of land to Omanis who had never held property before in their lives. The only stipulation was that they should immediately build on the land. Apartments and family houses began appearing everywhere. People flooded the banks seeking loans for building. At first borrowers needed the backing of a guarantor, but then the government itself became the guarantor for the people. A new date stick hut even appeared halfway up the Iron Clad mountain behind my house. Although inexpensive, the dwelling enjoyed a fine view and caught every breeze that wafted through the mountains! Later a stone, mud, and cement structure was built there.

In 1971, Dr. Roy Ebenezer, a Christian eye specialist from India, retired from the Vellore Medical Center and came to Muscat to be in charge of the Eye Department of Al Nahda Hospital. Shortly after he arrived in Oman he was asked to travel south to Salalah to examine the eyes of the Queen Mother of

Sultan Qaboos. Dr. Ebenezer was new to the country and the language, and I was asked to accompany him to the palace in Salala, about 700 miles west of Muscat.

In the royal palace we were first escorted into guest rooms where we waited for the royal summons. During the two-day wait I met one of the three men who had been with Sultan Qaboos during the coup. He had been shot in the stomach but had made a full recovery. He spoke beautiful English.

At an appointed time, a servant came for us and we were led to the royal quarters of the palace. On a stairway we met a handsome, bearded, distinguished looking Arab gentleman, whom we took to be the Sultan's secretary or member of his staff. He led us to a room in which a regal-appearing woman sat. We knew she was the Queen Mother.

There were six of us now in the room: three Omani men, the Queen Mother, Dr. Ebenezer, and myself. When the distinguished person sat next to me and introduced us to his mother, I suddenly realized that he was Sultan Qaboos bin Said himself. I lost my poise, regained it, and did my best to assist in the eye examination and answer questions. At one point, I remember, the Sultan asked us about our airplane flight over the famous Empty Quarter, the shifting sands of the interior. The Sultan spoke excellent English. We told him that the emptiness of the desert made us appreciate the coconut palms and vegetation of Salalah all the more. Dr. Ebenezer concluded his thorough examination and gave his diagnosis. The Sultan and his mother listened, and then he quietly left the room.

A few minutes later the Sultan returned with glasses of lime juice, which he served to us himself. The fact that the Sultan was willing to serve us in that manner told us about his own stature as a leader. It took a confident, secure man to put aside pretensions and serve foreigners as he did. I was deeply impressed.

Engaging us in conversation again, the Sultan asked Dr. Ebenezer about his background. Our doctor then told him the story of his life in India, why he was a Christian, and what the Lord had done for him. Among other things, he asked permission of the Sultan if he could tell him about his best friend. When he got his consent, Dr. Ebenezer told him quietly about Jesus; how in love he came to earth in human flesh to live among us; about his life on earth and how he had died and rose again; that God loved him in a very personal way.

Dr. Ebenezer added that he had made many friends in the world, because he had visited sixty-two countries for study, to attend conferences, and to give lectures. Among these friends were Muslims, Hindus, and people of other beliefs—but he considered God to be his best friend, his savior, and his guide.

The Sultan listened graciously and seemed to ponder the words. We closed by assuring the Sultan that he was in our prayers and that others in the Christian church were praying for him. The entire visit lasted almost two hours. We found Sultan Qaboos to be pleasant, humble, and easy to visit with.

Truly amazing things were happening during those exciting days. As missionaries, we rejoiced with the people. We coped as best we could with the new rise of nationalism and the rise of Islam. We loved and served the Omani in the Spirit of Christ, and we prayed that they saw Christ's love in us.

More and more oil tankers appeared in the waters off the coast; income for the country increased to make possible a massive development program. Schools, hospitals, clinics, and roads were built. Welfare aid was introduced. Girls who never thought to attend school were taking classes. New ports were created first in Mutrah and then in Dhofar. Radio and television were now taken for granted! News of the outside world flowed into Oman. A modern international airport at Seeb was built and began operations while the second international airport at Salalah catered to domestic flights. Postal services and telecommunications were established. The opening of an earth satellite station in 1974 put Oman in instant touch with the world. Color television was introduced. Foreign gardeners were brought in to seed grass, plant trees, bushes, and flowers. The sandy desert sprung to life.

The Omanis could buy new vehicles, travel abroad, build new homes, freely visit friends and relatives, plan for secure retirements, and even bring in servants from overseas.

All that happened within the space of just a few years! The country was catapulted from a way of life that was almost unchanged for thousands of years, right into the middle of the twentieth century.

By December, 1970, we knew that we could not, and would not want to, compete with the government hospitals that were springing up. The Omanis could then get free medicine, hospitalization, and surgery in these hospitals. Any kind of competition, even a semblance of competition, between the government institutions and our hospitals would have been unhealthy and counterproductive for the mission.

The minister of health and his assistant met with us in Mutrah one evening and gave us a plan for incorporating the Christian medical mission work into the new government programs. Briefly, the agreed upon plan included these three points:

1. The government would lease the mission hospitals with their equipment, for a nominal amount, for a period of three years. In 1974 the arrangements would be reviewed by both parties.

2. The Omani government would begin paying all salaries in the hospitals except those of the missionaries. The government would give the employees raises and absorb the resulting budget deficit.

3. There was to be free medical care for all Omanis, beginning January 1, 1971. (A nominal fee would be charged for obstetrical care, at least for a time.)

So from January, 1971, until December, 1974, the mission hospital would remain intact and we would run our own show, so to speak. The government subsidy took away the financial pressure, and we felt a new freedom to serve the people.

During this interim the Rev. John Buteyn, our field secretary from New York, Dr. Don Bosch, and the Rev. James Dunham approached the ministry of health with their offer to give our Mutrah compound, complete with hospital, equipment, residences, and property, to the government. This property would be donated as a free gift in the name of Jesus. The mission would retain the obstetrical hospital in Muscat with the understanding that the government could use the hospital, complete with residences and compound. Both compounds would be turned over to the government to use, but one of the Mutrah compounds, which is larger than the Muscat compound, would be deeded over to the government.

In November, 1974, the Rev. Buteyn would come again to Oman and set up another contract with the government. It went without saying that this next contract would radically change the way we conducted medical mission work in Oman.

We missionaries were caught up in the whirlwind. We watched developments carefully, realizing that we couldn't do much to alter things, even if we disapproved. The government, however, handled itself wisely and fairly and we had no cause for alarm. Our mission people used phrases such as "most cooperative," "even-handed," and "determined to succeed," to describe the actions of the government. RCA representatives who had struggled with hospital-government negotiations in other Middle Eastern countries in similar situations reminded us that the government of Oman was behaving with wonderful openness and fairness.

Still, we couldn't help but wonder: How will these changes affect our Christian witness? How can we hold on to the old goals of the mission, which were formulated in a different century? How can we remain true to our calling as emissaries of Jesus Christ in this country?

Jesus said, "You are the salt of the earth." The only way we had been able to function in previous years was as a closely knit band of believers, living together and working together. Out of necessity we missionaries had gathered into walled compounds. We had gone into the society as much as we could, but always we returned to the home base at night, or when a medical tour ended. We were like piles of salt, waiting to be scattered throughout the land.

I quoted Dr. Cantine in the beginning of this book: "The most effective way to open a Muslim's heart is through love." We had already seen that personal visits were very effective in building relationships with our Muslim friends. As the new government orders came to us, it became evident that we would be thrust out of our small group to scattered locations throughout the country. We would begin to work with Omanis in many different hospitals and clinics throughout the country. No longer would we be the bearers of special knowledge or skill. We would be just some of many medical workers imported from abroad. We would be put into positions of serving the Omanis, working under them, or being servant-leaders.

As we thought about these changes, we felt the Lord was working through them and we had been planted in the country for just such a time as this. As a group of missionaries, we discussed whether or not to put limitations or qualifications on the kind of work we would do for the new government. We voted to make ourselves available anywhere in the country without limitations, even if it meant living alone or being isolated from Christian groups. I think the new government appreciated that willingness to be of service.

Staff members who worked in evangelism, teachers in our mission schools and our ordained clergy, faced a different challenge. Part of my job involved evangelism, so this challenge affected me as well.

Nationalism gained strength in Oman. There was new zeal for the Muslim religion and less tolerance for Christian evangelistic work. The Ministry of Islamic Affairs was established to ensure the strength of Islam in the country and to prevent "proselytizing" by representatives of other religions. Public evangelistic work was not allowed. Dispersing evangelistic material, free of charge, was also forbidden. Muslims who observed evangelistic work taking place could report incidents to government agencies, and unwary representatives of non-Muslim religions could be asked to leave the country.

However, the new openness in the country led to an interest in religious books that were for sale in our book store. Since these books were sold in the marketplace for a fair price, they were not regarded as evangelistic tracts. Under Harvey Staal's direction, a new book store opened in a shopping district and there were other opportunities to sell our books as well.

The new openness also produced an acceptance of different religions, *as long* as they kept their place. The Sultan gave our church a beautiful piece of property perched on a hill overlooking a main highway. He also gave us property for a new Christian cemetery. Before that, we Christians had only the isolated "Cemetery Cove," which was not easily accessible, and the mission cemetery located behind the school/church complex on the mountainside.

The Christian community led efforts to raise money and build a new church on the property donated by the Sultan. People of many nationalities and denominations, along with the missionaries, donated money for the new church project. Women's groups held bazaars. Money flowed in. Eventually a beautiful edifice was built.

As students from our mission school were being drawn away by the new government schools, our teachers struggled to keep the schools running smoothly. The government allowed us to teach Bible and also allowed a chapel service every day. Teachers had the satisfaction of seeing their former students placed into the most advanced levels of the new high schools and into college and professional-level courses. While our former students moved rapidly into these positions, most students in government schools were still coming up through the lower grade levels. We were particularly happy to see our young women enter professional careers in the new country. How often we prayed that they would remember their Christian training in their important new positions!

Things were changing among the Omani Christians who had lived and worked with us for many years. Some remained true and faithful, despite the massive changes. But others—including some who had been closest to the mission—seemed to drift away. They had many different reasons. One woman obtained a good job, and with four small children she said she simply didn't have time to attend church services and prayer meetings. One of the older Christian women, who should have been a mature example for others, still struggled with a sharp tongue. Another Christian hospital worker could often be heard shouting at her fellow washerwomen. Still another dear friend who lived with us said she was too busy to attend all the church services, even though, as far as we could see, the changes in the country had lightened her workload rather than making her busier. An older gentleman, who for years had been a pillar of the church, began missing services and we knew he was spending most of his time at home. Some of the Omani Christians were not on speaking terms with each other.

There were times of discouragement. We sometimes asked ourselves, "Where have we failed them?" Or: "If we were not here, would the Christians do better or would they do worse?"

In times like these, we had to remind ourselves that our friends had indeed confessed Jesus Christ as Lord and Savior. In their talks in the Tuesday *mejlis* or in their prayers, we could see the work of the Holy Spirit. Sometimes we may have expected too much from them. After all, what church in the United States didn't have "problem children" in its midst, or members who were not on speaking terms with some other members? Sometimes we held up *perfection* as their goal, and we forgot to look back at the course of their lives and appreciate the tremendous distance they had come, through the grace of God.

And we missionaries always had to realize that being an Omani Christian in a wholly Muslim society was even more difficult than we could understand. Christian Omanis were not just a minority in their country, but a tiny, minute part of a minority.

Our job was not to make judgments, but to be faithful.

We were always to be firmly committed to sharing the love of Jesus, but we had to be more and more careful not to give offence.

If our efforts were perceived as "proselytizing" we could be asked to leave the country. We had to make some difficult decisions, as we longed to share the gospel openly, but we realized that a few gentle words and deeds of love and kindness were sometimes all we could do.

Meanwhile, there was an escalating need for deeds of love and kindness in our medical work. Occupancy in our women's hospital ran at 100 percent or sometimes 200 percent! In 1969 we had 2,300 deliveries out of 3,100 admissions. In 1970 the figures were 2,700 and 3,200. In 1971: 4,000 and 4,700. And in 1972, 5,200 babies were born in our hospital—100 per week. During one twenty-four-hour period we had twenty-eight births. Not all of the deliveries were easy. Hundreds of cesarean sections, emergency surgeries, breech deliveries, and other abnormal deliveries were included in the statistics. The recovery rooms were not adequate to hold the number of women who gave birth, so they spilled out onto the verandas and even into hospital offices. We threw mattresses on the floors wherever there was extra space.

"We have gone beyond our capacity," I wrote in a report to the Ministry of Health in 1972.

As the months passed the dispersion of our medical people began to take place. Dr. Bosch and Dr. Alice were transferred to the new and beautiful Khoula Hospital, seven miles from Mutrah on the way to the Batina Coast. Don was hired as the chief medical officer and was given a new, air conditioned home. Dr. Alice was in charge of the obstetrics work at El Khoula and later moved to the Mina El Fahal hospital. She, too, was given a lovely home.

Dr. Bosch was also given a unique responsibility in his new position—care of the Sultan in the event of an emergency. El Khoula Hospital was the main hospital in the country for surgery, trauma, and orthopedic work, so it was natural for the hospital to be chosen for royal medical care. The hospital was in constant touch with the palace, and every time the Sultan took a ride in a car, rode a helicopter, or traveled to another part of the country, the hospital was ready for virtually anything. "Whatever else can be said about this kind of life, it certainly is not boring!" one of the nurses reported to me.

An interesting thing happened to Don after his reassignment to the new government hospital. "I am now working with more Christians than at any other time in my missionary experience," he once remarked to me. The larger facilities required more people. The Ministry of Health assigned newly acquired expatriate staff from other countries and among these were Muslims, Hindus, Buddhists, and Christians. Many of them were Christians trained by our mission hospitals in India.

Tension in the outside world continued. On October 21, 1973, the Arab nations who participated in OPEC put an embargo on oil destined for the United States. People living in the United States at that time remember the gas shortages, the long lines at the pumps, rationing, and shortages of heating fuel. I should say that Oman was never a member of OPEC.

The day after the embargo was announced, Egypt and Syria attacked Israel in a fierce attempt to regain land lost in the 1967 war. In the middle of Yom Kippur, Egypt sent men, tanks, and planes across the Suez Canal. Syria, meanwhile, hit at the Golan Heights and recaptured Mt. Hermon. For a week or so, it looked like the Arab countries would carry the day. Israeli jets, however, knocked out bridges over the canal and cut off hundreds of Egyptian tanks and men. Then the Israeli jets bombed Damascus.

U.S. readers of this book may remember that President Nixon was seriously worried that the Soviet Union might move down and take part in the Yom Kippur War. In October he put U.S. military forces on alert all over the world.

In mid-November a cease-fire was declared and the fighting was over. The oil embargo, however, continued. In the United States by the spring of 1974 there was panic buying of gas, even longer lines at the pumps, charges that the United States' own Exxon company was making excessive profits during the embargo, and rationing in many towns. In March, Saudi Arabia became the first member of OPEC to suggest that the embargo be lifted.

I began to use portable recording equipment in my work and in visits to my friends. One of my supporting churches supplied me with tape recording equipment and playback units. I was able to make a number of recordings, one of which was a health talk which focused on the whole person, ending with a Psalm. This health talk included the dangers of using salt following deliveries. I put cassette players in several rooms in our mission hospital and let patients listen to the recording. This saved hours of time spent in teaching and explanation. Most of the women who heard these recordings could not read; a tape was the only medium that could reach them.

The modern world was inserting itself into almost every area of life in Oman, but the old ways remained. A marriage arranged by a father for a twelve-year-old daughter was still common. The girl could not go against the father's wishes if he wanted to impose his will on her.

I encountered this situation on the Batina Coast when I visited the home of Shawwanah, a woman who had been a good friend of the mission in Muscat and a personal friend of mine for many years. We had had some fine talks together. I respected her for her strength of character and wisdom.

A twelve-year-old niece who had been raised in Shawwanah's home was a week away from marrying a much older man who had been married before. The upcoming marriage was solely the will of the father and not Shawwanah nor the girl's. The girl had been doing very well in school, and Shawwanah had hoped her niece would continue her education and make something of herself. Shawwanah was really the only mother the girl had ever known.

But the dowry had been paid to the father and the marriage was planned for the following week.

Shawwanah drew us aside and presented us with a bold plan to disrupt the marriage and go against male authority in this matter. She said she would put the girl in our vehicle with the statement that we were going to a nearby hospital. We would, however, continue driving with her all the way to Muscat, a four-hour drive, and keep the girl in my apartment until Shawwanah came for her. In other words, we would kidnap the girl in order to thwart the marriage!

We strongly agreed that the father, who had not even raised the girl, was in the wrong. We saw some wisdom in the plan. But we also feared being a part of deceitfulness. We talked it over and over with Shawwanah, but she was desperate. In the end, we agreed to take the girl to Muscat, and I agreed to keep her with me for a period of time.

When we reached the bend in the road that led to the local hospital, we continued straight out toward Muscat. The girl became edgy and asked why we weren't going to the hospital as planned. I explained to her what we were doing and why. Understandably, she was upset. She began to cry because she feared her father. We feared him, too!

We stopped at a gas station for a fill-up. Two police cars were there and I almost gave the girl up to them, so they could return her to the father. Later I was happy that I didn't.

It was dark when we reached Muscat. It was good to be home. A little of the tension was over. After setting up a room for the girl and eating, we all went to bed.

The next day the girl went to the government school again, where she had been doing so well. Shawwanah came that evening, embraced the girl, and thanked us profusely for having the courage to carry out the plan. The girl stayed with me for several weeks, while Shawwanah returned to her home. Her adopted mother felt it was safer that she remain with me.

The incident could still flare up at any time, we knew. Shawwanah told me that the girl's father had already spent the dowry money, and since the marriage never took place it would have to be returned. She knew that it was just a matter of time before the girl's father (who had never done anything for the girl before) would come and demand possession of her.

Finally the father came. Shawwanah again had a plan. Sitting down and calmly reasoning with her brother, she asked if he would accept the full amount of the dowry from her, to be used to pay off the jilted bridegroom. That way the debt would be canceled and the father still got the benefit of the money.

Surprisingly, he agreed to Shawwanah's plan and took her money. The incident was closed. The girl continued in our school, graduated with honors, and went on to marry an educated man whom she loved and respected. As I write this, the girl is happily married and God has blessed her with four fine children.

My 1974 furlough was peaceful and good even with a non-stop, two-month speaking tour. I lived with my brother-in-law and sister, Ben and Harriet Veldman, in Palos Park, Illinois. Their lovely home, surrounded by a vast green lawn, was located at the edge of a forest preserve. I enjoyed the beauty and green of the area, the colors of the changing seasons, and Blackie, their dog, to whom I would give extra food treats beyond his normal table scraps! He must have been impressed, because when I returned five years later, Blackie remembered me and was happy to see me.

I needed to take the Illinois driver's license test on this furlough in order to renew my license. In former years any member of my family could renew the license for me. Now I needed a photo and had to take a written test, road test, and eye exam. I was accustomed to driving the heavy four-wheel-drive British landrover in Muscat, which required a lot of arm muscle. Now I would be driving a vehicle with power steering and power brakes! The power steering was easier to manipulate, but for me it meant driving a vehicle I was not familiar with. It would have been easier to have taken the test in my landrover! But the good Lord provided help. I passed the test.

I was a great-aunt many times over, and the family reunions were getting bigger. My parents would have been so pleased to see

God's manifold blessings to their children, grandchildren, and great-grandchildren. Psalm 103:17 tells us, "But from everlasting to everlasting the Lord's love is with those who fear him, and his righteousness with their children's children."

I took some refresher courses and spoke in various churches. My speaking tour took me around the United States in the winter months. Despite slippery roads, snowstorms, and almost every night in a different private home, the tour went well. These tours revealed the great interest our people have in RCA mission work. Though speaking still did not come easily for me, I was more practiced and God was blessing my efforts. When I could, I showed slides. The response and the giving were generous. I appreciated meeting the people of the churches. I was especially delighted to be on farms. I visited the farm animals and, when there was time, I roamed the fields.

Furloughs were always full of activities. When I wasn't speaking or taking courses, I would visit family and friends and attend church activities. There were also letters to write. I was happy to hear from my many friends in Oman and India, including missionaries, and I tried to respond to each of them. The letters to my Omani friends I wrote in Arabic.

During the furlough I wondered about my job back in Muscat. The mission's medical people were being reassigned to hospitals all over the country. Don, Alice, and Anne had already been transferred to other hospitals, and I could be too.

But I loved the Muscat Hospital! I knew its people; and the place that is familiar and known is always the easiest.

In a sense I was by this time more Omani than American. I had now been in the land of the Arabs thirty years—longer than I had lived in the United States. The Omanis were close to my heart and were more a part of me than my natural family. They had become my family. Their language was my language. As Ruth said to Naomi in Ruth 1:16, "Your people will be my people," but I could never say as Ruth said, "Your God will be my God," though many had said to me, "Become a Muslim like us. You are too good to go to hell." I now felt a stranger in America and at home in Oman. No wonder I shortened my furloughs when I could.

Like Esther, we missionaries were in Arabia "for such a time as this" —a time of tremendous change. Those of us who went out in the 1940 era knew the hardships and poverty of the people and with them we appreciated their new affluence. We were truly privileged to have lived through these changes with them.

One time Chaplain Vander Bilt, while visiting a Jewish patient in the University of Illinois hospital, mentioned God's many blessings to the people of Israel. The patient jokingly replied, "Yes, but God did not give us oil. Oil was given to the Arabs."

We missionaries were witnesses of the fulfillment of God's promises to the Arabs. In Genesis 17:20, God tells Abraham, "And as for Ishmael, I have heard you: I will surely bless him; I will make him fruitful and will greatly increase his numbers. He will be the father of twelve rulers, and I will make him into a great nation." Oil was instrumental in lifting the Arab nations from obscurity to greatness.

I must add here that God did not allow oil to be discovered until he first established his church in the Gulf. And the denomination that had the privilege of entering the Gulf was the Reformed Church in America, of which I am a part. One does not know how long oil lay under Arab soil ready to be tapped, while the Arabs continued to suffer desperate poverty, illiteracy, and lack of medical care. It was no accident that the establishment of the church was followed by the blessings of oil.

As I packed my bags to return to my adopted homeland, the terrible battles in Beirut were just beginning; airport security was being tightened around the world in an attempt to prevent terrorist hijackings; the pro-American Shah of Iran was about to lose his throne under pressure from Muslims in his country; and King Faisal of Saudi Arabia, a strong, stabilizing influence in the Middle East for many years, was shot to death by a deranged nephew.

X
New Work in Sur

See, I am doing a new thing! Now it springs up; do you not perceive it? I am making a way in the desert and streams in the wasteland.

Isaiah 43:19

When I returned to Oman I learned that Oman's director of nurses, Asiya Kharousi, had assigned me to the town of Sur, about 250 miles southwest of the capital. I was prepared for the change. I knew beforehand that I could be transferred from Muscat. I knew I would be happy wherever I was sent. I would go forward in the name and power of my Lord.

I learned, too, that the town of Somayil had actually been first choice for me, but that the people of Somayil refused to have me. When I had gone to this town a few years before, I had given out passages of scripture to residents there and got into some trouble. My actions were reported and I was called on the carpet by the Ministry of Internal Affairs. People in Somayil did not even want me in their hospital.

Before I continue, I should mention the Scripture Gift Mission of London, the organization which sent me scripture publications for so many years. During my span of time in Muscat, they sent me boxes of beautiful scripture portions on a regular basis. They were unabridged scripture portions taken directly from the Bible. The little publications were colorful, attractive, and beautifully done. We passed them out daily in our mission hospital to all the inpatients being discharged.

Even though the government decided where I was to be relocated, it was months before I could make the big move to Sur. There were problems lining up transportation. The ministry's vehicles were very busy and some were constantly under repair. In 1975 the roads in the interior were still bad. Along with my household possessions I had to transport frozen foods and other foods not available in the remote, seacoast town. I needed a sturdy, dependable lorry and a very careful driver to make the trip on the rough roads to Sur. While waiting, I returned to the routine of our mission hospital in Muscat. I assembled boxes and waited until the government had transportation lined up.

The telephone call came one morning that all was in readiness and I should prepare to go. The people in Sur were waiting for me and were impatient. I wish I could describe the truck that came for me. It was made in Great Britain, obviously for heavy duty. It was long, wide, high, and heavy; it was old and had seen better days! The advantage of the vehicle was that it was so heavy it would crush any rocks in its way! Shembi, the driver, was a strong, rough, and capable Balooshi. He had years of experience behind him and I trusted him.

The truck was too large to come through the passageway leading to my apartment, so the large drum of dishes and unbreakables, plus other boxes and suitcases, had to be carried by the male workers of the hospital more than a block to the truck. At the last minute I couldn't find the silverware, so Danish Nurse Emsy gave me her extras. Everyone who saw the truck marvelled at its colossal appearance! It had already been loaded with supplies for the Ibra hospital we would pass enroute, as well as with supplies for the Sur hospital. Everyone who could break away from the hospital came to say good-bye and to wish me well. They all laughed as my feet struggled to reach the first step high above the ground and as I pulled myself up by taking hold of two iron hand bars. I still had another step to make to get into the cab of the truck. Fortunately my mode of dress in Muscat consisted of long white cotton trousers under a cotton dress!

Dr. Alice had brought her camera and got some good pictures. Ayisha told me later that Shembi, the driver, didn't know what to make of it all. He had said to her, "Look, they're taking our picture so if anything goes wrong they will know who the driver is and will hold me responsible."

Jeanette in lorry leaving for Sur.

Word reached me later, too, that members of the royal family had seen me riding in this truck through town on my way to Sur. They put in a complaint to the Ministry of Health, saying it was a disgrace that I had to ride in such a vehicle—I should have been sent in a comfortable car!

We hadn't gone far down the road when something went wrong. Shembi opened the huge hood, moved this and that, and improvised as only he could do, and we were on our way. But this had to be repeated a number of times. Shembi cleverly maneuvered around the sharp boulders but couldn't avoid the rocky terrain. Travel was slow and hot. The cab was open and hot winds blew through it. We had left in the early morning and should have been in Ibra—the halfway point in our journey—by noon, but we didn't reach it until evening.

The Ibra hospital supplies were unloaded as the sun went down. Hospital mechanics worked on the motor long into the night. I was given supper by the nurses and a comfortable bed. Shembi was taken care of by the hospital. We left the next morning after a good breakfast. There were more troubles along the way as we bumped along the rocky, rough road, but Shembi seemed to know what to do.

We were happy and thankful finally to reach Sur around two o'clock the following afternoon, when everybody was napping. A British nurse from the organization "Save the Children" had heard the truck rumble in. She got up to welcome me and serve lunch. Shembi enlisted men from the hospital to help unload my things. I unpacked the cold box. The large six-cubic-foot refrigerator was in good shape. Later that afternoon the medical officer in charge, a doctor, and the hospital administrative officer came to my villa to meet the new "matron." We sat in the combined living/dining room to visit. I told them about our trip. They were very familiar with these episodes and knew what I was talking about. The medical officer, Dr. K. C. Mathews, had arrived the same way two years earlier. It had taken him *three* days to reach Sur.

Driver Shembi and I remained good friends. Every time he returned to Sur with supplies for the hospital, he sought me out to visit with me. I met him a few times at the ministry after that and he always greeted me with a broad, friendly smile. I wouldn't have missed that trip for anything.

I had never been to Sur before. The town was not often visited by outsiders because it was isolated from the rest of the country by the almost impassable roads. We had treated Suri women in the Muscat hospital. They came to us by launch and returned the same way. They spoke Arabic, but a different dialect. Their faces were always covered, and they were more aggressive than the women of the capital area. They were well dressed; the adults and the children wore beautiful gold jewelry. Also, they never seemed to have trouble coming up with the money to pay hospital bills.

Sur, in years past, had been one of the wealthiest cities in Oman—even wealthier than Muscat. According to historians, the wealth came from shipbuilding, exporting, smuggling, piracy, and trading in slaves. Several of our pioneer missionaries, Zwemer,

Stone, Moerdyk, Harrison, Storm, Van Peursem, and Sharon Thoms, visited the Sur area. Some of the Suri men still remembered them. The missionaries must have been discouraged by the lawlessness of the people. Dr. Harrison, in fact, felt compelled to report an incident of slavery to the British authorities, and shortly after that the missionaries were no longer invited to the area. I was told about a revolt of slaves in Sur that was punished by the beheadings of 500 slaves in a single day. (I'm told that the Ghailani tribe responsible for this massacre has slowly dwindled and has not had the blessings of God.)

Times had changed, however. The smuggling and slave trading had been stopped by the British and by the government of Oman. Our pioneer missionaries would have been happy to have seen these changes. They might also have been astounded to learn that an RCA woman missionary would be allowed to live and work permanently in the city.

When I first moved to Sur, it was more like a quiet country town than a seaport with a colorful, wealthy history. The residential and commercial areas extended right up to the Arabian Sea. I sometimes took staff nurses in my eight-passenger Toyota Land Cruiser to the seashore for tea and a walk on the beach. We would often find unusual seashells.

It was the new roads that finally opened Sur to communication with the rest of the country. Not too far inland were the ranges of barren mountains that separated us from the great desert and from the other parts of the country.

The weather in Sur was much more pleasant than in Muscat. The nights were cool and occasionally even the days. Winds would blow in from the sea, gently or with great force.

The Suri woman wore a rich black, transparent fabric garment over an expensive print dress. The latter was visible through the transparent black garment. The black garment had silver thread upon silver thread sown together in the bib and yoke to form an eight-inch square at the front and at the back. This was called a *monsooba*. The heavy silver stitching on the *monsooba* was sewn by the women themselves. It set them apart from other women in Oman.

I was aware of being observed. The people were polite and reserved. But I was a novelty, being the only white Western infidel woman in town, with my face uncovered. I would need to gain the people's confidence and prove myself before I would be accepted.

I was given a villa on the compound of the Sur hospital. The home had the living-dining room combination, a kitchen with an electric stove and refrigerator, a bedroom with walk-in closet, and a bathroom. There was a high-walled faucet for showering (no tub). Anne DeYoung, who had stayed in the same apartment for about six months, had left a washing machine. Each villa had an air conditioning unit in the living room and bedroom.

At the back, off the open veranda, was an open area for a garden inside a high cement wall that provided privacy and kept goats out. Later I grew my own vegetables and fruit trees in the garden. The bouganvillea bushes had pink blossoms that were poisonous to goats; I grew them in front of the house outside the wall. Anne had already planted some the year before, and I added to them. The bouganvillea bloomed all year round. I was welcomed by their beauty each time I approached the home. Date gardens and other fruit trees in the city were not far from me.

The first animals that welcomed me to my new villa were sorry-looking, shaggy, wild dogs. They were not exactly friendly, but they wouldn't hurt you either. They were more afraid of me than I of them. Each one had excavated a large hole in the dirt at the foundation of the house, into which he crawled to keep cool and have a sense of security. Whenever other dogs from the town would come near my home, the resident dogs would fiercely protect their territory. They scavenged their own food.

There was room in the back garden within the wall to keep chickens. After I had gained the respect and confidence of the people, as the years went by, I would sometimes be given gifts of chickens or a goat. I had a coop made to protect the chickens from foxes. I cared for them and fed them until I gave them to families or had someone clean them for my table. I didn't keep goats, but gave them to families with children.

Religiously, Sur was more conservative than Muscat, a fact which was to be impressed upon me as the years passed. The population of the city was 100 percent Muslim. The religious leaders enjoyed a great deal of authority and respect among the people. The foreigners on the hospital staff, mostly women from India, were the only non-Muslims I had contact with in town. The only time I had contact with the British in town was when they needed medical care or when we needed their blood for our patients.

The Sur hospital had full facilities for surgical, obstetrical, pediatrics, and medical inpatient care. There were separate buildings for male medical and surgical, and female medical and surgical; likewise for the male and female outpatient clinics. We had separate eye, pediatric, dental, and public health clinics. The Public Health Department handled immunizing newborn infants against tuberculosis and treating tuberculosis patients. The larger public health complex was separate from the hospital. Delivery rooms and surgery were also in a separate building. (We got lots of exercise walking from one building to another!) Between all the buildings were the bougainvillea bushes and date palms. There were always birds singing in the trees.

We had good X-ray equipment and a good laboratory set-up. And there was one building (a large office) for patient records. On the campus were facilities for laundry and cooking, dormitories for the nurses and staff, and villas for the doctors, matron, and the expatriate staff.

The Sur hospital was built in 1973, located in the wide open spaces on the sea; while our Muscat mission hospital had grown up like Topsy, squeezed in between mission-owned and town-owned property outside the city gate and alongside mountains.

Unfortunately we were overrun with cats, because of fish scraps in the area. As in Muscat, men gunned them down periodically—a terrible job.

It didn't take me long to realize that my position in the Sur hospital would be much different from that in Muscat. They referred to me as the new matron. This meant they had put me into the British medical system, in which a matron was much higher in the chain of command than a superintendent of nurses in the U.S. system. A matron, in fact, was one of three people in charge of a hospital, along with the chief medical officer and the hospital administrator.

In the early months I was uncomfortable with the new responsibility, and I worried about living up to expectations. I had never been given so much power and authority, as well as respect and responsibility. I didn't especially like it, because I didn't feel that I had been adequately trained for it. I was acutely aware of my shortcomings, and I worried about being accepted by the staff.

Each ward and department had a nursing supervisor or in-charge nurse. The laboratory and X-ray department staffs were under the medical officer in charge. We had many local Omani staff working in each department. I supervised the nurses and medical orderlies and taught the latter. I also taught new staff nurses

Arabic twice a week. Occasionally the hospital administrator and I would visit outside clinics run by private doctors.

I was often sent for hospital supplies to the Ministry of Health in Muscat, because it seemed I could get more supplies faster than others!

Most of the expatriate staff in Sur were Christians from India, many of them from the State of Kerala in South India.

Christians in Kerala believe that Jesus' disciple Thomas journeyed to India and established the first Christian community in Kerala 2,000 years ago. Christianity has been there ever since. Keralite Christians are strong in the Word, prayer, and fasting. They have a very personal relationship with their Lord. One of their denominations is the old Syrian Orthodox church, which is highly ritualistic. This was evident when one of their priests came from Kerala and conducted services for us in my villa. They used incense. There was also the Marthma church, whose services were much like ours. The faith of the Indian Christians remained strong throughout the centuries because they remained in the Word, strong in prayer and fasting.

The expatriate nurses came to Oman as hired laborers. Many of them came from poverty-stricken backgrounds. They had received nurses' training in their own countries, often in mission hospitals. Job opportunities were lacking in their homelands, and salaries were much lower than those in oil-rich countries of the Gulf.

These nurses made the sacrifice of leaving husband and children in order to make a better life for their families. They worked hard in Oman and lived frugally. A goodly part of their salaries was sent home to the families for the education of their children; they also set money aside for future homes. Many of these nurses worked as long as ten years, receiving only a month's vacation each year to see their husbands and children. Their travel expenses were paid by Oman's Ministry of Health.

Many of the Keralites came to Oman as young single women fresh out of nurses' training. As they worked in Oman, their families arranged suitable marriages for them. On one of their leaves they would be married. Even during their pregnancies they continued to work in Oman. The ministry took care of their medical needs. They could have their babies with us, receiving free medical care. Their immediate families in India would then care for the infants and children.

These nurses came for the betterment of their families. Few recognized that God was in the dispersion. But with the discovery of oil, out of necessity, the entire country opened up to foreigners, including Christians. These nurses and others were quiet witnesses to their faith. The Muslims with whom they worked side by side observed their lives. They were often asked questions about their faith. These women were very effective missionaries, in their own way. They too bore the name of Jesus.

It seems that Eastern peoples adapt more readily to languages than Westerners. The expatriates coming into Oman were good at languages. Most of them came already knowing two or more languages. It did not take them long to pick up the colloquial Omani Arabic and Baloochi. I was able to give the very new nurses just out from India (and the other countries) the rudiments of Arabic, so that they could speak, read, and write.

Because these Keralites were so important in my life and work in Sur, I'd like to introduce several of them.

Dr. Mary Mathews was the wife of the chief medical officer of the Sur hospital. She and her husband invited us to their home for gatherings on special occasions, especially at Christmas and Easter. Their home was open to us and they were very hospitable. When I could not be present to lead the Sunday worship service, she would take over. God gave her rich spiritual insights.

Rachel Thomas was a leader among the Keralite nurses. Rachel worked in public health in Sur: checking on babies in homes, giving immunizations to children, checking and watching the weights of these infants, and advising their mothers. She had an excellent command of languages and often translated Pakistani, Urdu, or Hindi into English for us, when a Pakistani pastor came to conduct a worship service. Although timid and humble, she was a quiet witness for her Lord among her fellow workers. She was the kind of person of whom you say, "The fruits of the Spirit were evident throughout her life." She had a husband and two children back home in India.

Jaya Paul came from the hills of Ootacamund, South India. She came from a fine Christian home and married a teacher. She worked as a teacher in Sur and later was honored in Sur as "teacher of the year." She heard of our Christian group at the hospital, sought us out, and was overjoyed when she found us. When her hostel was a distance from us, I drove her home; later she joined the teacher's hostel located on our compound. She was a real part of our group and attended each Bible study. Since she lived in a teachers' hostel, she had to be back by curfew time.

Anniyamma Varghese's husband lived and worked in the capital, so their separate lives weren't as difficult for them as for some of the others. God blessed them with a daughter while living in Sur. Anniyamma had a way of understanding when others were in a particular time of need. Several times when I was struggling with the powers of evil in very specific ways, she called me and prayed for me. She and her friend Vijaya (below) were prayer warriors with a keen sensitivity to Satan's wiles.

Vijaya had known Anniyamma since nurses' training in India and was a convert from Hinduism. She and Anniyamma had permission from the hospital to share a room in the dormitory together. I remember her as a deeply spiritual person, faithfully reading her Bible, praying, and fasting. She had an unfortunate experience with an unfaithful husband and a failed marriage.

Mary Isaac and Punnama Mathews were sisters, both of whom had husbands who worked in Muscat. They kept their children with relatives in India. Later Mary and Punnama were able to bring their two daughters to live in Muscat. As I write this, we are praying that Mary will be transferred to a hospital in Muscat, so their family can be complete. Both Punnama and Mary sang well and provided tuneful support in the singing of our hymns. They too were deeply spiritual, prayer warriors, and leaders in the Christian group.

Susie Abraham loved the Lord and was close to him in prayer. She was evangelistic and had a concern for the lost. As I write this, she has returned to India to rejoin her family after having been ten years in Oman.

Agnes Rufus enjoyed a close relationship with her Lord and had an active prayer life. In her prayers she had a way of offering a special kind of heartfelt praise to the Lord. She had deep spiritual perception. She might be called charismatic, as could some of the others within our group.

Immanuel and Jothi, husband and wife, were my confidants all through my term in Sur. I was always welcome in their home and could share with them some of my deepest feelings. When I came back late at night from a tiring journey, dinner was prepared and ready for me, at their table. They always listened to my tales and quietly offered their support. They went with me to places in which Satan was working in specific, frightening ways, and they prayed with me time after time. We often came together for prayer in either of our homes. May the Lord bless them and their loved ones.

The real ice-breaker in my introduction to the people of Sur came from the Lord in the form of a sickly, misshapen little boy named Yusef.

Yusef was a baby in a Bedouin family that lived near the mountains between Sur and Muscat. Bedouins are nomadic, self-sufficient, proud people who inhabit some of the wildest, roughest territory in the world—the interior regions of the Arabian Peninsula. They take pride in their skills as desert warriors, in their world-famous camels, in their ability to survive in virtually uninhabitable terrain, and in their fierce loyalty to traditional Muslim beliefs. Bedouin tribes helped spread Islam hundreds of years ago, and the Bedouin warriors helped the present ruling family of Saudi Arabia assume power a century ago. Tents, herds, and outdoor living are the Bedouin way of life.

A few months after I began working in Sur, a Bedouin father brought Yusef, a tiny, fifteen-month-old boy to our hospital. The boy weighed less than nine pounds when admitted. Our hospital policy was to permit a mother to remain with a child, but since Yusef's mother was dead, the father stayed with him.

Yusef looked and acted more like a wild animal than a human baby. His little body was shriveled and shrunken, and he stood clinging to the bars of bed yelling, "Yi! Yi! Yi!" every time we came near him. According to the old customs that were popular before modern medicine was practiced, the family had branded Yusef in several places on his chest with hot irons. This old folk remedy was called "cautery" in English and *wasam* in Arabic. Yusef's burns were infected. We saw that God's mercy was the only thing keeping the boy alive.

Yusef's father, Abdullah, truly loved the little tyke. Just the fact that he had come so far on his camel with the child, leaving his herds behind, meant that he cared deeply. Many men in his place would have let the child's condition decline to the point of death, sincerely believing that it was Allah's will.

Abdullah stayed in our hospital for three days. He told us that Yusef's mother had died three months earlier, when the child was a year old. Soon after her death, Abdullah remarried a former wife of his, Taeeba. Even though she remarried Abdullah, Taeeba was still angry with him for having divorced her before, leaving her with his two children. Taeeba was not interested in caring for this infant Yusef, the son of the dead wife. She also did not know about supplementary feedings for infants. Bedouin women always nursed their babies. Abdullah expected Taeeba to care for their goats as well as go out with them every second day. So Yusef was neglected.

During his first three-day stay in our hospital, Yusef did not eat or drink. We forced spoon feedings upon him with much strife, screaming, and fighting. He refused to have anything to do with us.

After three days of this, the father considered it to be a hopeless case and requested a discharge. He needed to return to his herds. We suggested that he leave Yusef with us for a time, but he refused. I pressed him: "The child won't live if you take him."

"Then he must die," the father said. "It would be his portion and as God wills."

I remember feeling some irritation: "No, Abdullah, it is *not* his portion, and I don't think it is God's will for him to die."

I dashed off a note on the bottom of the child's hospital chart: "Father insists upon taking the infant home. But the child will die, if this happens."

Our hospital's Dr. Ali, a Muslim, took it from there. He strongly urged Abdullah to leave Yusef with us. Abdullah still refused. He didn't know us or the hospital. This was his first experience in any hospital. We called Ahmed, the hospital administrator, to help us. Ahmed had the gift of tact combined with persuasive speech. Finally Abdullah agreed.

Ahmed said, "Get the father to sign a paper giving us permission to care for the boy and absolving us of responsibility in case the boy dies."

Since we could not keep an infant without an accompanying parent or guardian, a local woman at first agreed to take in Yusef. But her plans changed and she could no longer care for him.

Yusef then came to live with me. I didn't realize what a precious experience this would be for me and how the Lord would use it in unexpected ways.

Yusef was afraid of me at first, but he then began to respond to tender, loving care. I set up a bed for him in my bedroom. He began to eat cheese, cereal, and drink his milk, and he began to gain weight. A friend gave him a walker, and slowly he was able to manipulate it and move about in the living room. It was heartwarming to see the development of his singing and talking. As his body grew stronger he chattered, laughed, and sang. During the four months that I cared for him he began standing by himself, walking while holding onto my fingers, and then tottering around furniture in my home. He soon became everyone's favorite.

I was now a single mother doing double duty. I had the care of an infant at home, which meant his washing, bathing, feeding by spoon, spending time in play, and getting up in the night for changing. I also had my job at the hospital. God's grace and help were there. God gave me the strength to carry the work at the hospital and the infant in the home.

Though Abdullah lived a distance from us and did not have time to leave his flocks, yet he came to visit Yusef and see his progress. He did not come directly to my door and ring the doorbell. I would see him in the shadows creeping stealthily to the window to listen quietly and see if his son was being abused. But the father always found a happy child who was eager to talk to him. Abdullah had to sneak away again, when it was time to leave, because Yusef wanted so much to go with him. It was beautiful to see the love they had for each other.

I carried Yusef to the hospital every morning on my hip, placed him in a mattressed play-pen (given us by Save the Children) in the nurses' station, and carried him home again each afternoon. The hospital staff and townspeople watched and remarked about how matron cared for and loved this Bedouin orphan. In the East, "orphan" means bereft of either parent. Townspeople looked down upon Bedouins, and here was a stranger caring for this "hopeless tyke." It was amazing how Yusef opened their hearts toward me. They became interested in his progress and marveled at how well he was doing. It was truly miraculous; again God's grace was there. I began to be called *Umm Yusef* or the "Mother of Yusef," which name, along with matron, remained with me until my retirement.

Eventually Yusef weighed fifteen pounds and Dr. K. C. Mathews, now medical officer in charge, said he was ready to operate on the child's inguinal hernia. In mid-November, Dr. Mathews performed a herniotomy and circumcision on him. I carried him in my arms to our home immediately after surgery and cared for him night and day.

During this healing process I was Yusef's mother and private duty nurse. It was a difficult experience for both of us. It hurt me to see the pain on his face as I changed the dressings every time he urinated or defecated, day or night. He disliked this process as much as I did.

But he loved the seaside. He loved playing in the sand while I wandered around looking for shells (all the while keeping an eye on him).

I didn't miss a day of work. When I was busy in the hospital, the nurses on the ward took care of him. But every time I walked into the nurses' station, he held out his arms to me to take him. I only took him into my arms during our coffee break, when he ate cookies and drank milk.

The four-day Muslim religious holiday was approaching. Abdullah suggested I spend the holiday with his family, during which time I could teach them the care of Yusef, who now weighed seventeen pounds. Yusef was eating, walking, talking, laughing, and doing everything a normal one-and-a-half year old child would do, except he was not potty trained. But then, children in the desert didn't know what a potty was and wouldn't have used one anyway! (The hospital provided disposable diapers when he was with me.)

Yusef playing on my living room floor

I agreed to go to the Bedouin encampment with Abdullah and Yusef.

When Abdullah came to get me for the trek to the desert, I arranged for a taxi truck to take all of us. The eighty miles on the well-trodden dirt road was no problem, but the driver was not happy to drive on an unmarked road into the desert. There was not even a camel or donkey path, because the Bedouins could find their way anywhere without a road or even a path. It was a rough ride for the vehicle off the main road to their encampment, which was called Wadi 'Ar 'Ar. I could understand the driver's concern for his vehicle. It would have been better had Abdullah arranged camels or donkeys to meet us. At that time the Bedouins had no cars or trucks as they do today; they did not even know how to drive.

It was noon when we arrived. Many people came out to greet us. They were especially anxious to see Yusef. Yusef recognized everyone and just laughed. He was very happy to be back in familiar surroundings.

The people lived night and day in the wide open spaces, just as in the days of Abraham, Isaac, and Jacob. They sat under the shade of trees to eat their meals or snacks of dates with coffee. Each family's dwelling was constructed in the meager shade of a thorn tree. Blankets and matting were used for covering. The tree branches were clothes hangers. A date stick or thorn-brush fence with a door formed an enclosure around the home, keeping out donkeys, goats, and camels.

Abdullah cleared an open space and placed my mattress on the sand. The open desert was to be my guest room. When all the chores were finished, we spread out blankets and mats to sit on. Everybody relaxed and talked. This was a good time for me to read to them. The Bedouins listened attentively. On the third night, a friend of Abdullah's joined us. He said he had heard readings from the Bible before, when he had been a patient in "Thoms' hospital" in Mutrah. The Bedouins did not know me; nor did I really know them or their needs. If I'd have known more about them, I would have brought medicines with me. At night I slept with Yusef next to me under the stars, covered by a blanket.

One morning Jameela, Yusef's step-sister, accompanied me to a well some distance from the encampment. Many of the women had left early with their flocks. The men, too, were gone. We had the wide open spaces for bathing and washing clothes. Merium was attracted to the soap, which until then she had not seen nor used. I shared mine with her, and later gave her all my leftover soap.

After four days in the *wadi*, it was time for me to go. Three camels were brought: one each for Abdullah and me, and another for my luggage. When you ride a camel, you climb on him while he is kneeling on the ground. The camel is padded with blankets tied to his body with rope, which gives you something to cling to. You move with him as first the front legs stand to position and lastly his back legs come up. Having accomplished this feat myself, I felt far from the ground, as camels are tall animals. Then the animal's head turned and touched my left leg. I thought he was about to bite me! But everyone laughed. They assured me he would not hurt me and was only chasing flies!

The camel ride brought us back to the main road. I did not have to wait long for a passing vehicle to stop and take me to the town of Kamil. In Kamil I found Nasir from the hospital, with his cousin, at a gas station. They took me back to Sur.

God brought Yusef to Sur to give me entree into the lives of the desert people. I was now accepted by the townspeople of Sur and by the Bedouins of Wadi 'Ar 'Ar.

Meanwhile, outside Wadi 'Ar 'Ar and Sur, Oman was still changing. Better ports were built along the coast. Oman's navy was expanding. New government buildings sprang up throughout the country, accompanied by concrete roads, beautiful landscaping, fountains, and gardens. New restaurants began appearing in the capital area: first Indian, then Pakistani, then American-style fried chicken. People listened to local stations on transistor radios and distant stations on shortwave receivers.

In the capital, wives who had cooked over primus stoves began switching to bottled gas stoves, and missionaries changed too from kerosene stoves to bottled gas. City electricity brought electric lights, refrigerators, and air conditioning to offices and some homes.

Though the schools, hospital, and homes in the capital had electricity, the people of Sur got their first regular residential service in 1977. Those who could afford it bought refrigerators and air conditioners. Many borrowed money to buy these necessities.

Then came another major sign of progress when the 280-mile road from Muscat to Sur was completely paved. From the turn east at Kamil to the remaining thirty miles to Sur, five bridges were built over wadis that frequently flooded during rains, making the old road impassable. The twisting, turning road included long inclines over hills between mountains. It was an engineering feat designed by a French construction company.

Between 1968 and 1975 some of Oman's "oil money" went into getting the Communists out of the Yemen/Dhofar side of our country. The Omani army, with help from the Shah of Iran's military and British army officers, eventually drove them away. I remember the jubilation in December, 1975, when it was said that Oman was the first country ever to be able to dislodge Communists who had gotten a foothold in a country. About that time American aid was also given to Oman in return for permission to use Masireh Island as a base on the Arabian Sea.

In the mid-1970s, Sultan Qaboos visited Washington, D.C., and established firm political ties with the U.S. government. A few months after the visit, the U.S. government sent Oman a number of helicopters and military supplies.

As time passed, helicopter rides became part of my duties as the Sur matron. Since we were responsible for remote villages in our district, we sometimes were called out to conduct clinics or handle emergencies in isolated, mountainous areas. Typically, a call would come to Ahmed, our hospital administrator, from a sheikh or government official, informing him of a particular problem. It might be a serious injury, an illness, or an outbreak of illness affecting several people. I would hastily pull together my emergency supplies of medicines and wait for a government helicopter to land behind the hospital, or go to the police headquarters and accompany them in their helicopter. I would be accompanied by a staff nurse and an orderly.

The mountains, thousands of feet above the barren lowlands, never ceased to amaze me. Hidden in the valleys we would see lush green meadows, running streams, groves of date palms, green mango trees, and small villages. When the helicopter touched down in a clearing, people would gather and comment excitedly among themselves as we hurried to attend the sick. Sometimes we would bring a sick person back to the hospital with us. When the problem was not urgent, the helicopter pilots would fly us over scenic areas on the way back to the hospital.

One time I had to direct a British pilot and two American doctors to the Bedouins in Wadi 'Ar 'Ar. I knew the route only as a ground traveler, and I found that a dusty trail looks much different when you see it from an eagle's point of view!

In 1976, Sultan Qaboos married his cousin, who was a former student in our Muscat girls' school. The ruler celebrated by giving all citizens of Oman five days off from work. He also provided all his subjects with meals of rice and meat for three days straight. We could hardly believe the thousands of goats that went into these meals, as well as thousands of pounds of rice and spices. Then to add the final touch, he announced a thirty percent salary increase for all government employees in the lower pay ranges and a seven percent raise for all employees in the higher levels. Individual villages organized special dances, musical entertainment, and speeches.

The news from my home at that time was good mixed with bad. In 1976, I learned that my former mentor at RBI (now the Reformed Bible College), Miss Johanna Timmer, had passed away. Though I was deeply saddened, I knew that she had gone to glory. Founder, principal, and a leading teacher of RBI, she had lived a full and productive life for her Lord. She started her teaching career at Calvin College and later became the chief promoter behind RBI when it was being organized. (At that time I understand that she faced much opposition.) She willed her home in Holland, Michigan, to the mission board of the Christian Reformed church to be used to house missionaries on furlough or to reside in following retirement. (My friend Margaret Dykstra lived in Miss Timmer's home for a time following her retirement from work in Nigeria.)

In 1977 my brother Ted had a serious accident while working on a tire. A metal rim blew apart as Ted was pumping air into a big truck tire, and a piece of metal struck him in the forehead. Ted survived and was back on his feet in a few weeks, but the injury left him with a scar and other lasting effects. The accident was serious and could have been fatal, but the good Lord still had work for Ted to do.

The development of the church in Oman was a bit discouraging to us in the mid to latter seventies. On the surface, things were good. There were plenty of jobs. The children of the Christians were educated (thanks to our mission school); many of their parents had learned to read; most of the graduates had on-the-job training plus teaching in our hospitals; and the Ministry of Health hired our graduates to work in the hospitals that were mushrooming throughout the country. Thus our Christians were given responsible positions, promotions, and much larger salaries than we could give them.

Despite all this, we heard comments such as, "The mission never did for us what our government is now doing for us."

Some of the Omanis built two-story brick homes, with all the latest furniture, beautiful drapes, modern bathrooms, running water, electricity, refrigerators, and complete air-conditioning (which we never had nor have now). They imported servants; their children attended the best schools. We were happy for them. But like Israel of old, they forgot the God who gave them these blessings. They forgot to acknowledge God. The Christians had confessed Jesus as their Lord and Savior, they drank from his cup and ate his bread in remembrance of his death and resurrection; but then they forgot all Christ Jesus did for them, which was far greater than all the worldly goods they enjoyed.

A small minority remained true to the very end. Some have now died and are rejoicing in their Lord in heaven above. We give God thanks for them.

I believe that some of the Christians remain true to the Lord in their hearts; but because of the strengthening of Islam among them they had to be secret believers. They would have faced persecution if they would have taken a stand for Christ. Of these, there may be more than we realize.

As I have mentioned, we medical missionaries were always encouraged by seeing people get well physically. We had the peoples' gratitude, and many good things happened to us. Our missionary pastors, however, received little encouragement outside of our small group. Seeing people fall away hurt all of us, but it hurt our pastors most. They were deeply disappointed. They worked side by side with their people, they pondered and studied the Word to feed them, they gave their all for the people as Christ gave his all for the Church. Their hearts cried out when the people fell away. The prophet Isaiah wrote in chapter 55:9-11:

> As the heavens are higher than the earth, so are my ways higher than your ways and my thoughts than your thoughts. As the rain and the snow come down from heaven, and do not return to it without watering the earth and making it bud and flourish, so that it yields seed for the sower and bread for the eater, so is my word that goes out from my mouth: It will not return to me empty.

Jay, Midge, and the teachers at the school had the encouragement of seeing their students at work in high places in government and other responsible employment in the oil companies, businesses, and the military. Some were in charge of X-ray and laboratory departments in the hospitals; one became a steward in Gulf Airlines; some of the girls became wives of men in high offices. They increased their fluency in English and were influential with their husbands, their homes, and in society.

Several of our girls became registered nurses as Omanis were given leading positions in the hospitals. A male student was in charge of the blood bank at Al Nahda Hospital. Both male and female students became medical orderlies. Many others did very well in strategic places. They had learned strength of character with the rest of their education. More importantly, the Spirit of Christ was there to influence them and to change their lives more than they will ever know. They were not the same after coming into contact with Jesus and his emissaries.

During late 1976 and 1977 an incident caused me much anguish. I was teaching a large class of medical orderlies at the Sur hospital. At the close of one session I passed out to each one a small gospel portion with printed verses from the Sermon on the Mount (Matthew 5,6,7). I did not think the Sermon on the Mount would be an offense to them. On November 28 I returned from a trip to Muscat to be greeted by the news that the minister of health was very angry with me. I was accused of proselytizing. Ministers and others from Muscat came to Sur to investigate. Everybody was in an uproar. The bulk of the problem fell upon Ahmed, our hospital administrator, and Dr. K. C. Mathews, the medical officer in charge. During the investigations I packed a suitcase, should I be given a twenty-four-hour notice to leave the country.

I lived in fear and trepidation during this time. Ahmed informed me there would be some who would come to test me. And they did. They asked me for gospel portions or for a Bible, to obtain evidence against me. Dr. Mathews and Ahmed were my sole support during this time. God used them to keep me there. They told the ministers and others coming from the capital the truth, saying, "Yes, at one point the matron did pass out the *injeel* (gospel), but they would guarantee that this would not happen again." I give God thanks for both Dr. Mathews and Ahmed, who protected me and did not want me sent out of the country.

Before the incident ended, the governor of Sur requested Dr. Mathews, Ahmed, and me on a certain day to see him in his office. Again, I was fearful. I prayed much as did those of our prayer support group. The day came when we would have to appear before the governor. As per culture and custom, the men went in first and I followed. We shook hands and the usual salutations were offered. Dr. Mathews and Ahmed sat at the front, while I sat alone at the back. And they did all the talking and answering of questions. I did not have to say a word!

The outcome was the *wali* or governor put all the blame on the person who reported me! The governor was upset that the informer had reported the incident directly to the ministries in the capital, instead of first seeking a hearing in his office. The *wali* took offense in the fact that he had been bypassed. The plaintiff would be dealt with. (He would have received a good tongue lashing plus a warning. This encounter would not have been pleasant or easy.) So instead of me being punished, it was the one who had complained about me! Again it was God's grace to me and his help in time of need.

I had no idea that passing out a scripture portion would cause such an uproar, but I was ignorant of Satan's power and fury. He was going to fight us. In the parable of the sower, Jesus said, "When anyone hears the message about the kingdom and does not understand it, the evil one comes and snatches away what was sown in his heart. This is the seed sown along the path" (Matt. 13:19). Satan comes and snatches away God's Word.

Following the scripture distribution incident I became very cautious. I even worried about return addresses on letters I received through the public postal system. Return addresses having words like "church" or "Bible" or "Christian" displayed prominently could cause problems again. I wrote my supporting churches, institutions such as the Reformed Bible College, and other Christian organizations that mailed material to me, asking them to be careful about the words printed on their envelopes. Most of them understood and respected my concern. My churches began sending me letters in plain envelopes with personal names as return addresses. But the Reformed Bible College did not agree with me and refused to make this change! I later had to write them then that I could not receive their newsletters or promotional materials.

My fears may have caused me to be overly sensitive. I know I was very cautious during this time. It is not a comfortable feeling to be watched almost like a criminal, as if I had committed a terrible wrong. Parcels that came to me in Sur were opened and inspected for Christian literature. Later my letters were opened and read.

Then, just when I hoped the scripture problem was over, there
was trouble again. Through the mail, from England, came an old
order for scripture portions in Arabic! Always before, orders like
this had been directed to our mission headquarters in Muscat and
there had never been a problem. This time, however, someone in
the postal system directed the material straight to me in Sur,
where a local postal official opened the package, discovered the
offending material, and brought it to Dr. Mathews and Ahmed.
This was so irregular, and the timing was so embarrassing to me,
that I couldn't help but think that someone was again trying to
discredit me.

Dr. Mathew and Ahmed brought it to me the evening they
received it. It contained gospel portions that came from the
Scripture Gift Mission of London. I was terribly humiliated and
upset, because I had sincerely promised both of them that this
would not happen again. And here in front of my eyes was another
such box. I was very sorry and apologized, trying to explain
everything. I had written to SGM, explaining my situation and
asking that they not send me any more of their literature and
boxes. Dr. Mathew and Ahmed talked about it in my villa, and I
convinced them that I did not intend to flaunt their orders. I tried
to reassure them that it would not happen again. They were in a
precarious position, because they, too, were being watched. If this
continued, I would have to go. They would have to dismiss me.
They again stood beside me.

I held my breath as more time passed. No more back orders
appeared in the mail. There was nothing that could give offense.
Things died down. I know that my family, churches, and other
friends were praying for me.

My work at the hospital and the teaching of the medical
orderlies was not interrupted. Everything continued as usual, in
normal routine as before. The general staff and patients did not
know of happenings behind the scenes.

Every Tuesday and Thursday evenings at seven o'clock we met
for Bible study and prayer. Though everybody was invited, the
Christians mainly came. A good deal of time was spent in Bible
study, which I led. There was a time of sharing and discussion. We
recorded the prayer requests in a notebook and kept a record of
answers to prayer. Each week as we came together we shared
these and added other requests. The meetings continued until ten
o'clock or later.

Dr. Mary Mathews, wife of our chief medical officer, made the suggestion one time that we meet every morning for prayer before going on duty, as they did in Vellore Medical College in South India. We thought it might be a good idea, but we doubted that this would be possible in a government hospital in a Muslim country. We would need permission for this. I approached Ahmed, our Muslim administrative officer. To our surprise, Ahmed immediately agreed and even suggested we meet in the hospital nurses' dining room! This we did, gathering between 6:40 and 6:55 every morning. Some of the nurses stood, while others sat. We had hymn books and opened with the singing of a hymn. I read a few verses each morning from the Bible (following one book consecutively) and expounded on the verses. The power of the Holy Spirit came through with fresh, new insights and inspiration. We closed with prayer giving thanks and praise. We asked that God would give us wisdom and grace to care for the patients, strength for our day, and the ability to reflect Christ's presence in us. We prayed for the patients and the staff, and for Christ's healing presence in our midst. I believe that the Sur hospital was especially blessed because we began our day with God this way.

Just as Daniel's habit of praying three times daily became known in ancient Babylon, our times of prayer became known in the Sultanate. Once, when I visited a government hospital many miles away, in the town of Salallah in the Province of Dhofar, a British (male) government worker greeted me by saying, "I want to meet the only matron who dares to conduct morning prayers for the staff in a government hospital!" We gave God thanks that we were so privileged and that his grace and blessings were there.

Our Muslim friends took pride in praying five times every day. There was no denying that everything and everybody stopped when the call to prayer was issued from minarets throughout the town. The women would pray at home and the men would go to the nearest mosque. Should a Muslim be traveling, as I so often saw between Sur and Muscat, vehicles stopped at a place of water, for it is important that they wash. Passengers would get out and pray toward Mecca.

These people were critical of Christians for not praying. Many of them did not realize that Christians *did* pray, even though we didn't do it at a set time or place. When I could, I defended our actions by quoting what Jesus taught in Matthew 6:6, "When you pray, go into your room, close the door, and pray to your Father, who is unseen. Then your Father, who sees what is done in secret, will reward you."

There were times when we would be praying in my villa, and Muslim staff workers would ring the doorbell. They would have some business to report or they needed something from me. The nurses would be on the floor in various positions; on their knees or genuflecting with hands on the floor in earnest prayer and petition. I would invite the staff workers to come in and whisper to them, "Christians pray too." Then they would see Christians in prayer.

Our prayer and Bible study times in my villa were greatly enhanced by the coming of Alexander, whom we called "Alexander the Mechanic" because of his job. He came from Karachi, Pakistan, where he was part of a charismatic group. He had been recently married, never having left his family or homeland before. He knew little English and spoke in Urdu.

When Alexander arrived in Oman, he had no idea where his sponsor was going to send him to work. Knowing little Arabic, all he could do was go where his sponsor took him. He told us that he was extremely disappointed when his sponsor began driving away from the capital. His heart sank as his sponsor continued to drive the 280 miles to Sur. When they arrived, he learned he was the only Christian working in a garage. He told me he cried when he was told there was no church in Sur.

Then one day he met some Pakistani Catholic Christians and they told him about our group meeting in the hospital. With his limited knowledge of the language, it took him three weeks to find us. How elated he was finally to find our Christian group!

Alexander joined us in Sunday worship; he also joined our weekly Bible sessions. He was able to express himself more fluently in English day by day. Things were not always easy for him. He experienced ostracization in his garage. And he missed his family and church. But Alexander had a strong relationship with the Lord Jesus.

We became his family. He would come to me when he had a problem and ask for prayer. At our Bible and prayer sessions, he was eloquent in prayer in his own language.

Alexander had been given the gift of prophecy while still in his own country. God speaks of this gift in 1 Corinthians 12:10. The power often came upon him after we had been in prayer for some time or toward the close of our session. He would relate a message in Urdu to Rachel, who would translate it into English for us. As

Rachel interpreted, I would write the message in my notebook. The Lord would speak to each of us individually by name. He called me matron because that was what everybody in the room called me!

God always gave us words of encouragement and commended us for coming together in the study of his Word and in prayer. He was pleased that we prayed for gospel workers. One time he told us our names were written in the Book of Life. There were words of reprimand and words of advice, which we took seriously. In these sessions we experienced power in God's Word and power in prayer.

About twelve of us met each session. Jaya, Rachel, Alexander, and I were present at each session, while the others were in and out each week as their evening duty permitted. Agnes had the gift of praise, and Vijaya and Aleyamma had the gift of speaking in tongues. And surely the gift of healing was in our midst, because healing happened often. They were all Spirit-filled. Many years ago on one of our vacations together in Kodaikanal, my friend Anne De Young and I had sought the gift of speaking in tongues but the gift was not given us. I have sought it since, too, with the laying on of hands, but it has not been given me.

The Malayalam group from Kerala were with us on Tuesdays and Thursdays. Each of these nurses took their turn to lead.

We thanked our Lord that there were no restrictions placed on this kind of activity, even though we could not "proselytize."

I was especially happy that we could begin each day with devotions, because this had also been my custom each morning for twenty-three years in Muscat.

Male and female teachers from the government schools and workers in town joined us for Sunday night worship. Sometimes Pakistani Catholics came. Also, doctors and nurses from the hospital came, including the Filipino Catholic nurses.

The Filipinos were new to Oman. The Filipinos seemed to be less reserved and quiet than the Indian staff. But some of them were more loose in character, too. Dr. Mathews, Ahmed, and I were strict with the staff. Other hospitals reported loose morals, but this could not be said of Sur. (I understand that the Filipino Catholics stopped attending church in Sur after I left. Their faith meant much to them, but they did not feel comfortable in a Protestant gathering.) I think some of them had their own worship in their rooms. They attended services in the capital on special holidays.

Ahmed gave us benches from the hospital, which I kept on my back veranda during the week. We somehow managed to crowd thirty to forty people into my living/dining room complex. On special occasions, such as Christmas and Easter, or when there was a visiting pastor from Kerala, the group would be larger. Mr. and Mrs. Mathews then invited us to meet in their larger quarters. We had our special dinners with them, too.

On some occasions an RCA pastor, a British padre, an Indian pastor, or a Pakistani pastor would come from Muscat to lead us in worship. But most often this lot fell to me. Margaret Dykstra kept on praying in Nigeria that staff would rise up to help me and lead us in worship. Dr. Mary Mathews led the worship when I went to Muscat. Other staff people were too frightened and shy to lead at first, but once they started, they did very well.

An offering was taken each week. There were times when we had meetings after the service to decide how to divide and distribute the money. Many benefitted from this money, the poor, the sick, and many religious organizations in each of our countries. We also purchased cassettes of the morning and evening worship services of the Nazarene Church of Pasadena, California. These cassettes were first heard by me and staff, and then passed along to Christians working in other hospitals throughout the country. We also received Words of Hope cassettes and messages, which were likewise distributed.

Christians from other hospitals came to my villa on their days off for prayer, fellowship, cassettes, and Christian literature. I always had my *Church Herald, Decision, Guideposts*, and other magazines to pass on.

There came a time when it was decided that we should purchase an electronic organ from a shop in Ruwi for our church in Sur. One of the male teachers from the school, who attended with his wife, could play.

The group enjoyed the singing sessions at the beginning of our service. A Reformed church from Melvin, Iowa, sent us fifty used hymn books in response to our request in the RCA "Hotline."

I led the singing each week, *haiste leit* (Frisian for "lustily"), and the group responded in kind. We often began with the chorus, "Jesus, Jesus, Jesus / There's just something about that name!" and then went into, "We have come into his house and gathered in his name to worship him / Let's forget about ourselves and magnify his name and worship him / Let's raise up holy hands and glorify his name and worship him."

When we came to the latter verse, I would raise my hands and a few in the group would do likewise. I could always count on Charles and Alexander to support with uplifted hands! The reserved Indians found it difficult to do. The "Dutch Reformed" also find this hard to do! To me the raising of hands is a demonstration of the assenting and ascribing praise to God. After the singing of praise and worship choruses, several request numbers from the hymnal were sung. Then we went into prayer and the message.

The decade of the 1970s rolled on. On March 31, 1979, the Egypt-Israel treaty was signed. Eight months later, Iranians seized the U.S. Embassy in Tehran. Fifty-two Americans became hostages for 444 days and the Ayatollah Khomeini tied America's Carter administration in knots. The relationship between Iran and Iraq began to deteriorate, a prelude to the horrible Iran-Iraq war that was to last through most of the 1980s.

My relationship with the Bedouins of Wadi 'Ar 'Ar deepened as the years passed. There would be various reasons to drive from Sur to Muscat, and I always stopped to see them as I traveled. Each time staff nurses who wanted to visit husbands or relatives in the capital would accompany me, which was a blessing. These nurses kept me awake as I drove across the desert. They also helped me treat the sick along the way. And we prayed!

I always packed a couple of boxes of medicines for these trips and made sure I had eye drops and ointment from the eye department. We conducted little clinics for the Bedouins from the back of our Toyota Land Cruiser.

When the Bedouin children saw my vehicle approaching they would all run toward us. I stopped the car when they reached us and piled as many as possible into the vehicle for the ride to their home under the trees. Abdullah would direct me to some shade for parking. He would then run for a blanket, throw aside rocks to make a clearing, and seat me comfortably for coffee and dates. Yusef was growing, eating everything, and he appeared to be stronger. He was always so happy to see me.

Abdullah and the family came to accept me as one of their own. During those years Abdullah brought Yusef to Sur when he was not well. Dr. Mathews and the pediatrician would see him and treat him as necessary; Yusef's step-brother, Shafeeq, or his step-sister, Jameela, would come with the child. They would often stay with me a week or more. These were always precious times for us. I kept two extra mattresses in the closet, which I spread out on the living room floor with a pillow and blanket.

We would go to the seaside in the afternoon, if possible. It was amazing what the children found on the beach to take back with them to the desert! Sometimes we went to town for a new pair of sandals. I would buy cloth for a new *dishdasha*, the long ankle-length dress men and boys wore. Saeed, the hospital tailor, would take their measurements and have the garments sewn in short order.

One time the pediatrician diagnosed Yusef as having rickets—something I suspected all along. There were times when Yusef came to us with pneumonia. No stone was left unturned to give him the best medical care. When he was with me, Yusef loved to search my magazines for pictures of camels, donkeys, and sheep. He laughed with great glee when he found one and would mimic the animals.

Each time Yusef came he got much attention. He had endeared himself to the hospital staff. Ahmed would tease him and say that I was his (Ahmed's) mother. This upset Yusef. He would punch Ahmed and say, "No, she's my mother!" Each time Yusef had an illness he recovered well. The rickets, however, never left him. His body was stunted and dwarfed, but not his mind!

When a stay in Sur was over for Yusef and his brother or sister, I'd schedule a trip, pack them up, and head for the desert. Yusef often sat next to me on the front seat of the vehicle—barely able to see over the dashboard.

One time, when I was spending the night with the Bedouins in the encampment, a grunting noise could be heard in the distance. I asked Abdullah the reason for this unusual noise, which continued to come closer. Abdullah smiled and said one of Ali's camels was returning home after having been gone for several days.

"He is happy to return," Abdullah said, "those are sounds of joy. He is happy that he's almost home!"

Once home, the camel grew quiet and contented. It was beautiful to see the animal nudging up closely to its master and to see the broad grin on the face of the man. These camels wandered great distances for days looking for food. They could see at night as well as during the day and would roam in the dark. This made the roads dangerous at night, because a camel could be in the middle of the road and a driver would not see him until he was on top of the animal. Many of these car-camel accidents were fatal to both the driver and the camel.

Accidents happened more and more frequently on the Sur-Muscat road as traffic grew heavier. In 1980, my turn came. I had just returned to Oman after a furlough that had been cut short. Arriving in Muscat, I attended a late-night mission meeting. I was up early the next day to drive our new Toyota Land Cruiser to Sur.

I was moving along easily at about sixty-five miles per hour on the Muscat-Sur road. The road was clear; I was traveling alone and fighting sleep, thinking that if I could just hang on until I reached Ibra, I would get a cup of tea and some food. I had just passed a car with two men sitting up front.

The next thing I knew, the Toyota hit a bump, and I was waking up with a start. The car had crossed the road to the other side and was crashing through rocky terrain. I tried to get control of the speed, slow the car, and bring it to a stop. It all happened so quickly. The car went up a hill and came down in a shower of rocks and dust on its side. Everything stopped. My window was open, and my left arm was resting in an awkward position. I didn't know it then, but the impact caused a fracture of my left arm. I didn't feel any pain.

I regained my senses. "Thank you Lord," I breathed as I reached over and turned off the ignition switch with my good arm.

The two men I had passed earlier saw my car turned over and stopped. They rushed over to the Toyota while I was still trapped inside. They couldn't understand what had happened. I told them I had fallen asleep at the wheel.

"Are you all right?" they asked. I assured them that I was.

Twice they asked, "Shall we break the window and pull you out?" Both times I said, "No."

I was able to give them the car keys by reaching up to the upper front window. They unlocked the back and removed the suitcases and boxes. Since I was a female, they politely did not touch me, according to the custom of their culture.

With difficulty I extricated myself from the bent steering wheel and pulled myself out from the back. When I was out, I realized I didn't have my glasses. One of the men crawled in and found them on the floor unbroken.

The men then put the luggage back into the overturned vehicle, locked it up, and drove me to the police station in Ibra. I held and protected the left arm, which was beginning to hurt. The police were very kind and took me immediately to the Ibra hospital.

There I met several people I knew and received excellent attention. The nurses washed and prepared the arm; the surgeon sutured the cuts and put on a temporary cast. He told me to come back in a week for a full arm cast. I had tea and a snack with the hospital people that night, before proceeding back to Sur.

The folks in Sur were most sympathetic and helpful. They brought gifts of fruit and *helwa*.

One of the first people to see me after I returned to Sur was Ali Jameel, a staunch Muslim who served as the hospital's tailor. He gravely advised me on the care of my fractured arm, what food I should eat, and that I should get plenty of rest.

"It hurts to see you injured," Ali Jameel said. "I wish I could take the injury from you and carry it myself." Then Ali Jameel gave me a large basin of *helwa*. "You will probably have many guests," he said, "and you can share this with your guests in honor of God's care and keeping when you had the accident."

That afternoon an Omani male nurse brought me five dozen bananas (a fairly expensive item in those days!) and said I could also share them with people who called on me.

Then the people started to come. Before too many days passed, I think I shared more than a hundred servings of *helwa* and bananas. One person brought me a rooster. Someone else brought a hen. Someone asked if she could go to the bazaar to do some shopping for me. All of these warm, generous people were Muslims, and they all recognized God's hand in my recovery from the accident. I will never forget these kind people and their unselfish acts of generosity.

My Christian friends, too, expressed concern and gratitude. Every hour seemed to bring a new knock on my door and another smiling face. The accident brought out the best in my Omani and expatriate friends. I thank God for this outpouring of love and compassion.

I returned the next week to Ibra and had the cast put on. Then I continued on to Seh El Malah to stay with Don and Eloise Bosch. Swelling developed in my right leg, and phlebitis, due to the injury, was diagnosed.

At the Bosch's I received rest and much tender, loving care. There were many visitors there, too. The Bosches had a beautiful home. I enjoyed their garden, their collection of shells, and their budgie birds. I had plenty of time to read and write. I wrote up the account of my accident to send home to family and supporting churches.

I pondered the accident. I could easily have been injured seriously by broken glass flying around. But miraculously, not a window had broken in the vehicle. I had a thermos of cold water in the car. The glass container had come out of the metal enclosure, which was bent, but not even the glass container had broken. There was no broken glass anywhere.

The roof of the car had collapsed and the motor was extensively damaged. The car needed much repair. Would the insurance cover it? Fortunately, I had delivered some of the babies of the family who owned the Toyota garage and also carried the insurance for the vehicle. They repaired the vehicle and returned it to me some time later as good as new. Praise the Lord!

Lillian Huiskens, the RCA nurse in Assaada, our old mission obstetrical hospital in Muscat, later told me how she had been praying for traveling mercies for me the day I had the accident.

XI
Prayer and Fasting

I want men everywhere to lift up holy hands in prayer, without anger or disputing.

1 Tim. 2:8

The Lord detests the sacrifice of the wicked, but the prayer of the upright pleases him.

Prov. 15:8

Do not be anxious about anything, but in everything, by prayer and petition, with thanksgiving, present your requests to God.

Phil. 4:6

. . .Jesus went out into the hills to pray, and spent the night praying to God.

Luke 6:25

But when you fast, put oil on your head and wash your face, so that it will not be obvious to men that you are fasting, but only to your Father, who is unseen; and your Father, who sees what is done in secret, will reward you.

Matt. 6:17,18

Prayer is everything to me. Even before I was born, my life was shaped by my mother's prayer. The picture of my mother kneeling at her bed in Rhode Island remains imprinted on my mind. Prayer was the starting point of my career in missions ("Lord, I'll go where you want me to go"), and it was the main link between me and my loved ones in America for forty-two years. So many times we missionaries felt as if prayer was a lifeline in stormy seas. Some of the heartwarming moments on the mission field came when new Christians prayed aloud in Bible study groups for the first time. The short, simple prayers of these Arab friends were more than the sum of their parts; they were awesome testimonies to the life-changing power of the Lord.

In this chapter, I want to discuss prayer and fasting. Prayer is a vital part of other religions. There is something inside men and women that drives them forward, seeking God. Muslims, for example, literally drop what they are doing to pray five times every day. We missionaries were reminded of this first thing in the morning, when the *muezzin* atop the minaret of a nearby mosque would call the faithful to prayer. The first call to prayer came before sunrise. The second call was at noon; the third in mid-afternoon; the fourth at sunset and the final prayer was offered two hours after sunset before retiring. Every Friday and during the month of fasting called Ramadhan, special prayers and sermons are offered in mosques. One cannot help but respect the Muslim's devotion to this prayer ritual.

Mosque with fortress in background in Muscat

While in Sur I knew two Christian Indian gentlemen who took prayer so seriously that they risked their businesses to promote it. One was a shopkeeper who devoted his new, one-room home to prayer. I was invited one night to conduct the dedication of his new living facility, which he also used for worship. I drove the twenty miles to his home with some of our staff and found several Christian and Hindu men in attendance. We enjoyed the presence of the Lord in our midst. According to their culture, lavish refreshments were served.

Another Christian man dedicated the restaurant he built to the Lord. He asked me to be present at its dedication. I was delayed in the hospital that evening and was worried about arriving late. Jacob and Yohanna accompanied me. Each of us prayed by turn as we drove in the dark of night with only headlights lighting the road. In the distance I could see the flashing lights of a police car. As we neared we knew it was an accident. A passing car had hit a camel. Driver and camel were both killed.

Jacob, Yohanna, and I realized that had we not been delayed at the hospital, it could have been us that had hit the camel.

We did arrive late at the dedication, and our friends were worried about us. When we told them what had happened, they thanked God with us.

At the dedication the proprietor of the restaurant sincerely wanted the spirit of Christ to be present. A dedicatory service was conducted and the restaurant was given to Christ. The owner had soft Christian music in Hindi playing in the background in the restaurant. Prayers could be offered before meals. During off hours, when the restaurant was closed, it became a house of God, a place of worship for Christians.

These two men were expatriates who left family, friends, and homes to provide education for their children and, in time, homes for wives and children. They also could not forget, like Daniel and his friends, the God they loved and to whom they prayed.

In Amarah, I spent some delightful hours in prayer on the roof of my house in the warm sunshine with Arab friends. In Muscat our Christian call to prayer came every morning at 6:30, when the prayer bell was rung. The bell could be heard for miles around. In Sur we prayed every morning and Tuesday, Thursday, and Sunday evening in my villa. Our doors were closed, but our prayer time was not a secret. During times when the opposition was strong, we were occasionally interrupted by people who wanted to know if any Muslims were present. Sometimes there were annoying phone calls.

The Indian nurses and I learned much about prayer. Times of sharing were especially important. Emotionally and spiritually we strove to reach a point at which we were joined together in spirit. We were not isolated Christians who happened to be in the same room, we were "one in the spirit," and we were "of one mind." The happiness of one person became joy for everyone and the pain of one became pain for all of us. We talked about our deepest concerns and shared lessons we learned as we walked with the Lord.

Jeanette leading mid-week prayer meeting in Mutrah

We prayed for the presence of the Holy Spirit at the beginning of each prayer session. We often felt the presence of the Spirit in unmistakable ways, feelings of comfort and closeness to God.

We kept a prayer list, on which we recorded specific prayer requests. Then, as time passed, we also recorded God's answers to those requests.

There were some wonderful times of prayer as I drove down the lonely highway from Sur to Muscat. The ever-changing play of light and shadows over the mountains, the appearance of wild animals, the birds, the display of stars at night, all of this natural beauty drew me close to the Lord. It truly *is* easier to talk with God in the midst of his glorious creation.

Why does God seem to be closer in a natural setting? Adam walked with God in the evening in the Garden of Eden. David wrote about the firmament showing forth God's handiwork. Job was reminded to look in awe at the way God had established creation. When we get involved with nature, caring for a garden, crops, or for animals, we need a measure of compassion. The trees in my garden needed constant help because they tended to grow together and choke each other. To keep them healthy I had to tie them apart. Progress in a garden is always a quiet, patient thing. Deadly attacks come from the weather, insects, and disease. Injuries are healed. Harvests come after months of careful cultivation. Fruits are offered freely to the gardener, to insects, and to the birds of the air.

Chickens, I found, could be affectionate creatures when they trusted their keeper. I began caring for one of my roosters when it was just a chick—a gift from the Bedouins. In the late afternoon he would begin waiting for me to come home, watching the gate and listening for my footsteps. Then, when I came into the courtyard, he went wild with joy. When this happened the first time, I thought he was badgering me for food, but as time passed I realized it was just his way of greeting me. The rooster also would be full of anxiety when one of the hens accidentally got loose from the coop. It would take some time to calm him down. Then the two animals would peck at each other in a gentle, friendly way and clean each other's feathers.

But to return to my train of thought, I should say that I found it easy to commune with God in this setting. The loving care of the heavenly Father was constantly evident, and if he cared so much for the plants, animals, and birds, how much more did he care for men and women, boys and girls! I felt that God was indeed close to me in the beauty of creation.

This feeling of the closeness of God often accompanied me during my daily duties. Sometimes, in the moments before an operation, or at the bedside of a very ill patient, I would inadvertently move my lips as I prayed silently. (More than once I worried that people who opposed me would think I was having mental problems!)

During these years in Sur, I also kept up a network of relationships with other praying Christians. The good folks in the Mt. Greenwood church and in my other supporting churches prayed regularly for me, and I wrote periodic "Dear Friends" letters to them. My old friends, the "Musketeers," still prayed regularly for each other. During the times of change on the mission field there were fervent prayers between missionaries and mission-minded members of the denomination. Arab, Indian, American, and European Christians throughout the Middle East prayed for each other. My old friend Vivienne Stacey stayed in contact with me through letters.

I mention all these items of personal history as a preface to this statement: Through God's grace during these years I learned much about prayer. These insights came through practical, day-to-day experience. I offer them in the hope that the Lord will use these ideas to edify his people.

One of the most important things I learned about prayer was this: Christians can develop a healthy prayer life through *obedience* and *discipline*. The basic inclination to do this, of course, comes from the Lord, but God allows his children the freedom either to work toward a closer relationship, or to drift apart. God keeps our salvation secure but allows the *depth* of our spiritual life to expand or contract, to a great extent, on efforts that we initiate.

A strong prayer life grows out of simple *obedience* to God's commands. Throughout the Bible, God tells us to pray constantly. As committed followers of Christ, we should remember to obey these directives:

> Then Jesus told his disciples a parable to show them that they should always pray and not give up. (The parable of the persistent widow follows this verse.)
>
> Luke 18:1
>
> Be joyful always; pray continually. . .
>
> 1 Thess. 5:17
>
> I want men everywhere to lift up holy hands in prayer, without anger or disputing.
>
> 1 Tim. 2:8
>
> Is any one of you in trouble? He should pray. Is anyone happy? He should sing songs of praise. Is any one of you sick? He should call the elders of the church to pray over him and anoint him with oil in the name of the Lord. And the prayer offered in faith will make the sick person well; the Lord will raise him up. If he has sinned he will be forgiven. Therefore, confess your sins to each other and pray for each other so that you may be healed. The prayer of a righteous man is powerful and effective. Elijah was a

man just like us. He prayed earnestly that it would not rain, and it did not rain on the land for three and a half years. Again he prayed, and the heavens gave rain, and the earth produced its crops.

James 5:13-18

A strong prayer life grows out of self-discipline. I can testify to the fact that the business of day-to-day life can prevent spiritual growth, even for a missionary. We need to be very forceful about setting aside time to be with the Lord. If that time is nonexistent, we cannot draw closer to God.

In today's fast-paced life it is very difficult for Christians to set aside time for prayer and meditation. People in positions of responsibility, parents with young children, and church members with important things to do, all of these people are under pressure to use every waking moment to attend to their work.

But the lesson we learned (sometimes painfully) is that we must go off "into the wilderness" at times to be alone with God.

Our prayer group in Sur learned several lessons about this. We learned that the ticking clock can hinder a deep walk with the Lord. When we met for evening prayer, we were not ruled by the passing of time. Granted, we had more freedom than most people to ignore the clock, but the truth remains. We were always ready to invest extra time in prayer.

Prayer is more than a stream of thoughts directed toward heaven. It combines with meditation and "waiting on the Lord" to become an open, gentle, two-way ebb and flow. During our weekday evening meetings we would pray and wait for the Lord's quiet voice. I found that this gentle conversation continued into my everyday activities. Sometimes, for instance, a thought would come to me as I cared for an injured dog or goat, or as I picked cotton from one of my cotton bushes.

In one of my old notebooks I wrote down my frustration and insecurity in the form of a written prayer. As I wrote, the minutes passed. Then the Lord began speaking to me. Now, years later, I remember his gentle voice in the words I continued to write. This is what the page of my notebook looked like:

> God shows his love and encouragement to me and tells me he is with me. He has not left me. He does love me through the first ripe dates of the season given me by Sadeeq the plumber, the two hot *chappatis* given me by

Mariamma and Zuwainah the other night for my supper and the papaya brought me this evening by Khamis; also by the simple blessing of the insect spray that killed the cloud of mosquitoes in my garden. Even my little chickens, dogs, and cats reflect your love—they know my voice and come to me joyfully.

Then the Lord spoke to me as I wrote about the special blessings he gave me over the years:

God gave me the gift of respect amidst the great and small—from the Sultan to the beggar on the street. "You have mercy, you listen to us," my patients often say. "You are a true Muslim." [Literally translated, that means, "You are one who is surrendered to God."] The Bedouins claimed me as one of their own. Women from one end of the country to the other knew of my relationship with Jesus. Every now and then a stranger would come up to me and introduce himself or herself by saying that I had helped at his birth.

During these quiet moments, while I gave my attention to God, the Lord directed my thoughts. At one point in my stream-of-consciousness writing, the words of a song appear in my notebook:

What have I to dread, what have I to fear,
Leaning on the everlasting arms?
What a blessedness, what a peace is mine,
Leaning on the everlasting arms!

Yes, the Lord came to me in those times, through the Holy Spirit, bringing peace and assurance.

That brings me to another point: During my years in Sur I found the Holy Spirit to be a Comforter in every sense of the word, bringing encouragement and close communication with the Lord. We usually began personal or group prayer sessions by asking the Holy Spirit to come down and be in us and among us.

When times were hard, and as my prayer life grew stronger, it was easier to offer adoration and thanksgiving to the Lord. We knew how bad things would be without him. We were grateful for everything we had, every moment of the day, even for the simple privilege of being allowed to stay in the country.

The discipline of setting aside time for the Lord, following a pattern of prayer and meditation, listening for the Lord's voice, and sensing his power and beauty will naturally lead to other signs of a healthy prayer life. You begin to pray for particular needs with more confidence. As you grow more sensitive to God's voice and the many ways he works in human lives, you begin to see more *answers* to prayer. There are times when you thrill to see vivid, sometimes unexpected developments that are direct answers to your prayer requests.

In group situations, the idea of "coming together" in prayer is very important. In Matthew 18:19,20 we read: "Again, I tell you that if two of you on earth agree about anything you ask for, it will be done for you by my Father in heaven. For where two or three come together in my name, there am I with them." With my friends, I learned the value of coming together with hearts touching. We requested the Holy Spirit's presence, then joined our thoughts before God, striving to agree in items of praise, confession, and petition.

The subject of "power in prayer" leads me to the second half of this chapter: Fasting.

I believe that the Lord honors fasting as a worthwhile spiritual exercise and allows fasting to strengthen the effect of prayer.

The subject of fasting comes up again and again in the Bible. Twice Moses fasted without taking food or drink for forty days and forty nights (Deut. 9:9,18). Elijah fasted forty days and forty nights (1 Kings 19:3-9). Jesus also went without food or drink for forty days and forty nights (Matt. 4:2). Humanly speaking, we would say that there must have been a mistake, yet the scriptures are very definite about these events.

Children living in Eastern countries learn early from their parents that fasting is part of life. This is true for Christians, Muslims, and Hindus in Third World countries.

My Muslim friends fasted for an entire month, Ramadhan, once per year on a lunar cycle. Since Ramadhan moved forward a few days on each year of the Western calendar, it appeared during different seasons as the years passed.

The fasting of Muslims during Ramadhan called for rigid self-denial. I was always amazed at their dedication, especially when Ramadhan fell during the heat of the summer. Temperatures would often climb to 110 degrees, and a summer's day would be twelve or more hours in length. Some devout Muslims do not swallow their saliva during a fast day. All food and water were taken after nightfall, during the hours of darkness.

"How can you go without food or drink during the heat of summer?" I would ask my Muslim friends.

"The first few days are difficult," they would reply. "But then it becomes easier. Allah is our help and strength."

Children at age nine would begin a moderate kind of fasting during Ramadhan, and by the time they were twelve years old they were doing it along with grownups. Even pregnant women and old people joined in. Only the sick were exempt, and they were encouraged to make up for lost fast days at another time.

Nights were times of feasting and sharing. Food was prepared all day and distributed freely after dark. Neighbors strolled from one home to another in lamplight, sharing food, gifts, and alms for the poor. We missionaries were graciously invited to be part of the festivities. The Bedouins in Wadi 'Ar 'Ar invited me to share their celebrations every Ramadhan, and I often returned to Sur with roasted goat thighs, a great delicacy.

My Hindu friends also fasted. For them it was a means of self-discipline and self-denial: "We don't need all that food." They also fasted for health reasons, believing fasting cleansed the inside of the body. Hindus generally were very conscious of cleanliness. They bathed frequently. If you were present in a Hindu household early in the morning, you would hear loud noises of the mouth and throat as they were thoroughly cleansed.

Hindus have four *ashrams*, or main beliefs: childhood is a time of freedom without undue restrictions, the discipline of study is valuable, the householder is responsible for his family, and a devout Hindu will consciously renounce worldly trappings. This last belief, especially, involves doing without. Devout Hindus generally fasted once or twice a week.

My good friend Nijaya, a Hindu woman from Bangalore, expressed the following ideas about fasting: "Fasting emphasizes a simple way of living that enables a person to think properly and attain happiness. Eating lavishly may make a person spend more and seek unnecessary pleasures. In order to keep physically fit, a person must watch his or her diet and make sure it does not contain excessive amounts of some foods or a lack of others."

"Fasting is healthy for the following reasons," my friend Nijaya continued. "It enhances prayer for a particular need. It leads to self purification. It clears your mind of thoughts of self and allows you to pay attention to the needs of others."

Each Hindu decides what form of fasting is best in his or her situation. Some may follow the weekly fast with great diligence; others may skip a meal once in a while. Nijaya also noted that after a fast there was the satisfaction of having accomplished something on both spiritual and physical levels.

I am indebted to my Christian friends from India for teaching me much about Christian fasting. Like many Indians, they had observed their own parents fasting and they had begun fasting themselves at an early age. To them, fasting was an accepted part of the Christian life, as necessary as scripture reading, witnessing, and prayer.

Keralite Christians fasted for several reasons: when praying for healing for a loved one, during times of stress, when parents were selecting a spouse for one of their children, prior to a marriage, when seeking guidance or deliverance, and in repentance for sin. During these times they would go without food and drink for an entire day, and upon breaking the fast in the evening they would eat a simple meal without meat or sweets.

I knew other Keralite Christians who made a practice of fasting once or twice weekly on a regular basis, regardless of particular life events. Members of the Marthomite Church of India fast every Friday to commemorate Christ's death; fifteen days in August (abstaining from certain foods); eight days in September; forty days during Lent; and twenty-five days during the Advent season. Many of them fasted Sunday mornings as well.

Indian, Russian, Greek, Armenian, and Orthodox churches around the world also fast in various ways. Fasting for them is a very serious matter and each denomination has its own set of rules.

In summary, fasting has different meanings for different people. A strict fast means no food or drink. A less strict fast might allow water or juice while avoiding food. Moderate fasts might deny certain kinds of food or "vices" such as candy, alcohol, or tobacco. Time periods vary.

Like most people from the Reformed church, I knew of the Bible's references to fasting. I also realized that it was an important part of life in the Old Testament and I knew Jesus referred to it in the New Testament. But it was not part of my denomination's tradition, so my knowledge was at first limited to scattered biblical references. As time passed, I came to the conclusion that there might be something valuable in it, at least in the Christian form of fasting. I studied it with fellow missionaries and with my Omani and Indian friends. There was no denying the sincerity of my Indian friends and the closeness of their walk with the Lord. They seemed to receive spiritual strength from fasting.

I knew the verses in the Sermon on the Mount: "Blessed are those who hunger and thirst after righteousness. . . " I began to realize that Jesus chose those words about hunger and thirst because they were such primary needs, and he wanted his followers to subjugate those needs and direct that same kind of urgent attention toward him. In the same sermon, Jesus said, "When you fast, do not look somber as the hypocrites do. . . . But when you fast, put oil on your head and wash your face. . .and your Father, who sees what is done in secret, will reward you" (Matt. 6:16-18). So often we concentrate on the negative aspects of being a somber hypocrite that we miss the positive things Jesus said about fasting. He acknowledged the practice and even gave us some directions on how to do it in a God-glorifying way.

As I encountered the different kinds of fasts and the different religious reasons for doing it, I asked many questions and kept an open mind.

I first tried fasting in Muscat in 1973, at the encouragement of my friend and colleague Nancy Rouwhorst. For several years I thought about the practice and engaged in brief (mornings only) fasts in a limited way. It was in Sur that I really became serious about it.

By sharing with you some further thoughts from my diary, you can see the effects of my first day-long fasts:

> 10/23/77 I have thought about fasting for some time and have tried it at different times, not even reaching midday. But now I have completed my first partial fast yesterday by taking only liquids—something to drink about six times. I had a poor night's sleep the night before and should have been tired during the day, but on the contrary, I felt vigorous and accomplished much—more than usual. I think I will try some form of fast once a week.

> 10/29/77 I fasted my second time today by drinking only liquids four times. Felt tired in the morning, but felt good in the afternoon and enjoyed good fellowship with God this evening.

11/5/77 My third consecutive week's fast day today, taking only liquids—four glasses of juice—in a 24-hr. period. My workload was the same as other days, busy and full. I was hungry in the early hours of work, but after the second glass of juice, mid-way through the morning, there was a lessening of the hunger and my work went very well. My mind seems to be sharper on fast days.

I appreciated Dr. Malefyte's devotional today from "Words of Hope." In spite of the hostility others may feel toward the gospel, in him we shall find peace. Indeed, "The joy of the Lord is our strength." I felt great power of the Holy Spirit while I was praying in bed last night. The Lord is confirming that he is with me and will use me. His will be done.

11/12/77 "I turned to the Lord God, pleading in earnest prayer, with fasting, sackcloth and ashes. I prayed to the Lord, my God and confessed. . ." (Daniel 9:3,4).

11/16/77 Fasted again, drinking only water. Went to Qa'ab, Wadi Beni Jabir, by police helicopter and then walked over rocky terrain to visit some homes. Worked at a good pace for about three hours and did not find it difficult. This evening I broke my fast in a friend's home.

1/27/78 Not doing too well with my plan to fast once a week. In fact, I have been eating more than usual!

3/4/78 I'm fasting again on a weekly basis. I find that when I am rested and fast on liquids only that my mind seems more clear and alert.

(My diary entries at this time are filled with verses of scripture, notes for talks in my "house church" gatherings, and stream-of-consciousness prayers. I was not living in "flowery beds of ease" at the time, but my diary shows plainly that the Lord was very close and by God's grace the spiritual side of my life was gaining in strength.)

My fasting in Sur was over a twenty-four-hour period. I would start the evening before the fast day. Then I would have liquids, including a cup of coffee at breakfast, a cup of tea with the nurses mid-morning, and juice at noon. After duty and a rest, I would spend time with the Lord and break my fast in the evening. Prayer and scripture study are always important parts of my fast day.

The powers of evil knew of our fast days. There was opposition: many interruptions, disturbances, and problems arose. Mornings were always the most difficult.

I was always concerned that a time of fasting would take energy away from my daily work. But I found that as long as I got a good night's sleep, the fast was no hindrance, even when I traveled to distant villages or to Muscat. My schedule in Sur allowed me to take some quiet time with the Lord in the afternoons, and I spent much time in scripture study and intercessory prayer on fast days. God gave special strength during these days and encouraged fasting. I was not unique. I was one of many who did this in Sur. I found also that I accomplished more work on fast days and was inspired to write letters. My mind was active and quick.

Since retirement I have continued my fasting faithfully once a week over a twenty-four-hour period. This day is an important part of my life. It is my "special" day with the Lord in the Word, in prayer, and exorcisms. During this weekly twenty-four-hour period, I take about three or four glasses of liquids.

Satan tries to bully me on these days by sending attacks of drowsiness. At the name of Jesus Satan has to flee. Fasting is a spiritual discipline in the Holy Spirit, along with prayer and the study of God's Word. These disciplines give renewed strength and power, insight, enlightenment, and inspiration to the Christian.

In my experience, fasting is closely related to spiritual power. It helps produce a strengthening of my Christian life. It is a means to come into a closer relationship with Jesus my Lord. It is time spent with him alone. It is a time of spiritually feasting in Christ's presence. And it is a time when I am available to be used by God.

The Lord has honored the discipline of fasting in my life and I would recommend it to other Christians.

Your experience may be different from mine. People approach fasting in many ways, and they engage in it for varying time periods. If different Christians were to discuss its benefits, there would be a variety of stories.

XII
Golden Years

*...a land where bread will not be scarce and you
will lack nothing; a land where the rocks are
iron and you can dig copper out of the hills.*
Deut. 8:9

Through God's grace, I suffered no lasting effects from my 1980 car accident.

Following weeks of convalescing, the cast came off. For quite a while after that I kept the arm in an elastic bandage. One of the hospital workers suggested that I massage the arm with olive oil, adding that this treatment had been used in the Middle East since the time of Christ. I tried it and found that the oil did indeed help. Later I recommended olive oil to others.

The injury took the usual time to heal, but when all was finished it never bothered me again. Months later, when I was functioning at peak capacity and using the arm fully, I became a bit irritated when people continued to ask about my recovery. But the question opened the door for me to tell them of God's protection, care, and the complete healing he gave to me. I befriended the family of one of the men who stopped to help at the scene of accident. This friendship continued until I left Sur. It was interesting, too, that the other man at the scene of the accident told Ahmed, our administrator, "This woman is better and stronger than ten men." They seemed to appreciate the calm spirit, and the fact that I did not become overly upset. They knew, too, that none of their women would drive alone between Muscat and Sur. What they saw was the strength God gives us in time of need. "God is our refuge and strength, an ever-present help in trouble. Therefore we will not fear. . ." (Psalm 46:1,2).

Later that spring I resumed my trips to Muscat to get supplies from the Ministry of Health—always with a traveling companion. I also began visiting my Bedouin friends in Wadi 'Ar 'Ar again. Yusef, at age seven, was about as tall as his four-year-old friends.

Yusef became very excited when he saw the Toyota coming. When the older children heard my vehicle grinding through the sand and dirt in the distance, they would run from the encampment to greet me. Little Yusef always tottered along in the rear, far behind the others. But when he finally made it, he would push his way through the others, cling to me, and look up at me with a big grin. "My mother," he would say.

Bedouins at well.

He would join me in the car, while the others ran behind. Sometimes he was carried out to meet me by his sister.

I encouraged Yusef's father and stepmother to put Yusef in school the following autumn. His brother and friends were attending a new government school several miles from Wadi 'Ar

'Ar, and they agreed that Yusef could probably benefit from it. A neighbor transported the children to school on the back of his truck.

As it turned out, Yusef did not last long in the school. But even this failure spoke to Yusef's sensitive and loving nature. The schoolmaster, a very strict fellow from Egypt, was not averse to using corporal punishment on his students. Occasionally he could be heavy-handed. Apparently, little Yusef witnessed this teacher physically punishing a student, and the shock affected Yusef's ability to function in the school. After that he told his family that he could not go back to school. His teacher agreed that Yusef was not ready for school emotionally, and he suggested that we wait for another year before enrolling him again. I went to Saik, where Yusef was attending school, to talk to his teacher one morning. I saw too that Yusef needed to be at home a while longer.

The modernization that swept through Oman's population centers came slowly to Yusef's family and the other Bedouins. The value of their precious camels rose steadily. By selling a single desert camel to a person of wealth, Abdullah could obtain enough profit to purchase a pickup. His main income, as in days of old, came from his flocks. Since Bedouins were now driving and owning vehicles, they would take their flocks to Abu Dhabi in the United Arab Emirates, where they would get a better price.

Abdullah, Taeeba, and the children began wearing sandals instead of going barefoot. Some of their homes were improved, with canvas coverings replacing the thorn bush enclosures under the trees. Some of the Bedouins purchased flashlights; formerly their lights at night were the moon and stars. Slow to change was the centuries-old custom of sitting on the ground eating dates, drinking strong coffee, and discussing news of the day. I was glad this custom remained. I sat down with them and appreciated the joys of simple living in God's great out-of-doors under the shade of a tree.

Parts of the country that had been strictly off-limits before 1970 were open now to everyone. My friends Jay and Midge Kapenga had eyes on the interior of Oman when they returned after a three-year leave in 1975.

"We dreamed of an assignment in the interior since 1947, which is when I met Jay," Midge once said. "But we didn't really get to the mountains or the interior until nearly thirty years later."

The Kapengas began working on behalf of the government in the interior. The government of Oman, in those days, was concerned that cotton weaving was becoming a dying art in the interior villages. Potential weavers' apprentices left the villages for higher paying jobs in construction, road building, the military, or even in other countries. The minister of heritage was a friend of Jay's. He asked that they work with the Bedouins in a certain locale. (Not the Bedouins of Wadi 'Ar 'Ar.) The minister encouraged Jay and Midge to go to the villages to study weaving and introduce new, more efficient looms. People from the interior also came to the old mission compound to be instructed in new weaving techniques. Jay and Midge also had opportunities to discuss life and faith with the people in the villages.

The Kapengas often brought beautiful pieces of cotton or wool weaving back to Muscat for commercial sale, with the proceeds reverting to the weavers.

The Kapengas retired earlier than I did, after devoting about eight years to the people of the interior. When they announced their retirement plans, word reached the Sultan, who invited them to his chambers. Jay and Don Bosch were then presented with the "Order of Oman" by the Sultan. Eloise and Midge were also given gifts. I felt that this award spoke well of the Sultan. He was generous and open-minded in giving this recognition to missionaries. The two couples were thrilled to have been thus remembered. As Jay wrote, "The Sultan knows what we do and he knows we are Christians. He knows we are missionaries...but he still gave an award. You have to respect him for that."

I was very happy to hear of the special recognition. It was a fitting climax to Jay and Midge's long years of service in the country. They were so faithful in their school duties as the school's student population went up and down in the early 1970s. Also, like our other padres, Jay had to work long, hard hours and see little tangible fruit from his labors.

Midge and I were so different, but in God's providence we were ideally suited to be friends and next door neighbors for all those years in Muscat. The Kapengas presently live in retirement in Penney Farms, Florida. Not only do I remain in contact with them, but I also hear from their children: Peter, Margaret, and Barbara, who live in diverse places around the world.

I continued to make occasional visits to the interior to treat the sick. We flew in government helicopters that took off from the police helipad in Sur. Government people would inform us by telephone of a tour to an inaccessible place in the mountains. We met the helicopters with our boxes of medicines an hour or so later and in a cloud of dust we would lift off from the platform, speed up into the mountains, and ease down on rocky terrain near isolated villages. Sometimes the pilots tossed out smoke bombs so they could see the direction of the wind before they landed. Villagers cleared landing areas for us.

The mountain people continued to welcome us graciously. They always served us coffee, dates, tea, and pomegranates. Cases of pneumonia, trachoma, malaria, and complications of pregnancy were among those that were taken back to the hospital.

The Ministry of Health, meanwhile, continued to move the nation into the twentieth century. The government built more hospitals, hired skilled medical personnel from abroad, hosted training sessions with medical experts in various fields, and encouraged native Omanis to train for professional jobs in the medical field. Again, I have to say that I was impressed by the wisdom of the nation's leaders, as they managed progress in a rapid but careful way. It was good to be part of it. The RCA should be proud of its role in providing medical missionaries to help the country at this critical time in its development.

Our new hospital in Sur doubled in size to 120 beds, and my duties as matron increased correspondingly. In 1981 we hosted a dedication celebration for the hospital's new addition. Staff members were up early and worked until late to clean the new wing, set up the medicine and dressing cabinets, make beds, decorate, and dress in their finest. We wanted everything to be perfect. On the morning of the dedication, Ministry of Health officials from Muscat helicoptered in to inspect the facilities and meet us. Some of the local townspeople played their goatskin drums and danced. A TV crew from Muscat showed up. The governor of Sur and his retinue were also present. There were several speeches. That evening we saw the events replayed on television.

Christian singing groups began traveling from Muscat to Sur to share evenings of worship and praise, with guitar accompaniment. There were also visits from lay Christians from Nigeria, India, and Pakistan. They left Muscat in early morning to reach us before noontime. They led us in a worship service, brought messages, and presented music. We usually prepared dinner for them.

Grace Shaw joined our group of Christian nurses in Sur. We got to know Grace well and appreciated her work and her love for her family. As the months passed, Grace was afflicted with an eye problem that slowly took away her sight. Little by little the problem increased, until finally she could work no longer. How we prayed for her!

I took her to Muscat to see specialists there, and later she went back to her home in India to seek more help. The news was bad: doctors said the optic nerves had died and she would never see again.

We were much in prayer for Grace. Her friends in India also prayed for her. We boldly prayed that God would restore her eyesight, for we felt that Grace could still do much in his kingdom. Months passed. Then it was almost a year since she had left Oman. One day a letter came from Grace saying that the Lord had restored the sight in both of her eyes. "It was only God's miraculous power that did it," she affirmed. "Even my Hindu doctor said that it was a miracle and an act of God."

Grace did not return to Oman, but took a nursing position in India. She and her family continue to give thanks for the miracle God wrought in her life.

About that time triplets were born to a family that had already lost five children. One of the babies had a problem retaining her feedings. The baby began to decline. Mrs. Mathews suggested we try soy-bean formula. It was noontime when I rushed to the bazaar, only to find the one pharmacy in town that would stock up on such supplementary feedings closed.

The pharmacy would not open again until four o'clock. I was upset because I knew Khoula was loosing ground. The Lord heard my cry, and a gentleman asked me my problem. He immediately said, "I know where the pharmacist lives. I'll go call him." The pharmacist soon returned to give me the precious formula. The baby was able to retain the formula for the first time of her young life. I know the Lord sent that passerby to me that day.

We also recognized miracles in the little things. Fatoom, a Christian nurse, worked with us several years. She had a likable personality and usually attended prayer meetings on both Tuesday and Thursday nights. Then I noticed that the quality of her work began to fall off. She did not seem to be happy. Something was troubling her.

In my concern for her, I telephoned her on my day off and invited her over for a visit. Since we were used to reading the Bible and praying in the group, I read a meditation in "Words of Hope" and told her that I would like to pray with her and for her.

We began to talk. Personal problems were weighing her down, she said. She was drawing into herself and feeling depressed.

I began to pray for Fatoom. But I also prayed for others who were experiencing problems. One of our nurses, Punnamma, was married to a young electrician. The two had a handicapped child. "Her husband was recently transferred to Muscat," I mentioned to Fatoom. "Punnamma is worried about living alone in Sur with their child. They're in a very difficult situation."

So Fatoom, despite all of her own problems, began to pray with me for the young family with the handicapped child.

While we were still in prayer, my doorbell rang. There stood the young electrician himself! We invited him in and asked him how he came to be back in Muscat.

"It's my day off," he explained. "I came into Sur late last night to be with my family for a short time. We still haven't worked out a solution to the problem, but there are sympathetic people in Muscat who are listening to me. I think something may work out in our favor. I just wanted to let you know that there is hope."

After the young man left, Fatoom and I realized that the Lord had brought him to my door almost as if to say, "Trust me. I hear your prayers. I am in control. In my good time, I will send an answer."

By the time Fatoom left my villa that night, her burdens were much lighter. She said she was glad she had been able to share her problems, pray about them, and for a few moments focus her attention outward, on the other family. "I feel real joy and peace now," she said.

An Indian Christian laborer, Mr. Mathew, was another good friend that we continually lifted up in prayer. Mr. Mathew was hired to drive for a wealthy merchant sixty miles from Sur. He felt called to be a lay evangelist, and when he visited our weekday meetings he often shared with us the ways that the Lord was helping in his ministry.

One evening I drew him aside and asked him how his work was going. "I had an interesting incident this week," he replied.

"I was driving my employer on the open highway in the interior," Mr. Mathew said, "when suddenly the man had a severe pain in his side. He was afraid and said we must go to a Muslim priest (Mullah) for healing.

"I am a priest," Mr. Mathew said.

The merchant thought for a moment. He was aware that Mr. Mathew was deeply committed to God's service, and he had seen him pray to his God during Muslim prayer sessions.

"What kind of priest are you?" the merchant asked.

"I believe in the prophet 'Esa (Jesus), and I would pray for you in his name."

"Do it," the merchant said.

Then, following a routine that was practiced by Muslims and was known to the merchant, Mathew took a glass of water, prayed to Jesus as he held it, and gave it to the man to drink.

"The pain left him immediately," Mr. Mathew said.

During a period of time we prayed often for the nine-year-old daughter of Lakshmi, one of our nurses. Lakshmi, a Hindu, was alone in Oman while her husband and relatives raised her children in India. Lakshmi told us that her daughter suffered from emotional problems and a learning disability. Again and again we prayed for the girl. Then Lakshmi left us for a stay with her family in her homeland.

Imagine our excitement when Lakshmi returned several weeks later and testified that her daughter had been healed. Lakshmi was so excited about the answer to our prayers that she immediately gave us the names of others to pray for. Lakshmi, through her attendance of our Sunday worship services and prayer groups, became a Christian and left Hinduism.

Sometimes God answered prayer in a mighty way, but other times he used regular medical treatment as the means of accomplishing his will. This happened once when a fellow named Umraan brought us his child, Ali, who was writhing in convulsions. Traditionally, Omanis regarded convulsions as irrefutable proof of demon possession. Laboratory tests soon proved that the convulsions came from bacterial meningitis (not viral). The case was severe, but not demon-inspired.

Umraan listened to us describe the sickness, but then said he wanted to take the boy to a religious healer who would cure the child by reading verses of Koran over him. I carefully and patiently explained that the diagnosis was sure, there were standard medical treatments that would probably bring about a cure. Yes, God would bring about the cure, but he probably wanted to work through modern medical techniques.

Umraan was adamant. The traditional healer had to conduct a reading. Finally I relented enough to allow Umraan to bring the healer to the hospital, where he could do his work.

Umraan left, only to return later with the announcement that the healer could not come to the hospital. Ali had to be taken out of the hospital and transported to the healer's home.

The child's situation was becoming grave. I called three public health officials—men that Umraan knew and respected—to meet with us and emphasize the need for medical treatment. The five of us spent an hour in intense discussion.

Reluctantly, Umraan agreed to keep Ali in the hospital and let us begin treatment.

Then we began three stormy days of intravenous fluids, ryles tube feedings, antibiotics, and sedation. Not once did Umraan leave the side of his child. His face was drawn and tense. We spread the word through the Christian staff to pray earnestly for little Ali.

On the morning of the fourth day Umraan met me in the hall at seven o'clock, just as I came out of the morning prayer meeting. He was smiling broadly. Ali was responding! During the early morning hours the boy spoke to the father, he shook hands with the nurses, and he was conscious of his surroundings.

I checked him immediately. Ali's fever was down and he was eating breakfast. Yes, medical procedures were instrumental in effecting this recovery, I told Umraan. They were the instruments used by God, who is still the Great Physician. The Christian staff and I, who had been praying for Ali those three days, gave God thanks and praise.

When we spoke of our faith to men such as Umraan, we always needed to be careful. I was being watched.

Sometimes I would be stopped in the hallway. I knew people were looking at a "suspicious" book I was carrying. I know that my villa was being watched to see if any Omani Muslims were worshiping with the Christians. Informants might come in during a worship service on the pretense of using the phone. We passed along "Words of Hope" messages, cassettes, and Christian literature only to Christians.

Sultan Qaboos was not behind the problems. He was a good and just man, and every time our missionaries had contact with him they came away with a highly favorable opinion of him. There were many diverse forces in Oman, and in the government itself. We do not fault the Sultan for the existence of things that we missionaries considered to be inconvenient or troublesome. The "bottom line" for us, year after year, was the fact that we were allowed to stay in the country even though we were known to be missionaries.

The feelings of the Sultan became apparent when he donated land near the capital for a Protestant and Catholic church. Beautiful Protestant and Catholic edifices were built with a large parking lot. The Christians coming into his country were given the freedom to conduct worship services there. The Rev. Rodney Koopmans and the Rev. Richard Westra were two of the church's first pastors. Their wives, Janie and Maja, as well as their children, were a blessing to the mission and the community. I am ever grateful to Jay and Rodney for their help in getting my badly damaged car to Muscat for repairs after my 1980 accident. This involved the police and took considerable effort and time. The Rev. Roger and Lee Bruggink, John and Lynne Hubers, and Alfred and Yvonne Samuel are serving Christ and his church in Oman today.

So even though there were problem areas, as far as mission work went, we could also see areas of growth. We all marveled at the way groups of expatriate Christians were springing up in the country. Years before, we had prayed unceasingly for a Christian influence in the interior. Now, without much stress or strain, Christian workers, most of them Indians, were quietly establishing worship services, prayer groups, and Bible study groups wherever outside laborers were needed.

In October, 1982, Abdullah brought Yusef back to me. "He has been asking for you," Abdullah said as we walked from the hospital to a shade tree near my villa, where he had left the boy. "He doesn't complain, but I think he is very sick."

I took them into my house for a cool drink and rapidly examined Yusef. The glands in his neck were swollen, he had a fever, and he complained of a headache. I brought him to Dr. Mathews, who admitted him to the hospital. He ordered several tests on him.

Early tests indicated that Yusef might be suffering from a flare-up of his tuberculosis. Yusef himself was quiet and stoical. It was not like him to complain much. He just watched us with his big brown eyes.

Three days later Yusef went into convulsions, and we could see that something more deadly was at work in his body. We ran more tests. A spinal (lumbar) puncture gave us the truth. It was viral encephalitis. This was the worst possible news. Antibiotics are effective in bacterial diseases, but not viral. This kind of illness offered only a small chance of recovery.

Yusef had the complication of internal bleeding along with the disease, which lowered his hemoglobin. He needed blood transfusions along with intravenous feedings, oxygen, medications, and the Ryles tube in the nose. Actually, these treatments could do little but alleviate the symptoms. There was almost nothing we could do to attack the virus. Everybody prayed for Yusef.

For a time it actually seemed that Yusef improved. We wondered if the Lord might have further plans for the little boy. I spent many hours sitting beside Yusef's bed, praying for him. Abdullah, his father, stayed in the room with him continuously. Other Bedouins came too, making the one-and-a-half-hour trip from their home to the hospital to see him. Lines of anguish on Abdullah's face grew deeper each day.

Then the boy's kidneys began to fail. His breathing was rapid. There was more internal bleeding. Other complications set in. I knew that unless the Lord sent a miracle, it was just a matter of time.

Yusef's father was filled with fear. "I must take him home to one of our healers," he said. Other men from the family clustered around me and agreed with Abdullah. "Nothing here will help him anymore," they told me. "The only chance is to take him to a person we know who has healing abilities. He might help. We must do this."

I disagreed. To me, it was a struggle between modern medicine and Christianity on the one side, and superstition and the powers of evil on the other side. Even though there was almost no hope for Yusef, I didn't want to give him up to the wizard and his powers.

But I was exhausted from the late nights at Yusef's bedside. The men were determined to take the boy. I felt overpowered. Finally Yusef was released "against medical orders."

Abdullah and the others immediately took Yusef to the healer, who, for an exorbitant fee, pulled out a crystal ball, read some magic in it, and prescribed a strenuous hot treatment for the boy. He also told them to sacrifice a male camel.

The family then took Yusef back to their encampment, wrapped him in several blankets, and placed him next to a blazing wood fire. Sacrificing a camel would have created serious financial problems for the family, and they decided not to follow that part of the advice.

Meanwhile, I could not concentrate on my work. I was so tired and upset that I wasn't even able to pray diligently for Yusef. The only thing I felt I could do was drive out to the *wadi*. One part of me knew that the end was near for Yusef, but another part of me refused to accept the seriousness of his condition. I hoped the Lord would still give him healing.

The next afternoon after duty hours, I loaded some medicine, pillows, and blankets in the back of the Land Rover and headed out to the desert with two staff members.

When I approached everything was quiet, but when they saw me, they began to weep and wail. I knew then that Yusef was gone. Everyone was worn out from the ordeal.

"Yusef died last night," they told me.

Full of grief, I got out of the vehicle. "We're sorry we didn't send a messenger to tell you," they said.

I understood. I hadn't really expected them to. Following the custom of the desert, Yusef had been buried immediately after his death.

I walked over to Abdullah, who lay wrapped in blankets on the ground. The long, sleepless nights had taken a toll on him. I offered my sympathy and asked if I could help. He looked miserable. It was obvious that he did not have the kind of faith in Jesus Christ that gives hope and comfort in such a time. I wondered if our friendship would remain firm after the spiritual and cultural clashes of the last few days and nights.

"It is over for Yusef," Abdullah said, "but please, matron, don't leave us."

By God's grace I had become part of the family in the *wadi*. I could never have left them.

Why did the Lord take Yusef from the earth?

On a spiritual level, perhaps the Lord took Yusef to spare the family further hurts. Yusef had rickets and probably would never have grown. At eight years of age, he weighed a mere twenty-nine pounds.

Or maybe the Lord took him so Yusef wouldn't need to face a very difficult life. Yusef had a very sensitive nature. Emotionally, he couldn't even stand problems in school.

Had I failed Yusef during those last days? Could I have prayed more? Perhaps. During his illness the Christian staff had prayed for him and me. Did I give in too soon when I allowed the family to take him to the healer? There wasn't much I could have done. I pray that the Lord will forgive me for shortcomings that were my responsibility.

Yusef had been baptized and dedicated to God years before. I felt I could do that because Abdullah had put his life in my care. He was a lost child when he first came to me with matted hair and severe malnourishment. God brought him back to life. I just thanked the Lord for the pleasure of caring for him and knowing him those seven years. My hope and prayer is that some day I shall again meet him in heaven.

It was a long trip back to Sur that evening. The Rev. Alan Gates, an Episcopal minister, took the Sunday worship service the next day. I was grateful for release from that responsibility. I was very tired.

As months went by, I missed Yusef very much. I still miss him and think about him.

Two months later in 1982, Abdullah's wife Taeeba, Yusef's stepmother, gave birth to her third child. She had come ten days earlier with her son, Shafeeq. They stayed with me. I had the privilege of delivering her. It was a healthy little boy, and at first they said they would give the infant the same name, Yusef. Then, for superstitious reasons, they decided not to. They gave him the name of Amr. Amr grew to look surprisingly like Yusef. When I left Oman for retirement, Amr was healthy at four years of age and growing.

To the hurt of Taeeba and the family, Abdullah later took another wife. (The Muslim may legally have four wives plus concubines.) I, too, was most upset that he would do this, and Abdullah knew I disapproved. Before I left for America, his new wife had given him two sons. The two families were living separately at first for some time, because Taeeba would not have the second family near her; but in time Abdullah won. He built another structure next to Taeeba's for his convenience, and they all lived together. Abdullah later began farming a plot of ground. "The desert spaces belong to God, the government, and the Bedouins," as the saying goes. The Bedouins have free access to whatever they walk on and choose. Abdullah walled in a plot where he grew alfalfa for his camels, goats, and donkeys. He also planted a few vegetables for the table.

In the quiet of my home, during rest time, I thought about fellow missionaries my age who were retiring, one by one. Jay and Midge retired in 1983 and were back in the States. My good friend Anne De Young retired a year before the Kapengas at age 66. Lillian Huiskens retired in 1976. Don and Eloise Bosch were about to retire, although they were able to return to Oman every winter to the beautiful home the Sultan had built for them on the sea.

Edwin and Ruth Luidens, with whom Harriet Wanrooy Boyce and I traveled to Arabia, had left the Arabian field in 1964 for other work. Ed became involved in radio outreach in the Middle East out of Cyprus; later he became responsible, as executive secretary, for Far East mission under the National Council of Churches. (Ruth died in December 1977 and Ed passed away as I wrote this book, in May 1989.)

Like many missionaries before me, I thought about retirement in terms of the continuance of the Lord's work. The people in the hospital needed another matron who was bilingual and could take responsibility for a staff of sixty-five people. Then there were the Bedouins who had come to depend on me. Yusef's stepbrother and stepsister were growing up. Shafeeq has a good mind and was doing well in school, but unfortunately he did not finish high school. His parents could not convince him to continue his studies. He joined the Sultan's army. There would be thoughts of getting Jameela married. Of Yusef's two siblings, I was closest to Jameela. She was my pal and helper during my visits to the desert. Abdullah was looking for marriage partners for these two teens, and I hoped I might have some influence on his decision. Abdullah was looking for a family with a marriageable son *and* daughter, so an "even" exchange be made, and there would be no exorbitant dowry or bridal fee to pay.

In 1983, I was sixty-five years of age. It was also my furlough year. I had completed four years since my last furlough in 1979. Should I retire at the time of my furlough? I looked to the Lord to help me make the right decision. Physically, I was fine and still going strong, and my love was with the people in Oman. It was just that I was approaching that age when most people retire. So many of my friends had already retired. But I had been in Sur nearly nine years and away from the mission and my colleagues. My thoughts and my people were now in Sur. I wasn't yet ready to leave them.

Ahmed Khadhoury, our hospital administrator, didn't want me to retire. He said I walked faster than anyone in the hospital! Besides he added, "Your president, Mr. Ronald Reagan, is still going strong at seventy-two years of age. Why must you retire?"

One afternoon, while having my quiet time with the Lord, a thought came into my mind loud and clear. It wasn't a voice, but it

*Ahmed Khadhoury, Sur hospital administrative officer,
Dr. Matthews, medical officer in charge and his wife,
Dr. Mary Matthews, with Jeanette.*

was so clear that it could have been. "Why don't you go on your regular furlough in 1983 and then return for three more years of service before retiring?" I believed the Lord was behind the sudden thought and was directing me through it.

I was relieved to have more time to finish my work in Oman. I threw myself into daily duties and wrote letters to my family, friends, and the Mission Board informing them of my decision. God willing, I would be home at the end of May or early June.

The days flew by. Before long it was furlough time.

As usual, I began my furlough with a physical exam, courtesy of the Associated Mission Medical Office in New York. My reports were all good. The only advice the doctors gave me was, "Put on a little weight while you are back here in the States." I'd heard that before.

One of the first things I would have to do when I reached the Midwest would be to renew my driver's license and buy a used car.

Ben and Harriet had moved from Palos Park, where I'd stayed on my previous furlough. They were now living in a condominium in Orland Park (without my good friend Blackie). They graciously invited me again to spend this furlough with them. They now were the grandparents of Kelli. I spent some delightful days in Orland Park walking and talking with one-and-a-half-year-old Kelli, who was delighted with the wonders of birds and flowers. (As I grew older, birds and flowers held a renewed fascination for me, too!)

Back in South Holland, Illinois, I spent time with Cornelia Dalenberg, whose life story, *Sharifa*, had just been published with the help of a group of friends in South Holland. Cornelia, who was almost ninety years of age, was beginning to fail. She was always a living link to the very first generation of RCA missionaries. Her mind was clear, and we would reminisce about life on the mission field. She had known Samuel Zwemer personally, had worked side by side with Dr. Paul Harrison for many years, had been on some of the first excursions into Saudi Arabia's interior, and had been one of the first Western women to go into the famous marshes in Iraq. She had been a single nurse who had devoted herself to her calling.

My brothers Ted and Mel had lost their concrete block hauling business, with its ten trucks and drivers, through no fault of their own. When the mayor of Chicago made a change in the Chicago building codes at the end of 1981, concrete block was no longer needed by contractors, as it had been before. The demand for their product dropped and the business had to be disbanded. Ted then drove an Ozinga Brothers cement truck and Mel found work with McAllister Heavy Duty Equipment.

Throughout the years Harriet used her musical ability in church, and at this stage in her life she continued to use her talent to serve the Lord. As she and Ben traveled and spent time in other towns, they would come across churches without an organist. Harriet would play for them. They spent six months of each year in Texas, where Harriet played for the church they attended. Back in Illinois, Harriet played the organ once a month at Rest Haven Nursing Home. As I write this Ben and Harriet enjoy visiting the sick and shut-in.

Mel, like dad, was a "constant" elder in the church, and, like dad, vice-president of the consistory. They were *in* for their term of service, *out* a term, and then back *in* again. When Mel began to work at Mc Allisters, his hours of work changed from day work to the noon-to-nine shift, and he could no longer attend consistory meetings. For that reason he could no longer serve as an elder. However, he still is a strong influence in the church and active where he can serve.

During that last furlough I thanked God for my family. We truly had a goodly heritage. "But from everlasting to everlasting the Lord's love is with those who fear him, and his righteousness with their children's children" (Psalm 103:17). God brings out this promise and admonition time and again in his Word. As the five of us pondered God's blessings to our family, we knew that our parents and their ancestors for generations had followed the precepts of the Lord. We were blessed through their walk with the Lord. We praised and thanked God for his faithfulness. I felt (and still do) that the blessings of this heritage will follow the children of my siblings, if they too will obey and walk in the ways of their Lord.

That fall I began speaking in churches again. I always found this encouraging, because our people wanted to hear about the work in Arabia. I was overwhelmed by the size of the gifts coming from the churches in the midwest farming areas. They shared the bounties the Lord gave them.

When I spoke, I gave a personal plea for young women to enter medical mission work in Oman, as so many missionaries were scheduled for retirement.

Churches in New York, New Jersey, Michigan, Illinois, Wisconsin, Minnesota, Iowa, Arizona, and California invited me to speak and show slides. As usual, meeting with the folks in these churches inspired me. They were interested in our work and were most hospitable. The meals they prepared were so good!

One of the additional benefits of speaking in churches around the country is having extra time in various towns to visit old friends and former missionaries. I can't possibly write about all the old friends I saw during that furlough, but to name a few, in California I saw Dr. Mary Allison and Mary Kuik; in New York I saw Anne De Young; in Michigan I saw Margaret Dykstra; in Wisconsin I saw the Pennings; in Arizona I visited George and Christine Gosselink; in Fulton, Illinois, on the Mississippi River, I visited Cornelia De Witt VanderPloeg; and in Florida I visited Jay and Midge Kapenga and Lillian Huiskens.

Millie, my sister, lived in Holland, Michigan. On trips to western Michigan, I always found time to stop and see her. The Lord had blessed John and Millie with seven children and fourteen grandchildren. Both were still very active in the church. Millie became the artist in our family and was studying art in her latter years. John was handy in wood carving.

Times were changing in the RCA. As I traveled about, I couldn't help but compare the audiences I saw with the crowds of people who used to attend mission emphasis gatherings years before. I remembered the exciting mission fests in Render Aggen's grove. Now interest in missions and in giving was down. The General Program Council informed the churches that they were facing a deficit. Giving among many of the churches was down. I felt sad, because I knew a giving church was a growing church, as is a church interested in mission and missionaries. But I knew the folks at the General Program Council at 475 Riverside Drive in New York continued to work hard on our behalf. They never let us down.

During my furlough I kept hearing about more problems in the Middle East. To many Americans, the devastating Iraq-Iran war was something so far away that it was on another planet. But my heart bled for hundreds of thousands of young men and civilians who were being killed. Many good people, both Muslims and Christians, were among the dead. Many of the families I knew in Basrah and Amarah were losing their children in the so-called "holy war" between the countries. Lebanon was being devastated and our people held hostage. Harvey and Hilda Staal were holding on tight to do the work of the Lord in that country. Harvey could no longer go out for fear of being kidnapped. Hilda went out to do the shopping for them. A bullet had even crashed through a window of their home.

One commentator reported that the Iran-Iraq war, interestingly, was an event that kept the United States close to Oman. As trouble flared up in the Persian Gulf, U.S. presidents saw the strategic value of having a friendly nation in control of the Strait of Hormuz, Oman's point of land guarding the oil shipping lanes out of the Gulf.

Sultan Qaboos was hosted in Washington by U.S. President Ronald Reagan, and we often read that Secretary of State George Schultz was conferring with the Sultan in the Middle East.

When I saw headlines in which the Sultan was prominently featured, I was proud of him, and amazed at the long way Oman had come, with God's help, since the revolution of 1970. I caught myself referring to Sultan Qaboos as "our ruler"! I was more Omani than American by then, because so many more of my years had been spent in Oman. If the climate were not so hot, I would even have considered retirement in Oman. (When I was ready to retire three years later, Omanis invited me to stay and live with them. This would not have been hard to do, were it not for the weather.)

My furlough neared its end. Reports from my opthamologist and dentist were excellent: no need to obtain new lenses in my glasses or new fillings in my teeth. My dentist, Dr. Albert Tanis, had cared for my teeth for forty years without charging me a cent. I told him that many of my friends marveled that I still had my own teeth. (I thank God for this special blessing.)

Then I was on the plane again, on an eight-hour flight from Chicago to London and another eight-hour flight from London to Oman. The flight was uneventful, for which I was thankful. I arrived in Muscat January 6 and was again in familiar territory. I stayed with Nancy Rouwhorst in the old mission house, and soon left for Sur in the old, faithful Land Cruiser.

Back in Sur, my generous Omani friends welcomed me with boxes of Danish cookies, bowls of sweets, and a freshly baked cake. Immanuel and Jothi prepared my first meal in Sur, one of the Indian nurses invited me over for supper, and an Omani laborer brought me a box of grapes that I could distribute to callers who were sure to come. Between welcoming visits with dozens of friends, nurses helped me wash dishes and put my villa in order.

I was very conscious that this was my last term of service. I very much wanted to make the most of it. I had decided that my next vacation would not be out of the country, but a tour on behalf of the hospital within the country of Oman. I had the advantage of using ministry of health vehicles in my travels, so there was little expense involved. I needed to take only one bus and that was between Tanam and Behla; in each of the other places transportation was provided.

My travels during this term took me from Sur to Rostaq, Sohar, Tanam, Behla, Nizwa, and Muscat in one extended trip. Upon reaching the various towns, I stayed in the hospitals, where food and lodging were provided me. Everybody knew me as the matron from Sur. And in each of the hospitals there were nurses who had worked under me. Most thrilling to me was the opportunity to lead worship and study groups. I found that in most places the Christians were meeting regularly for worship. I could encourage them in their walk with God.

In Rostaq, a woman named Joan Cooper met me. She was a Christian matron from Scotland whom I knew from Muscat days. I also knew several other folk who worked in Rostaq.

The matron in Sohar was a Christian from Ghana, and a practicing Catholic. She arranged for me to visit the local copper mines not far from the Sohar hospital. A British Christian couple lived in the mine community and opened their home for Christian fellowship and Bible study. They gave us a tour of the mines. On Sunday evening in Sohar, I led the worship service. Many Christian staff had gathered, plus Christians from the town. The Sohar hospital was a busy place. They had a fine set-up and staff. I especially remember their outpatient department, which was well organized with special rooms for special needs.

A hundred and eighty miles from Sohar, traveling on to Tanam, I met with another cell group of Christians. I remembered that Anne De Young had been matron here. A new matron had come shortly before and was struggling with the language. She was a Buddhist from Sri Lanka. They too had a good set-up and a congenial staff. I was happy to see some of our Sur nurses that had been transferred to Tanam. They were happy to meet me and assured me that they would pray for our group in Sur.

In the town of Behla, the matron was Rachel Thomas, the sister of our first mission nurse (with Punnamma) in the Mission Hospital in 1958. Rachel Thomas, like her sister, worked in the Mission Hospital before the coup and was now working under the Ministry of Health, as I was. The only difference was that she was salaried by the government of Oman, while my salary came from my denomination at home. Her husband was the hospital clerk or secretary. There was no Christian gathering of staff in Behla. Rachel said there was disunity in their camp and no cooperation between the Protestant and Catholic staff; and there was no interest in meeting. I spoke to a few of them and encouraged them to meet together. (Today Rachel and her husband are living and working in New York. She followed Yohannan and Elizabeth to the States.)

Behla was famous for its pottery. I was able to stop and see a large pottery shop and see how the different kinds and sizes of pottery are made. Omanis were very dependent on the large water *hubbs* used as water coolers and water pitchers and jars before the days of electricity and refrigerators. The pottery of Oman is still turned on a hand-and-foot-operated machine as in the days of yore. But the finished products are beautiful. The shop had a large display with white pots of many sizes, used for many functions. The potter was proud to show how he operated the treadle and molded the clay by hand as it spun round.

The Nizwa hospital was large and well run. The British matron was on leave; an Indian Christian from Kerala was nursing supervisor. The hospital there was strong in the care of infants and children. I was inspired and took many notes. Going through the hospital was a learning experience for me. In the afternoon, the administrator of the hospital (an Omani Muslim like Ahmed) sent his chauffeur and the hospital car to take me on a personal tour of Nizwa's famous old fort, underground waterways, old homes with beautiful archways, and leather works at which they made sandals, water bags, and other articles. The administrator's driver was well informed on the history of his town and people. The nursing supervisor accompanied me. That evening I met for Bible study and prayer with the Christian staff, brought them greetings from the other groups, and encouraged them in their ministry in Nizwa.

I was given a hospital vehicle and driver to take me to Muscat, where I visited the Annahda Hospital in Ruwi. This hospital was not new to me, of course. Annahda Hospital carried the blood bank for all the hospitals in the sultanate. Either by telephone from Sur or by personal visit, I was in constant touch with them. The people were most hospitable, caring for personal needs, and giving utmost respect. People I had never met before told me they knew me and knew of my long years of work in Oman. The matron was a Zanzabari Omani, who was educated in England. She was pleasant and most capable. Her assistant was a Christian male nurse from Kerala. Again most capable. They were a good team and had a fine staff. Adaaba Mahmood, one of our school girls, whom we sent to India for a three year nursing course, was working in pediatrics.

The following year during my vacation, I continued my travels in Oman and flew to the Qaboos Hospital in Salallah, Dhofar, 700 miles west of Sur. This was another memorable experience, with a tour of the largest hospital in Oman, furnished with the latest equipment. This hospital had to be self-sufficient for it was almost isolated from contact with the other hospitals. I found it to be very well staffed. The staff had fine housing.

I spent a few days with them and again was furnished food and lodging and utmost respect. The respect people showed for a matron and for my years of service in Oman always overwhelmed

Jeanette under a frankincense tree in Dhofar, Oman.

me. I consciously strove, with God's help, to channel this attention for God's purpose. Not that I always succeeded—yet everybody knew what I stood for and why I was there. They knew that I had come out as a missionary and this missionary had been promoted to be a matron in a strategic hospital in Oman. I, with them, was a part of the Ministry of Health of Oman. We had some fine Christian meetings there, good Christian fellowship, and many opportunities for prayer as several invited me to share their meals with them.

Later I visited the Bilad Beni Bu Ali Hospital and public health clinic in Ja'laan. We had a good public health set-up in Sur, and this hospital needed guidance and help. Our public health nurse from Sur accompanied me on this one-day trip out of Sur. We showed them where improvement was needed and left our recommendations. One Indian female doctor, who was a recent Christian, felt she was alone in her faith and longed for Christian fellowship. I was able to send her Christian literature and cassettes from time to time. In Sur we remembered the needs of this hospital and staff in our prayers.

These Christian groups, spread out in various places throughout the sultanate, were Christ's lights in this Muslim world. It was so encouraging to me to see their faithfulness to their Lord; their desire to worship him even in a foreign land away from home; and Christ at work in and through them.

Wherever I went, even to shops in Nizwa, Suhar, Kamil, and Bilad Beni Bu Ali, I found Christians. And I found them remaining true to their faith; even witnessing to this faith to Hindus and others. This "dispersion" was only possible because of God's love shown to the Arabs and God's faithfulness to his promises. Psalm 145:13b says, "The Lord is faithful to all his promises and loving toward all he has made." How true this is.

I continued to stop at Wadi 'Ar 'Ar to see the Bedouins every month or two, and our relationship remained close. My brother-in-law Ben had given me an old sleeping bag to use when I slept in the desert. I carried it and a mattress with me. At age sixty-six I could still get a good night's sleep under the stars. The mornings came all too soon. Bedouins rise before daybreak. The hungry sheep wanting to get out of their sheep-cote awakened them.

Abdullah also showed up now and then in Sur. He continued to see himself as the liaison between his people and the matron, and many times he would bring a sick person to my home, prior to admission in the hospital. Formerly they would stay with me in the villa, but more recently a hospital was built closer to them. The women now had their deliveries in the Bedee'a hospital.

They were ever faithful to their five prayers a day. When they came in for the day or to spend a few days with me, my villa was their place of prayer. The garden hose was used for their ablutions. They bowed toward Mecca on the mat or carpet on my living room floor. My home was truly a "house of prayer."

During this time an incident happened which showed them the power of Christian prayer. One of the Bedouin women who lived in Wadi 'Ar 'Ar had been taken over by evil forces. Her husband Salim told me that his wife, eight months pregnant, had gone to the well for water one day when demons pounced her. Mahfoodha was in great distress. They had taken her to traditional healers at exorbitant costs—to no avail. Salim had great difficulty in caring for the family, the flocks, and his other work.

I was filled with anger at the forces of evil that were destroying the family. I knelt down beside Mahfoodha and taking her hand I commanded the demons to leave her in the name of Jesus and upon the authority of the blood and the Word.

When I returned to Sur, we continued to pray for the woman. When I visited Wadi 'Ar 'Ar I would pray with her. On the third visit, all praise to God, the demons left. Mahfoodha got up and was all smiles and so thankful. She said she could care for her family again.

On the next visit there was no doubt about it. The husband greeted me immediately with the statement that his wife was back to normal. He was full of joy. The woman, too, affirmed that the cure was complete.

"Your prayers to Jesus were the reason," the husband said. He wasn't reluctant to say that the money spent on the healers had been worthless. "I thank God for giving my wife back to us and I thank him for your prayers in the name of Jesus."

In the months that followed, this branch of the Bedouin tribe was more open than ever before to discussions about Christ. They asked me to talk to them, read scripture with them, and pray with them. I responded to their inquiries. I did not push my religion on them. The Lord simply brought things about as he willed. I praise God for the opportunities he brought about, first through our contact with Yusef and second through the healing provided for the Bedouin woman, Mahfoodha.

On March 20, 1986, I visited my Bedouin friends for the last time, accompanied by Nancy, a Filipino nurse from Sur. It was three days after a heavy rainstorm, and the rains had packed the sand so hard that we could drive over it without any trouble. We arrived in the vicinity of Abdullah's encampment late in the afternoon and were shocked to find the place deserted. Cast-off remnants of the camp were visible, but the family had obviously moved out. For a moment I feared I might have to leave Oman without a final, farewell visit.

I saw a car track going into the desert, and Nancy and I decided to follow it. Further along, we spotted a little garden near an old well. A water pump brought water up for the garden and a plot of alfalfa. Nancy and I got out to stretch our legs and look around. Then, in the distance we saw two women walking along.

We called to them and they answered. One of the women was Yusef's stepmother, Taeeba. We told them of our desire to see the family. "I need to wait here for a friend and escort him to our camp," she told us.

Then she decided to take us instead. "I can leave a message," she said.

With the toe of her bare foot, she made a line in the sand to indicate the direction of the camp. "Ali, the driver of the car we were waiting for, is good at reading tracks in the sand," she said. "He will recognize the tread marks of your vehicle and will know immediately why I am not here to meet him. It will be all right."

We arrived in camp later that evening and were greeted by Abdullah, Shafeeq, Jameela, little Amr, and other old friends. Shafeeq, almost full grown at seventeen, was home for a few days from the army in Muscat. I complimented Abdullah on the new location of his camp.

I told of my coming retirement, and the Bedouins were devastated to hear that I would be leaving them. The husband of the woman who had been cured so miraculously came to the camp when he heard I was there. He asked me to talk about God's Word before they went to bed. So there in the desert I again had the privilege of sharing my faith with my friends the Bedouins.

Then as the stars came out in the clear, crisp sky, we bedded down under the trees. The night was cold, but Ben's sleeping bag kept me warm. I gave it to the Bedouins when I left the next day.

At sunrise we were up with the others and ate breakfast near a little fire. A camel race was held early in the morning, and the people made sure we were on hand to see the magnificent animals perform. Over the years I had come to appreciate the camels more and more. I could even spot some of the finer points that made the animals such valuable property throughout the Persian Gulf. We intently watched the race and learned that Abdullah's camel had lost. His friends laughed at him and taunted him, saying he had given his favored camel too much to eat! I suspected that this was true, because every time I turned around in the night I could hear the animal chewing the alfalfa near me. Like professional athletes, the animals usually ate less before a performance!

Following the race we conducted a little clinic for the sick. Then, with Abdullah, we moved along to another encampment. On the way we met a truck full of people from the camp. We stopped to talk for a few minutes and learned that their *wadi* had filled to overflowing during the recent rains, and they were grateful to be alive and safe.

"A flash flood was so bad in our *wadi*," they told Abdullah, "that we had to flee for our lives. It happened all of a sudden in the dark of night. Amidst the screams of the children and the cries of the women we threw our possessions together and ran with our flocks to high ground. We are glad to be alive. Now we are on our way to make a sacrifice of thanksgiving."

"What will your sacrifice be?" I asked.

"Fresh slaughtered meat, rice, vegetables, and spices—all in great amounts. Very costly," they replied.

"What will you do with all of this food?" I asked.

"We're going to the town of Bedee'a with it," they said. "There we will give it to our friends and to the poor."

These people had made a vow that should God bring them to safety, they would sacrifice in thanksgiving. Psalm 50:14,15 brings this out so well: "Sacrifice thank offerings to God, fulfill your vows to the Most High, and call upon me in the day of trouble; I will deliver you, and you will honor me."

There was not much point in continuing to their encampment, since most of the people were in the truck en route to Bedee'a. We completed our mission, however, and gave some medicines to the few people who remained. Then it was time to go back to Sur.

"Matron, we will miss you," Abdullah said. "You have been good to us. We thank you. Think of us when you are living in Chicago, U.S.A. Do not forget us."

"God is gracious," I said. "I will pray that he will be close to you and your family. I will never forget you."

And so, that chapter of my life came to a close. I do not cry during moments of emotion. That has never been my way. But as I drove away from the desert that afternoon, I felt as if I were leaving a piece of my heart behind.

Sometimes when you live in the middle of a situation, you lose your ability to see things objectively. So many wonderful things happened in my life, by God's grace, that it is hard for me to identify some events that may be more important than others. My friends in the Mt. Greenwood Reformed Church who helped me put this book together, Dave and Barb VanderWoude, Beverly Renz, and Angie Fisher, tell me that the contact with the Bedouins stands out in their minds as a highlight of my career.

Perhaps, like Queen Esther, I was placed in Sur for a particular purpose—working with the Bedouins. It all came about through the Lord's leading, because of a father's love and a misshapen little boy named Yusef. I was simply a missionary who was able go through the door that was opened by the Lord.

The weeks ran forward toward the day of my retirement. It was all ending too soon. There were so many things to do.

In the spring of 1986, brother Mel called me to let me know that my parents' old house on St. Louis Ave., two blocks south of the Mt. Greenwood church, was about to go up for sale. The people living there had called to let him know. If I were interested in it, Mel said, I could have it for a reasonable price.

I didn't have to think long about it. It was almost as if the Lord were speaking directly to me saying, "This is the place for you, Jeanette." I had decided that I wanted to live in a house in a city neighborhood, rather than in a retirement complex of some kind. I still loved the people of the Mt. Greenwood church dearly, and there was no congregation I would rather be associated with in the States.

The matter of a place for retirement had been in my mind for some time, and with my friends in the prayer group I had prayed often that God would make his will known to me. A number of ideas were in my mind, but none held more promise than this.

"I'll take it," I told Mel. "It's an answer to prayer."

In April the Sur staff gave me the nicest party I had ever attended in that town. The Omani staff drummed, danced, and marched according to the traditions of their regions. The expatriate staff also presented skits, songs, and folk dances from their homelands. Two small Indian girls performed a dance in native costume. This was followed by a delicious dinner catered by the kitchen workers. The hospital staff then presented me with a three-foot-long scale model of a typical Sur *dhow*—a ship made famous by generations of Sur's sailors. All of the boards, masts, sails, and fittings were complete in miniature. A tailor-made packing box was included with the model.

The next day, just before I was scheduled to go to Muscat, I was visited by an army of well wishers. I shook hands with everyone and tried to explain that I really did need to finish packing boxes, cleaning the villa, and filling my suitcases. "We won't go until you're ready to leave," the visitors said. All I could do was get help from some of them while I did what had to be done. With the extra help I filled the back of the land cruiser and was able to say a last good-bye.

I remember not shedding tears that day. There was so much to do that I didn't have time to feel sorry about leaving. I hoped my friends didn't misunderstand me and think I was happy to go. Just before I drove away I shared a final prayer in my living room with the visitors. I committed them to the Lord and asked God to provide for the needs of the hospital and prayer group. Then I left. I remember that it was an extremely hot day.

Back in Muscat (as in Sur) farewell gifts began arriving at my door. The Ministry of Health presented me with two gold pens and a fine leather wallet. The pens carried the emblem of the country and were especially made for the Sultan. (Someone in the States later estimated the value of the set at around $2,000.) One member of the royal family gave me a check for R.O. 100, (about US$ 300). A very dear friend gave me a finger ring and matching earrings of rubies and diamonds. Someone else gave me a wide, heavy bracelet made of 24-karat gold. Then there were two other gold bracelets, a gold watch, a gold necklace, a gold chain with a cross, and many other things.

I was upset and embarrassed by these gifts. I felt like the Israelites leaving Egypt. I didn't need more money, and wearing such lavish jewelry was not my style. Then I decided to give away the gifts, all but the model *dhow* and the ruby-diamond ring and earring set (which were gifts from very close friends). I wanted the proceeds to be used on behalf of other missionaries and ministries. I didn't feel that the givers would take offense at this.

By the time I left the country, almost all the gifts had been put to work for the Lord. I am grateful to have had a chance to do this in his service. To this day I don't know the value of all the jewelry that passed through my hands during those days.

Farewells among the missionaries in Muscat were not as permanent as those I shared with the Omanis and the expatriates, because missionaries had ways of bumping into each other at church gatherings, at General Synod meetings, while traveling in the States, and at conferences. We knew we would see each other again. We shook hands, embraced, and promised to look each other up on such-and-such a date. At the Ruwi church, the new Arab pastor prayed for me and commended my travel plans to the Lord.

Thus, on a hot summer's day in Oman I completed forty-two years of overseas mission work. I left a land and people that had become my own. The greater part of my life had been spent with them. They will always remain part of me. Jesus said, "So you also, when you have done everything you were told to do, should say 'We are unworthy servants, we have only done our duty'" (Luke 17:10).

XIII
New Paths of Service

Praise the Lord. Praise the Lord, O my soul.
I will praise the Lord all my life;
I will sing praise to my God as long as I live.
Psalm 146:1,2

He brought out Israel, laden with silver and gold,
and from among their tribes no one faltered.
Psalm 105:37a

When I came back to the United States in May, 1986, I had an additional three months of full-time service to complete for the mission board. During this time I traveled extensively, just as I did on previous furloughs.

Wendell Karsen of the Speakers' Bureau cleverly arranged a speaking tour on the West Coast for missionaries who were invited to attend the General Synod and the Women's Triennial during the month of June. In cooperation with the Robert Schuller ministries, we stayed in the beautiful Rancho Capistrano Renewal Center, a secluded and peaceful conference center. The synod was being held in the Crystal Cathedral in Garden Grove.

Wednesday at the synod was visitors' day for women. This gathering was held in Rancho Capistrano. Five missionaries spoke—each for five minutes. We told of our work on our fields. It was interesting for me to hear of the work in Africa, Japan, and Mexico. Eloise Bosch and I spoke of the work in Oman. There was an applause after each speaker.

Friday morning the Board of World Missions gave its report and all the missionaries in attendance were called to the platform by the Rev. Warren Henseler, the area secretary for the Middle East and Africa. When the report was over, the group was dismissed from the platform—all except Beth Marcus and me. Both of us were retiring that year.

While we stood before the delegates, the Rev. Henseler spoke about my service and presented me with a beautiful plaque acknowledging my work for the Lord in the Arab world. A similar plaque is given to all retiring missionaries. Mine read:

> In recognition
> of the faithful and dedicated service of
> Jeanette H. Boersma
> to the Reformed Church in America,
> which she served as a missionary nurse
> in the Middle East from 1944-1986.
> Presented by the General Program Council/Division
> of the General Synod, RCA, June 14-20, 1986.

It was signed by four men, including the Rev. Henseler.

Then it was my turn to respond. It was the first time I had appeared in front of such an important church body. I don't remember all that I said, but I began by giving thanks to God for his grace and faithfulness to me those forty-two years; for good health and strength; and for his special care and keeping.

I then mentioned the fact that I had left for the Middle East in 1944 with twenty-eight teeth and had returned with twenty-seven.

(Let me add here that at seventy-one a wisdom tooth was added in my mouth, so I now again have twenty-eight teeth!)

The place filled with laughter! Then I started laughing, too! There was applause. And I told them that while on the field my eye glasses were never broken; God had protected and faithfully provided for me all those years. I should have thanked them for their support and prayer, because without the denomination behind us the missionaries could not function. But I don't remember that I did.

As I turned to go back to my seat, the delegates applauded and then stood and continued to applaud. It was the first standing ovation I had ever received. The applause, I know, was for God and what he had done. "When we are weak, then are we strong" (2 Cor. 12:9,10).

During the month of June I was privileged to speak in several churches in California and to attend the Women's Triennial, also held at the Crystal Cathedral. The Folmsbees from Mexico, the

Van Wyks from Japan, the Herbelins from Bahrain, and myself were there. There were others who came and went. Gordon and Birdie Van Wyk and I remained. The Van Wyks and I had been commissioned in the same group in Buck Hills Falls, Pennsylvania, in 1944, and until then our furloughs had never brought us together. It was fitting that we should be together in Capistrano as we began our retirement. We had never had the opportunity to become acquainted, but did so then. When not out speaking, we went on daily walks, had our meals together, and swam in the pool. Between our going out and coming back from speaking in the California churches, we could relax at Capistrano.

En route back to Chicago, I stopped to speak in the Longview Reformed Church in Phoenix, Arizona. They had long and faithfully supported me. I knew many of its members now and they were "family," because on every furlough I went to Phoenix to speak. I also went on to Tucson to visit George and Christine Gosselink, with whom I spent my first Christmas in Iraq in 1944.

On July 14 I returned to Chicago and moved into my parents' former home. It was sparkling clean; my brothers and sisters and their spouses had cleaned it from top to bottom in preparation for my return. I felt that the home was a direct gift from the Lord.

Originally my parents had willed it to me. But in 1975 when property values seemed to be going down, my brother advised that I sell it, saying it might not be a place where I would want to live in retirement. My young nephew Ted, and his wife, Lynn, bought it. Their payment was placed into a Certificate of Deposit and gained interest for me at a time when interest rates were in the range of 10 to 16 percent! Ted and Lynn sold the home to Chuck and Debbie Boomsma, members of my church, in 1978. Debbie's father, Rudy Beukinga, is a carpenter and he made many improvements on the home: archways, a beautiful open staircase, a new bedroom, shower, and new insulation. The home had been well maintained all those years. (Had I rented it, I would have had much expense in repairs.) It was the Lord's leading, speaking through my brothers, that I sell it. And it was the Lord's leading in 1986 when Chuck and Debbie Boomsma informed Mel that they were about to put the house on the market.

I didn't give much thought to money during most of my life, because the Lord through the church wonderfully provided. And now, as I again see the way God has provided the house and retirement income for me, it is truly amazing. Despite the fact that I disliked taking time away from mission work to correspond with bank officers about my finances (and without really understanding how the savings accounts worked), the Lord kept interest rates working for me. My savings eventually were enough to provide the house, a car, and an income.

I knew that I would again be speaking in the fall, and I needed a dependable car to travel the roads alone to Wisconsin, Michigan, Indiana, and throughout Illinois. On furloughs I bought used cars; but I knew I should now buy a new car. And, praise the Lord, the money for a new car was there! I appreciated the Toyota on the field; but it seemed best to buy an American-made car as my dad and brothers had always done. I purchased a 1986 Nova, which was just the right car for me.

I was also able to furnish my home. One evening women in the Mt. Greenwood church threw a surprise party for me and contributed many items for my home: sheets, towels, lawn chairs, a table, kitchen utensils, a clock, coffee urn, glasses, electric beater, artificial flowers, and so many, many things I would need to start up housekeeping.

The month of September technically ended my career as a missionary, but the Speaker's Bureau asked me to continue to speak, which I was happy to do. Wendell Karsen was developing mission fests throughout the country. I knew they were often short of speakers and I conveniently lived in the Midwest. I began speaking again in earnest in September and continued for another two and a half years. During this time I crisscrossed the country. I spoke at morning services, Sunday schools, women's groups, and at New Brunswick Seminary. I got so that I rather enjoyed speaking, though I never lost my nervousness just before getting up to speak. As always, it was a joy to meet new people. It was the start of work on this book that made me put my speaking aside. I don't think I'll be speaking again. God may have other work for me to do.

A beautiful Wurlitzer organ that had originally been owned by my sister Harriet came to me from a woman who bought it from Harriet. The woman gave me a bargain price which I couldn't refuse. As I mentioned before, organ playing had interested me ever since I played at St. Peter's Anglican Church in Basrah and in the mission church in Muscat. In 1965, while at Barrington College, I had taken some organ lessons. I am again taking lessons.

My home was furnished, but I needed a desk. A little ad in a weekly "throw-away" paper caught my eye and a fellow gave me a good price on a well-made desk. He even delivered it to my house.

I attended a writer's conference at Moody Bible Institute, with the intention of exploring my skills as a writer. It was announced that a Moody student was selling a computer/word processor at a discount. That night the greater portion of a dream was about purchasing a computer, and I felt it was a message from the Lord. At age sixty-nine, he wanted me to learn word processing and start "writing" on a video monitor.

The patient people who helped me write this book can testify that learning to use a computer wasn't always easy for me. There were times when I put out an SOS call of distress to Henry Boersma (grandson of Sietje Boersma, my dad's uncle), and he and his good wife, Joyce, would come to help me. I would also ask Dave and Barb VanderWoude to come and rescue chapters of this book that were in danger of being swallowed up by my computer! But as the months passed the mistakes became less frequent. Now I feel comfortable with this new way of writing. I thank God every day for the computer. I especially think how clever it is (and almost think it to be human) because it reminds me when I want to go out that I haven't saved what was written. I have to say to it, "Thank you for reminding me!"

I have many books, and my one small bookcase was insufficient for my needs. My friends Stanley and Johanna DeYoung heard that I needed a large bookcase and began scanning classified ads and making calls for me. None of their leads worked out. Then one day an old friend of Stanley's called him with an offer of a well-constructed bookcase without cost. This person was moving and had no place for the bookcase. "Would he be interested?" It was soon in my home. Stanley suggested I give him a mere five dollars for its delivery. God is so good.

My home does not have central air conditioning. For the most part I would not need air conditioning, but when temperatures reach the nineties, with ninety percent humidity, Chicago can feel as hot as the Persian Gulf. Also, there is no breezeway and the house is hemmed in between the north and south sides, so I get the sun's rays in the afternoon. I said to brother Ted that should he hear of a used window air conditioner, I would be interested in it. Again, it wasn't long before an excellent used air conditioner, suitable for cooling three rooms, became available at a very reasonable price. Ted found it and helped brother-in-law Ben install it.

As I write this my best dishes are arranged in a cabinet in my home. I received them from my parents in 1951, and they are very precious to me. In 1951 they were shipped from Chicago to Muscat, in 1975 I shipped them from Muscat to Sur, and on my retirement we packed them in Sur; they traveled from Sur to Muscat by truck; and from Muscat to Chicago by air-freight. During all those miles in the arms of longshoremen, on docks in international ports, on board trucks, boats, airplanes, and who-knows-what-else, not a single piece was broken. Thank you, Lord.

I must thank Brother Mel for taking care of my bank accounts and on one occasion writing a stiff letter to the U.S. Internal Revenue Service, when they began hounding me unnecessarily for taxes. The Lord used people and systems to work things out for my good. May he be praised!

I can testify (as so many others can, too) to the following verses:

> Whoever sows sparingly will also reap sparingly, and whoever sows generously will also reap generously. Each man should give what he has decided in his heart to give, not reluctantly or under compulsion, for God loves a cheerful giver. And God is able to make all grace abound to you, so that in all things at all times, having all that you need, you will abound in every good work. You will be made rich in every way so that you can be generous on every occasion, and through us (says Paul) your generosity will result in thanksgiving to God. (2 Cor. 9:6-8,11)

During my retirement years I have remained in constant contact with people in Oman and other Persian Gulf countries. A stream of most welcome letters still comes to me from expatriate nurses in Sur, Muscat, and other cities. I have hosted some Omani friends and their children here in Chicago, when they come to the United States for a visit or go to school. We missionaries keep in contact through letters and phone calls, and some call me by phone from Oman.

In 1987 one of my good friends in the royal family flew me back to Muscat for several weeks. The invitation came by telephone from Oman. All travel arrangements were made in Oman and the ticket sent me. I left in November.

I was met at the Seeb Airport by a long, black limousine driven by the personal driver of my friend. I had planned to stay in mission facilities, to avoid being a burden to my friend, but I was informed that she was expecting me to stay in her palatial home, have one of her late-model automobiles at my disposal, and receive a gift of spending money amounting to about $300. I had learned long ago that I could not refuse such gifts and invitations!

I had first met my hostess thirty-six years before, when I was new to Oman. Her status was less than it became in later years. Royalty too lived in poverty in earlier days. What I always appreciated about my friend was her spirit of helpfulness to women and children in need. Many women felt free to come to her. I had been present at the death of her stepmother, who was the mother of the Sultan. In the earlier years she would seek my help in her medical needs. The Thoms, Kapengas, and Bosches were also friends of her family. She appreciated a small black kitten I brought her from one of Pussy's litters.

Now our roles were reversed. She was a woman of immense wealth and power. I was just a retired missionary from Chicago, living simply. I hadn't packed suitable clothing to be with her. Since I thought I would be living with my fellow missionaries, I brought simple, casual clothing and a Sunday dress!

My friend, however, was as warm and gracious as ever. We sat, talked, and caught up on news from the previous year. I inquired about her health, and she asked about my family. We shared a wonderful meal from her kitchen. In a kind way, she indicated that she would need to dress me according to my status as her house guest. She gave me three pieces of expensive, beautiful cloth for dresses, and another piece for a long skirt, and then sent me to the tailor to have long dresses made. She also gave me a pair of sandals and a flannel robe.

Then she gave me an itinerary. I was to go with her to dinner functions in prominent homes. There were a number of special performances and celebrations to attend during the national holidays.

I also had free time to visit my old friends and drive down to Sur. Lee Bruggink, wife of the Rev. Roger Bruggink, accompanied me. On the way to Sur and upon my return from Sur we stopped to see my Bedouin friends. They were overjoyed to see me. "You have been away too long!" they said. I found Abdullah and the family well. Abdullah's children were growing. His daughter Jameela had grown and matured. Shafeeq was working in Muscat. Little Amr, born not long after Yusef died, was five years of age, almost old enough to begin school. I passed out little gifts, but this time I was not able to dispense medications. We sat on the sand and enjoyed being together. My visit was a big surprise to them, because they never thought to see me again.

It was good to see all my friends at the hospital, both the nurses and the Omani staff. I walked through the entire hospital and greeted everybody. I met with the nurses for prayer and Bible study. It was like old times again.

Later I went one more time to the Sherqeeya with Mary Anne Murphy (whose husband is a professor in Qaboos University), her young son, and a brother in-law. They had never visited the Bedouins before and were thrilled to meet them and to learn how they lived. It was the brother-in-law's first visit to Oman. My guests and I were served the traditional coffee and dates.

Back in the Muscat area I had a chance to see Don and Eloise Bosch, and in their company I attended the grand opening of the Royal Qaboos Hospital in Qala. Oman's director of nurses, my former boss, asked me to sit with her in the front row of the assembly.

After the ceremony, a few of the guests were ushered into a special room adjoining the assembly area. Due to tight security, only a few people were given this honor, and I was one of them.

When we got into the room, the lights and TV cameras were focused on the Sultan himself in a receiving line. Along with many dignitaries, I had the chance to shake hands with Sultan Qaboos. As was his custom, the Sultan was restrained and rather quiet as he greeted his subjects. But when I shook hands with him and said to him, "We give God thanks for you and for all you are doing for your country," he recognized me and smiled. That evening we were shown on television! A number of people told me later how surprised they were to see me in Oman. Ahmed Khadhoury, my old friend from Sur, said, "It looked like you were talking to the Sultan longer than anyone else."

Another surprised friend said, "The Sultan almost never smiles on TV, but I noticed he smiled when you spoke to him!"

Later I was invited to attend a *henni* party sponsored by a high government official for his daughter. The government official, who also was very wealthy, was married to a lady I had delivered and who later attended our mission school. Eloise Bosch also was invited and attended the party with me.

A *henni* or "henna" party is a grandiose affair put on for a young woman just before her marriage. The name comes from the red dye, henna, that is used to paint designs on the feet and hands of the bride. More than 200 women were present, all dressed in their finery. Thousands of colored lights surrounded us, a band played, special women dancers were brought in, and lavish refreshments were served to us while we sat on expensive Persian rugs.

In the middle of all this excitement sat the bride on a highly decorated bridal bed. She was completely covered except for her bare feet, which were being painted by attendants with little brushes. The designs consisted of dots, flowers, vines, and symmetrical patterns. Tips for the attendants—Omani riyalls—were tossed into a tray.

At one point the father, the groom, and his brothers formed a line and walked through the women to put a contribution in the tray. They carefully kept their eyes straight ahead, so as not to accidentally look upon the unveiled faces of the women.

Later I met Norman Thoms, son of Wells Thoms, and the two of us went through the city looking up old friends, dining together, and generally enjoying good fellowship.

I found the church and prayer groups to be very active throughout the country. The Rev. Roger Bruggink (RCA) and Ray Skinner (Church of England) seemed to work well together in the Protestant Ruwi church. There were many denominations sharing the facilities, with a couple of thousand worshipers (almost all of them expatriates) each week. The church in Salalah was served by the Rev. John Hubers. Land for a third Protestant church had been donated by the Sultan not far from a new hospital that had just been dedicated. The Sultan had also donated land for a new mosque, a Catholic church, and a Hindu temple.

All of the prayer groups that I had seen in Oman during my last years of work appeared to be functioning. Many Hindus were turning to Christ and nominal Christians were becoming alive in Christ. But still there were virtually no Muslims willing to give their hearts to Jesus.

There was much that encouraged me, however. I felt more than ever that missionaries should stand firm and give themselves fully to the work that had begun so long before. "Let us not become weary in doing good, for at the proper time we will reap a harvest if we do not give up" (Gal. 6:9).

The end of my visit came much too quickly. Then it was back to the United States. From the land of rocks, sea, and sand to

Pastor Grawburg and Jeanette at Tenabrae service at home in Mt. Greenwood church.

springtime in the American Midwest. It was like shuttling between two different worlds.

When I came back, I had time to continue my involvement in the activities of the Mt. Greenwood Reformed Church. I enjoyed my church and its activities and was happy again to be a part of it. "I was glad when they said unto me: Let us go unto the house of the Lord!"

Even in retirement, *especially* in retirement, God was teaching me new dependance on him and leading me into new paths of spiritual growth.

One of the pathways went through the valley of the shadow of death. My health and strength were good and I felt like everything was going full speed ahead. My schedule was busy with things I enjoyed doing, and I was working hard on this book.

Then came a doctor's report, tests, and the announcement that in six days I would need to have surgery for cancer. Tests indicated cancer cells in my abdomen, but it was not known how widespread the cancer was. If surgery couldn't get all the cells there would be chemotherapy. I remembered Wells Thoms, who died of cancer just after he retired. Walt Carlson, one of my favorite announcers on WMBI, died of cancer at age seventy, three months after retiring.

At first I resented having my strong, serviceable body cut up by a surgeon's knife. I struggled to submit to God's will. Things were going so well! All the little blessings had helped settle me in the house and living just two blocks from my home church! What was to become of it all?

Yet my desire was to serve the Lord. It took some time, but I reached the point of submitting to his will. On WMBI, Dr. Charles Stanley spoke about disturbances entering a person's ordered life. He said that they are like grains of sand in an oyster. Out of the oyster's irritation, a beautiful pearl is made. Then Dr. Stanley gave five points to consider when serious problems enter a person's life: (1) submission, (2) thanksgiving, (3) praise, (4) forgiveness, and (5) service. I prayed earnestly about those points, particularly the first. I admitted that the Lord might want to take me home, but there also might be further glory for him in my remaining on earth. I let God make the decision.

I knew I had nieces and nephews in the States and friends in Oman who had not yet made a commitment to the Lord. It was conceivable that if the Lord took me, it might help them think about life and death and finally make a decision.

My friends in the church's Monday morning prayer group organized a twenty-four-hour prayer vigil on my behalf, and after a worship service one Sunday evening, pastor Phil Grawburg and the consistory conducted an anointing service as God recommends to us in James 5:13-18. Many friends and my family gathered for the service.

I wrote my friends in the States, my missionary friends in Muscat, and the nurses and friends in Sur, and they all prayed for me. Family and friends around the globe prayed. Then came the surgery. Yes, it was serious, but the Lord saw fit to use it to remove the cancer completely. There was no worry about further complications. A specialist in radiation therapy said radiation was not necessary. The Lord honored the anointing service and he heard the prayers. He gave me complete healing. In God's providence, I was given more time to serve. God had more work for me to do. My heart was filled with gratitude to the Lord and to all the people who stood with me. I thank God for returned health and strength and complete healing.

My brother Ted, who was injured so seriously years ago, continues to be an influence for good among his eight children, twenty-one grandchildren, and in his church. One of his sons is now studying for the ministry. God thought of me, too, when he gave Ted recovery, because Ted mows my lawn and helps in the care of my garden. Tree branches need removing, bushes need trimming, and sidewalks need shoveling in the winter. (My neighbors also help me.)

And now my book is almost at an end. I feel the story has been told sufficiently. The Lord has taken care of me all my life, wherever I have been. Does God not promise in his Word that he cares for the fatherless, widows, [and singles]? God is true to his promises.

I again thank God for his clear calling in my life. I knew for certain where I was meant to be. The calling was strong, of which this book is a witness. This was a wonderful gift, given to me before birth in answer to my mother's prayer.

My own prayer is that the Lord will give this same calling to young people in a new generation. It might be said that mission work is changing and this is true, but there still are many, many openings and opportunities for service for missionaries around the world. They are still needed. I pray that the Lord will raise up talented, dedicated young men and women to fill these positions, and give them the strength to obey and serve faithfully.

May the good Lord rekindle in a new generation the fires that burned so brightly in people like Samuel and Peter Zwemer, Paul Harrison, Sharon and Wells Thoms, and Cornelia Dalenberg. I also pray that the Lord will provide renewed life in his Spirit to our Reformed Church in America.

I am asked, "What is the main idea you want to leave with a person who reads your book?"

What I want most of all is for the reader to know that the Lord led me throughout my life. If it had not been for the vow and prayers of my parents, and the Lord keeping them to their vow, I know I would not have been a missionary and this book would not have been written. It awes me to think that God would not give them a child or children until they had come to this point in their lives.

God leads us to make commitments and then holds us to these commitments, promises, and vows for his purposes. My parents made theirs and then forgot. But God would not let them forget. When reminded they made a new commitment, which they followed through with great sacrifice.

The Lord held me also to my commitment, made when I was eight years old and forgotten until God reminded me of it at Moody Bible Institute Founder's Week session, when I was twenty. Two years later he again reminded me when Dr. Mylrea was speaking.

The Lord's faithfulness comes through in his keeping us on the path chosen for us. The Lord works in miraculous and wondrous ways to bring about his purposes.

God's leading is for each of us, because "God so loved the world that he gave his one and only Son; that whoever believes in him will not perish, but have eternal life." He led my colleagues as I was led. God has a purpose for each of his children; not just for special ones, but for each of us. We are all one in Christ Jesus. It is for us to hear, know, and obey. Then come God's guidance, help, and provision. And then we have the peace that passes all understanding; his special blessings. Our God is faithful; we must be faithful, too.

RAS EL HIKMA MAKHAAFET ALLAH transliterated:
"The fear of the Lord is the beginning of wisdom"
(Ps. 111:10 and Prov. 1:7) courtesy of Jay Kapenga.

Appendix A

Jeanette Boersma's supporting churches. Thank you one and all!

Mt. Greenwood Reformed Church, Chicago, IL
Warwick Reformed Church in Warwick, NY
Mohawk Reformed Church in Mohawk, NY
First Reformed Church in Scotia, NY
Colonial Church of Bayside in Long Island, NY
Second Reformed Church of Rotterdam in Schenectady, NY
Longview Community Church in Phoenix, AZ
Trinity Reformed Church in Pella, IA
Ebenezer Reformed Church in Morrison, IL
Ferry Memorial Reformed Church in Montague, MI
Jamestown Reformed Church in Jamestown, MI
Reformed Church of Palos Heights in Palos Heights, IL
Hope Reformed Church in Kalamazoo, MI
Trinity Reformed Church in Grand Rapids, MI
Union Reformed Church in Paterson, NJ

Appendix B

I give respect and honor to the following who worked as nurses on the field during my span of service.

There were six single nurses on the field during my span of service: Cornelia Dalenberg, Christine Voss, Jeannette Veldman, Anne De Young, Lillian Huiskens, and myself. Louise Essenberg Holler, Joan Olthoff Buckley, Elaine Sluiter Lester, Mary Bonnecroy Coulter, Allene Schmaltzriedt Lee, Marilyn Tanis Franken, Marianne Walvoord Sundberg, Margaret Koeppe Pennings came out as single nurses, most of whom (if not all) met their husbands on the mission field and were married. Most of them remained and served the Lord with their husbands as career nurses, while Dorothy Scudder, Elinor Heusinkveld, Marjorie Vander Aarde, and Verla Van Etten arrived as career missionaries with their husbands. They too worked full time in the hospital and made valuable contributions.

There were the short-termers: Harriet Wanrooy Boyce, Nellie Hekhuis, Hazel Wood, Judith Zuidema Dallal, Elaine Fieldhouse DeVries, Marcia Newhouse Bull, Carolyn Johnston Lukas, Cynthia Byker Kennedy, Gloria Rottenberg, Mary Schepper Moore, Nancy Hoger, and June Herbelin. Each of these came out as single nurses and were married with the exception of June Herbelin, who served with her husband, Dr. Ted Herbelin, and Nancy Hoger, who is still serving her Lord in a busy hospital in Chicago. With the exception of Harriet Boyce, Nellie Hekhuis, Hazel Wood, Judith Dallal, and June Herbelin, who worked in Bahrain, the above short-term nurses worked in Oman. These short-termers normally stayed for a period of three years, though a few stayed five years or more. They were a great part of our work and such a blessing.

Index